A Bohemian Brigade

Other Books of James M. Perry

Arrogant Armies: Great Military Disasters and the Generals Behind Them
Us & Them: How the Press Covered the 1972 Election
The New Politics: The Expanding Technology of Political Manipulation
Barry Goldwater: A New Look at a Presidential Candidate

A Bohemian Brigade

The Civil War Correspondents— Mostly Rough, Sometimes Ready

James M. Perry

John Wiley & Sons, Inc.

New York • Chichester • Weinheim • Brisbane • Singapore • Toronto

This book is printed on acid-free paper. ∞

Published by John Wiley & Sons, Inc.
Published simultaneously in Canada

This publication is designed to provide accurate and authoritative information in re-gard to the subject matter covered. It is sold with the understanding that the pub-lisher is not engaged in rendering professional services. If professional advice or other expert assistance is required, the services of a competent professional person should be sought.

Library of Congress Cataloging-in-Publication Data:

Perry, James M. (James Moorhead)
    A bohemian brigade : the Civil War correspondents—mostly
rough, sometimes ready / James M. Perry.
        p.   cm.
    Includes bibliographical references and index.
    ISBN 0-471-32009-9 (alk. paper)
    1. United States—History—Civil War, 1861–1865—Journalists.
    2. War correspondents—United States—History—19th century.
    3. Journalism—United States—History—19th century.   I. Title.
    E609.P47   2000
    973.7′8—dc21   99-39101

Printed in the United States of America
10 9 8 7 6 5 4 3 2 1

For the women who keep an eye on me —
Peggy, and Greta and Kathie

Contents

Preface ix

Acknowledgments xiii

1 The World's Greatest War Correspondent 1

2 Bull Run from the Rear 19

3 Bull Run from the Front 31

4 The Three Graces: Greeley, Bennett, and Raymond 43

5 Out West 59

6 Afloat 86

7 A Very Angry General 110

8 The Court-Martial 135

9 Prisoners of War 156

10 Grant Finds a Reporter 174

11 The Jolly Congress 184

12 Gettysburg 204

13 The Reporter Who Was Kissed by Lincoln 223

14   "There Is to Be No Turning Back"   237

15   The Fall of Richmond   260

Epilogue   278

Bibliography   287

Index   293

Preface

EARLY ON THE MORNING of May 24, 1861, just a few blocks from my home in Alexandria, Virginia, Colonel Elmer Ellsworth, a close friend of Abraham Lincoln, tore down a Confederate flag flying over the Marshall House hotel. As he walked down the steps, the flag in his hands, he was shot by the angry proprietor, James W. Jackson. Corporal Francis Brownell retaliated by shooting Jackson.

Alexandrians continue to debate which of the two men was the real hero, Ellsworth or Jackson. When Union sympathizers laid down a memorial in a city park to Colonel Ellsworth a year or so ago, Confederate partisans were so outraged they paid for *two* memorials to Mr. Jackson. Our bloodiest war still stirs deep emotions.

I have been a newspaper reporter for more than 40 years, the last 20 with the *Wall Street Journal*. In 1973, I wrote a book called *Us & Them*, examining how the press covered the 1972 presidential election (not terribly well, I concluded). In 1996, I wrote a book called *Arrogant Armies*, recounting some of the great military disasters of the last 250 years.

This book grows out of both those earlier books. It's about military history (the Civil War) and it's about journalists (the men who covered the Civil War). But it's not a history of the Civil War and it's not a book about journalism. It is, instead, the story of a fascinating group of men who tried to make sense of the most dramatic event in American history. If it sheds some light on Civil War history and American journalism, so much the better.

A number of books have been written about reporters in the Civil War, most of them by scholars. One of these books, J. Cutler Andrews's *The North Reports the Civil War*, represents a lifetime of work. Andrews introduced hundreds of reporters in this 813-page work, and no one can write about this subject without referring to his book, again and again.

But Andrews wasn't a journalist. He didn't really understand what makes newspaper reporters so controversial, so infuriating—why generals hated them, why readers often mistrusted them, why so many of them were dishonest and inaccurate. He didn't really understand, either, why some Civil War reporters stood head and shoulders above the rest. I have singled two of them out in this book for special praise—Charles Carleton Coffin of the *Boston Morning Journal* and Whitelaw Reid of the *Cincinnati Gazette*. But others—a dozen, perhaps—were almost as good.

The modern American journalist emerged for the first time in the Civil War. It was the world's original instant-news war, made possible by the telegraph—the "lightning," they called it—a tremendous breakthrough in communications technology. Steam made a big difference, too—steam driving the big new presses, steam driving the locomotives that moved journalists and armies from place to place at speeds no one had ever contemplated before.

I have resisted the effort made by so many others to paint Civil War reporters in black and white, all devils or all saints. Most of the time, they were simply trying to do a very difficult job under harsh working conditions. It didn't help that the generals despised them. William Tecumseh Sherman called them "buzzards of the press." He arrested one of them and tried him as a Confederate spy. George G. Meade strapped one of them backward on a mule and rode him out of camp with a sign on his back reading, "Libeler of the Press," and the band playing the "Rogue's March."

They were rowdy and boisterous. They competed hard to be the first with the news, and got it wrong more often than they should have. They were frequently arrogant and pompous. They lied; they cheated; they spied on one another and on the generals they wrote about. They made up battles they had never seen. They speculated in cotton. They drank too much.

They did a lot of things reporters are still doing today.

We are now bombarded by wild tales from web sites on the Internet, so juicy they are picked up by cheap and irresponsible newspapers, magazines, and radio and television talk shows. Mainstream journalists wring their hands and wonder what they should say. Too often, they go along, printing the "news" with a caveat or two. The "lightning" worked very much the same way.

Too many mainstream editors and reporters still tend to be arrogant and pompous. With the arrival of celebrity journalists pontificating on television, we have a new class of highly paid reporters who think of themselves as the peers of the people they interview and talk about. We had one or two of them in the Civil War, too—but they tended to be editor-proprietors of the great metropolitan dailies. Horace Greeley was the best-known of the lot; he was as familiar to Americans during the Civil War as Dan Rather is to Americans now.

Reporters today are accused of being biased politically (in fact, we'd rather get on page 1 than score an ideological point). That was hardly a problem in the Civil War. *All* the reporters and editors, with the possible exception of the *New York Herald*'s James Gordon Bennett, who cared only about selling papers, were biased. Reporters supported their armies in the field, and most of the time they supported their newspaper's politics back home. Readers expected nothing else.

But out of all this turmoil and chaos came distinguished reporting. There were reporters who cared, and cared deeply, about what they wrote and how they wrote it. These reporters put their lives at risk on the battlefield; they took terrible chances in galloping across guerrilla-infested territory to get their stories published. They were often cold and hungry.

I have tried to bring these reporters, rogues and heroes alike, to life. I have tried to tell how they lived and how they survived. I have done that from the perspective of a long career working for newspapers myself. I know about rushing stories prematurely into print.

I have done that. I know about arrogance; I have happily denied making mistakes that were there for all to see. I have done my own fair share of pontificating. I belonged to my own Bohemian Brigade, the national political press corps, and I may even have been rowdy, once or twice. I have known moments of triumph, too, stories I wrote that I would never change—John Kennedy's assassination, Winston Churchill's funeral, nine presidential campaigns. I *know* these Civil War reporters. I have been there myself.

One part of the story is missing. This is basically a book about Civil War correspondents from the North. Reporters covered the war for newspapers in the South, too. The problem is we simply don't know very much about them. Too often, copies of the papers they worked for have disappeared, so we can't read everything they wrote. What's left is incomplete and impersonal. They didn't write about themselves very much during the war and none of them wrote a helpful book after the war. Northern reporters, on the other hand, babbled all the time in their stories about one another and a score or more of them wrote their memoirs when the war was over.

Two English journalists, Francis Lawley, a reporter for the *Times* of London, and Frank Vizetelly, an artist-writer for the *Illustrated London News,* fell in love with the "Lost Cause." We know a lot about both of them. They traveled in the company of several colorful European military officers, who wrote books about their experiences. They saw a great deal of fighting from the Confederate side and called themselves the "Jolly Congress." I have used them as surrogates here.

Alexandria, Va.
July 1999

Acknowledgments

I T IS NOT POSSIBLE to write a book like this one without access to a great library. It is my good fortune to live eight miles and a dozen Metro stops from the Library of Congress. I have spent hours hunched over its cranky microfilm machines looking at copies of more than a dozen newspapers published during the Civil War. I have wandered happily through its collections of Civil War photographs, maps, and manuscripts. Elisabeth Barna was a big help in tracking down a number of elusive nineteenth-century magazines.

I have also used my own library in Alexandria to make interlibrary loans. And when I have been in upstate New York at my summer cottage, I have spent hours with Owen Frank, the interlibrary specialist at Steele Memorial Library in Elmira, running down obscure books from cooperating libraries all over the eastern United States. Helpful, too, were the volunteer librarians at the Woman's Study Club and Library in Dundee.

We know most generals disliked war correspondents. They said so, frequently. It's harder to know what lower-ranking officers thought. That's why the letters of Captain Edward P. "Ned" Brownson about the *New York Times'* William Swinton are so interesting. They were kindly loaned to me by Dennis and Mary Kelly.

Several of the chapters in this book are illustrated by maps that appeared during the Civil War in Northern newspapers. These maps were provided by the Clements Library at the University of Michigan. Like the stories written by the correspondents themselves, these maps are not always entirely accurate. The Gettysburg map, for example, identifies Round Top as Sugar Loaf Mountain. But these are the maps that thousands of newspaper readers studied with intense curiosity as the war progressed. It seemed to me they were almost inseparable from the stories that were written to accompany them.

I would like to thank Alfred A. Knopf for generously allowing me to quote passages from Sylvanus Cadwallader's *Three Years with Grant,* edited by Benjamin P. Thomas.

I once again owe my thanks to my agent, David Black, and to my editor at John Wiley, Hana Lane. And, finally, I raise a glass of their favorite wine (Catawba, unfortunately) to the memory of the men of the Bohemian Brigade. They have been lively company for more than a year.

1

The World's Greatest War Correspondent

A CONVIVIAL WILLIAM HOWARD RUSSELL spent his last night in London before sailing to America at his favorite haunt, the Garrick, the liveliest of all the city's respectable clubs. He dined with his friend William Makepeace Thackeray, the magazine editor and novelist. Two days later, in Cork, in Ireland, he boarded "the good steamship *Arabia,* Captain Stone, and at nightfall we were breasting the long rolling waves of the Atlantic."

The educated classes in both Great Britain and the United States had reacted with keen anticipation to the news that Billy Russell had accepted an assignment from the influential and widely respected *Times* of London to report what appeared to be the breaking up of the American Union.

On March 3, 1861, the day the *Arabia* set sail for America, the forty-year-old Russell was at the height of his fame, if not yet his fortune. His greatest achievement—perhaps the most remarkable achievement by any war correspondent, ever—was his reporting of British blundering in the Crimean War in 1854 and 1855. In long, discursive "letters" to his editors in Printing House Square (news stories of the who, what, when, where, and why variety were still to evolve), he described the terrible suffering of the poorly clothed and poorly fed British troops, dying by the thousands with almost no medical attention. The letters had usually appeared on page 12, following the classified advertisements and the parliamentary reports, but they

1

were still a sensation. No one had ever seen reporting like this before, so powerful that it played a role in the fall of Lord Aberdeen's government. Russell had next appeared, again for the *Times*, in northern India in 1857 and 1858 to report the rebellion of the Sepoys, the native troops. Here, too, he created a sensation by criticizing the cruel treatment of the captured mutineers. Some of them, Russell had noted, had been strapped to the muzzles of cannon and blown to bits. "The Anglo-Saxons must . . . abate their strong natural feeling against the coloured race," he had written.

Russell was an Irishman, born in Dublin on March 28, 1820, but by 1861 he was a thorough Englishman, and a London man at that. Most important of all, he represented the *Times*, the greatest newspaper in the world, edited by John Thadeus Delane, who was right about lots of things but almost always wrong about affairs in the United States. "Delane had a few well-worn principles (or slogans) that seldom varied: the vulgarity of Americans, the inevitability of Southern independence, the desirability of peace," Hugh Brogan wrote in the introduction to *The Times Reports the American Civil War.*

Russell was a genial man and a great storyteller, and maybe just a bit of what we would call today an elitist. Delane, on the other hand, was truly a snob, spending his holidays hunting deer and game birds in the company of earls and dukes. Russell said he came to America— this was his first visit—"with no theories to uphold, no prejudices to subserve, no interests to advance, no instructions to fulfill. I was a free agent." That's a bit of a stretch, for Russell did hold some views about the United States, and chief among them was his strong distaste for slavery. For that and other reasons, Russell tended to sympathize with the Northern cause. That would put him in direct conflict with Delane and the other proprietors at the *Times*, for they were already making a complete about-face in their views on the South. In January of 1861, the *Times* compared Southerners to Irish peasants, "a poor, proud, lazy, excitable and violent class, ever ready with knife and revolver," and deplored the whole idea of secession. Two months later, on March 26, the *Times* reported that the Confederate Congress meeting in Montgomery was simply an admirable collection of statesmen. "Not one member has appeared in his seat under the influence

William H. Russell of the *Times of London*. (Library of Congress)

of liquors or wines, not a harsh word has been uttered in debate and all exhibit the most unflagging energy and determination." About the same time, the *Times* carried a leader—a lead editorial—blaming the North for evincing "a determination to act in a narrow, exclusive, and unsocial spirit, while its Southern competitor extends the hand of good fellowship to all mankind, with the exception of its own bondsmen." Delane's furious and shameless campaign against the North would nearly destroy the paper's hard-earned reputation.

The *Times'* own official history noted that "Englishmen in the mid-nineteenth century were neither close nor sympathetic students of American history." The *Times'* historian—he remains anonymous— suggested that America called up to the "ordinary English mind nothing but a vague cluster of associations, compounded of Mrs. Trollope, Martin Chuzzlewit, and Uncle Tom's Cabin. The British public was at once without knowledge and without understanding of the problems and situation of the United States." The British public needed an entire education about the old colonies.

Russell never really had a chance. Readers on both sides of the Atlantic expected far too much from him; they hoped he would be the man to make sense of what seemed to them to be a compelling, but immensely confusing, story. Russell was a fine descriptive reporter, but he made no claim to being a deep thinker (few reporters, then or now, do). The best he could do was what he had always done—write what he saw and heard, clearly and honestly.

In the stories he filed during the twelve months he spent in America, and in the book he called a diary that he published in London in 1862 and in Boston in 1863, he may have disappointed some of his contemporaries. But, to a surprising degree, Russell did just what he said he would do. He provided a clear and candid picture of the United States, especially the South, on the eve of a war that he predicted might be long and bloody.

Russell's Cunard steamer, the *Arabia*, hauled up alongside a wharf on the New Jersey side of the New York harbor early in the morning on March 16. "Ere the sun had set," he wrote in his diary,

> I could form some idea of the activity and the industry of the people from the enormous ferry-boats moving backwards and forwards like arks on the water, impelled by the great walking-beam engines, the crowded stream full of merchantmen, steamers, and small craft, the smoke of the factories, the tall chimneys—the network of boats and rafts—all the evidences of commercial life in full development.
>
> What a swarming, eager crowd on the quay-wall! What a wonderful ragged regiment of labourers and porters, hailing us in broken or Hibernianized English! "These are all Irish and Germans," anxiously explained a New Yorker. "I'll bet fifty dollars there's not a native-born American among them."

Russell accepted an invitation to attend a bibulous Saint Patrick's Day dinner organized by the Friendly Sons of Saint Patrick on his second night in New York City. Asked to speak, he rose to defend a free press—predicting it would flourish under the American form of democracy—and went on to call for the preservation of the Union.

Reporters from a number of New York's eighteen daily newspapers covered the Saint Patrick's Day dinner and took note of Russell's speech. One of them, writing anonymously, was awed by the great man's presence. Here, he said, was "the most famous newspaper correspondent the world has ever seen." He wrote:

> You must imagine this portly and pleasant looking gentleman, dressed in the extreme elaboration of Piccadilly full evening dress, his massive throat encased in the neatest and most dazzling of snowy ties; his broad chest making an immense display of fine linen; his waistcoat a miracle of embroidered silk, dark in color save where illuminated by flowers or traversed by his heavy watch-chain—another thinner chain running round his neck, meandering over his cambric frills and terminating in a pair of eye glasses which he is very fond of fiddling with while speaking. This substantial and slightly protuberant figure may stand about five feet seven inches in his boots; and such is the true picture of Mr. Russell as we saw him at the Astor Hotel dinner.

When news of Russell's impromptu speech got back to Printing House Square, heads began shaking. Delane and Mowbray Morris, the paper's manager, despised the American press and weren't much impressed with American democracy. "I am *very sorry*," Morris wrote, "that you attended the dinner and made that speech."

In one of his early letters—it was written March 29 and published three weeks later in London—Russell said New Yorkers didn't seem very serious about the crisis. New York, he said, "would do anything rather than fight—her delight is to eat her bread and honey and count her dollars in peace. The vigorous, determined hostility of the South to her commercial eminence is met by a sort of maudlin sympathy without any action, or intent to act."

When steamships brought back copies of the *Times* containing Russell's dispatch, patriotic New Yorkers felt betrayed. They had looked forward to reading Russell, and here in one of his very first efforts he was criticizing them. They hadn't expected that.

During his brief stay in New York, Russell met the most famous of all the New York editors, Horace Greeley of the *Tribune*. Russell was not impressed. Greeley, he wrote in his diary, "is the nastiest form of narrow minded sectarian philanthropy, who would gladly roast all the whites of South Carolina in order that he might satisfy what he supposes is a conscience but which is only an autocratic ambition which revels in the idea of separation from the South as the best recognition of its power."

Greeley did offer one useful bit of advice to Russell: Go south (not mentioning, one supposes, that he had never visited any of the slaveholding states himself). "Be sure you examine the slave pens," Greeley said. "They will be afraid to refuse *you*, and you will be able to tell the truth."

His stay in New York had simply confused Russell. "Such diversity of assertion and opinion extending to even the minutest matters of fact I never encountered before now, even in the House of Commons or in a meeting of the Geological Society," he wrote in a letter dated March 26, the day he arrived in Washington, D.C., to his editor, Delane. "As far as I can make out, there is no one with any faith in anything stronger than the march of events. Every man is an atom in a gale."

So, not a moment too soon, Russell packed his bags and began his first reporting trip. His first stop was Washington, the capital, with Abraham Lincoln, newly elected, in the White House, the nation's attention riveted on Charleston's Fort Sumter, still flying the national emblem but hemmed in now by shore batteries manned by fledgling soldiers intent on forming a new government.

Russell was such a celebrity that doors closed to most reporters swiftly opened to him. The very first night in Washington, he had dinner with Secretary of State William H. Seward. As the representative of the *Times*, Russell was important to Union interests. Seward desperately wanted Russell to relay to Europe assurances that the Federal government would weather the secessionist storm. He admitted to Russell that Regular Army and Navy officers were resigning their commissions "en masse" to sign on with the growing resistance in the South. But it would all blow over, Seward insisted. What Seward feared most, of course, was that Britain and the other leading powers in Europe might misinterpret events and recognize the rebel government already being set up in Montgomery, Alabama.

The talks must have gone well, for the next day Seward introduced Russell to President Lincoln. The meeting took place in a small room at the State Department.

The Civil War was the first in history in which photographs played a prominent role. But newspapers during the war couldn't publish those photographs, because the photoengraving process hadn't yet been perfected. So reporters took great care in describing famous men. Russell stretched his descriptive skills in painting this picture of Abraham Lincoln:

> Soon, there entered, with a shambling, loose, irregular, almost unsteady gait, a tall, lank, lean man, considerably over six feet in height, with stooping shoulders, long pendulous arms, terminating in hands of extraordinary dimensions, which, however, were far exceeded in proportion by his feet. He was dressed in an ill-fitting, wrinkled suit of black, which put one in mind of an undertaker's uniform at a funeral; round his neck a rope of black silk was knotted in a large bulb, with flying ends projecting beyond the collar of his coat; his turned-down shirt-collar disclosed a sinewy, muscular, yellow neck, and, above that, nestling in the great black mass of hair, bristling and compact like a ruff of mourning pins, rose the strange, quaint face and head, covered with its thatch of wild republican hair, of President Lincoln.

Russell liked what he saw. There was an "expression of kindliness" and "sagacity" to the man, with the eyes "dark, full, and deeply penetrating, . . . full of an expression which almost amounts to tenderness."

Seward took Russell by the hand and introduced him to the president. Lincoln put out his hand in a very friendly manner, and said, "Mr. Russell, I am very glad to make your acquaintance, and to see you in this country. The London Times is one of the greatest powers in the world; in fact, I don't know anything which has more power, except perhaps the Mississippi. I am glad to know you as its minister."

Russell was a keen observer and a good judge of character. The first time he met him, Russell saw a Lincoln that many Americans and most Englishmen refused to recognize. He saw in Abraham Lincoln a man who might one day really amount to something. "I left agreeably impressed with his shrewdness, humour, and natural sagacity," he wrote.

He failed, though, to persuade his own editors in London. They never understood Lincoln, and, in time, came to see him as a tyrant. It was all part of their campaign to vilify the North and defend the South. "Is Lincoln yet a name not known to us as it will be known to posterity, and is it ultimately to be classed among that catalogue of monsters, the wholesale assassins and butchers of the world?" the *Times* asked, in one of its most ill-tempered leaders. Russell, from the first moment he met Lincoln, knew better.

Russell stayed at Willard's Hotel in Washington—Willard's Menagerie, he called it. It was "a great pile, . . . a quadrangular mass of rooms, six stories high, and some hundred yards square; and it probably contains at this moment more scheming, plotting, planning heads than any building of the same size ever held in the world." These, of course, were Lincoln supporters—or men who said they were Lincoln supporters—looking for jobs in the new administration. "Place-hunters," Russell called them. The hotel served meals to twenty-five hundred guests every day. Russell said he overheard one of them order a breakfast that consisted of black tea and toast, scrambled eggs, fresh spring shad, wild pigeon, pigs' feet, two robins on toast, oysters, and a quantity of breads and cakes of various denominations. The hotel, Russell noted, was liberally provided with spittoons, but most of the guests didn't bother to use them.

It was, of course, just the kind of place that caused Delane and so many well-bred Englishmen to shudder. Vulgar, it surely was.

Russell met with a number of Southern sympathizers, including the Southern commissioners trying without much enthusiasm to end the crisis. Russell's biographer, John Black Atkins, said these Southerners emphasized again and again the differences between North and South. "The Southerners," Atkins wrote,

> spoke of the Federals rather in the manner that English country gentlemen might speak of prosperous manufacturers. They talked of Lincoln with contempt; they regarded Seward as the ablest but also as the most unscrupulous of their enemies; and the tone in which they alluded to all the Northern people betrayed their conviction that the pursuit of the mechanical arts had so demoralised them that they would not really fight for what they professed to prize.

Russell, during these early weeks in America, was impressed with the depth of the Southerners' distaste, amounting to hatred, of the North. He wrote:

> Whether it be in consequence of some secret influence which slavery has upon the minds of men, or that the aggression of the North upon their institutions has been of a nature to excite the deepest animosity and most vindictive hate, certain it is that there is a degree of something like ferocity in the Southern mind towards New England which exceeds belief.

Most educated Englishmen—surely the ones who came to America to observe the war—sensed that the South was more familiar terrain, peopled by gentlemen and gentlewomen. That foreign strain that Russell had observed when he landed in New York—all those Germans and Irishmen—was a Northern phenomenon, they fervently believed. This, of course, was nonsense. The major cities in the South, New Orleans being the largest, teemed with foreigners, too, and many of them found their way into the Confederate army.

Russell, still confused by all the babble, set off for the rebellious states on April 13, boarding the steamer *Georgianna* at Baltimore, en route to Norfolk, Virginia. "Late for the fair," he admitted in a letter to the *Times'* New York correspondent, J. C. Bancroft Davis (soon to be replaced for his pro-Union views). The Confederates, he had learned, had opened fire on Fort Sumter the day before. "The news [that Sumter had been fired upon] will be a great blow to

Seward and the people at Washington unless they are consummate hypocrites," he told Davis, in what seems to be a striking example of British understatement. Sumter surrendered the day after Russell set sail for Norfolk.

After a terrible night of "disturbed sleep, owing to the ponderous thumping of the walking beam [engine] close to my head, the whizzing of steam, and the roaring of the steam-trumpet to warn vessels out of the way—mosquitoes, too, had a good deal to say to me in spite of my dirty gauze curtains," Russell and the *Georgianna* ran alongside the jetty at Fortress Monroe. The fortress was a great Federal bastion, and it would remain so throughout the war. "The place looked dreary and desolate," Russell said in his published diary. "A few soldiers were lounging on the jetty, and after we had discharged a tipsy old officer, a few Negroes, and some parcels, the steam-pipe brayed—it does not whistle—again, and we proceeded across the mouth of the channel and James river towards Elizabeth river, on which stand Portsmouth and Gosport." The *Georgianna* pulled up at a

> dirty, broken-down quay, on which a small crowd, mostly of Negroes, had gathered. Behind the shed there rose tiled and shingled roofs of mean dingy houses, and we could catch glimpses of the line of poor streets, narrow, crooked, ill-paved, surmounted by a few church steeples, and the large sprawling advertisement-boards of the tobacco stores and oyster-sellers . . .
>
> An execrable, tooth-cracking drive ended at last in front of the Atlantic Hotel, where I was doomed to take up my quarters. It is a dilapidated, uncleanly place, with tobacco-stained floor, full of flies and strong odours. The waiters were all slaves; untidy, slipshod, and careless creatures. I was shut up in a small room, with the usual notice on the door that the proprietor would not be responsible for anything, and that you were to lock your door for fear of robbers . . .

After an unsatisfactory supper, Russell ventured into the streets. There, for the first time, he encountered a reasonable cross section of the populace that would support the Confederate cause and serve in its armies. "The people, I observe, are of a new and marked type, very tall, loosely yet powerfully made, with dark complexions, strongly-marked features, prominent noses, large angular mouths in square jaws, deep-seated bright eyes, low, narrow foreheads,—and all of them much given to ruminate tobacco."

From Norfolk, Russell pushed on by train to Goldsboro, in North Carolina. Now, at last, he was deep inside rebel territory, and he didn't think much of it. "[Three] N.C. hogs to make a shadow," he wrote in his diary. "N.C. here is most miserable, but people at [train] stations are wondrous respectable. The poor whites here are rabid to have a class below them, ergo they are all for slaves."

In Wilmington, North Carolina, he tried to send a telegram to Bancroft Davis in New York, but members of the town's Vigilance Committee "would not permit my telegraph to go. They were all drunk. I refused to see them." He set off for Charleston the morning of the sixteenth, arriving at the Mills House late that night. "Get a decent dinner late at night in hotel and am introduced to Governor [John Laurence] Manning and [former] Senator [James] Chesnut," husband of Mary Chesnut, author of the most celebrated of all Civil War diaries. Even later that night, he called on Brigadier General Pierre Gustave Toutant Beauregard, the Louisiana Creole and commander of the Confederate forces at Charleston. Beauregard cautioned Russell not to expect to find "regular soldiers in our camps, or very scientific works."

The next morning, he boarded a tug steamer with a number of local dignitaries and a reporter named "De Fontaine of some N.Y. paper." The reporter was Felix Gregory de Fontaine, still working for the *New York Herald* but soon to switch sides and join the staff of the *Charleston Daily Courier.*

Their first stop was Morris Island and its Confederate batteries. The soldiers

> wore the universal coarse gray jacket and trousers, with worsted braid and yellow facings, uncouth caps, lead buttons stamped with the palmetto tree. Their unbronzed firelocks were covered with rust. The soldiers lounging about were mostly tall, well-grown men, young and old, some with the air of gentlemen; others coarse, long-haired fellows, without any semblance of military bearing, and burning with enthusiasm, not unaided, in some instances, by coarse stimulus.

It was like a beach party.

Officers were galloping about as if on field day or in action. Commissariat carts were toiling to and fro between the beach and the camps, and the sounds of laughter and revelling came from their tents. These were pitched without order . . . many being disfigured by rude charcoal drawings outside, and inscriptions such as "the Live Tigers," "Rattlesnake's Hole," "Yankee Smashers," etc.

In every tent was hospitality, and a hearty welcome to all comers. Cases of champagne and claret, French *pates*, and the like, were piled outside the canvas walls, when there was no room for them inside.

Russell and his party returned to their tug and sailed for Fort Sumter. Russell took the standard tour and concluded the damage done to the installation by the Confederate gunners was "trifling."

In his letters to London, Russell repeated most of these stories and hit hard upon his belief that "nothing on earth will induce the people [of the secessionist South] to return to the Union. I firmly believe their present intention is to march on Washington." So wide was the breach between North and South, he concluded, "that the Union can never be restored as it was."

In one of his letters from Charleston—the second—he raised the intriguing idea that these Confederates might want to become subjects of the British Crown again. Failing that, perhaps a British prince could be recruited to rule the new nation. "The admiration for British monarchical institutions on the English model, for priveleged classes, and for a landed aristocracy and gentry is undisguised and apparently genuine," Russell wrote.

Russell couldn't help himself; he liked gentlemen, and these South Carolina planters were obviously gentlemen—"well-bred, courteous, and hospitable. A genuine aristocracy, they have time to cultivate their minds. . . . They travel and read, love field sports, shooting, hunting and fishing, are bold horsemen, and good shots."

But, said Russell—and a big but it was—"Their state is a modern Sparta—an aristocracy resting on a helotry, and with nothing else to rest upon."

Russell had spent too much time talking to these rich planters. In fact, most Southerners were republicans, and would remain so. When they read his letters, these South Carolinians were puzzled by his talk of a Confederate monarchy. Writing in the *Southern Illustrated News*, Constance Cary called Russell "snobbish," and she was an aristocratic Virginian. And as for Russell's views on the institution of slavery, Southerners were at first alarmed, and then outraged.

Russell's next stop was Montgomery, the Confederate capital. On his way to listen to a debate at the capitol, he witnessed his first slave auction, being held right outside his hotel. In a letter dated May 6, published in the *Times* on May 30, he described faithfully what he saw and heard:

On leaving the hotel, which is like a small Willard's . . . my attention was attracted to a group of people to whom a man was holding forth in energetic sentences. The day was hot, but I pushed next to the spot, for I like to hear a stump speech or to pick up a stray morsel of divinity . . . in strange cities. Three or four men in rough, homespun, makeshift uniforms leant against the iron rails enclosing a small pond of foul, green-looking water, surrounded by brickwork which decorates the front of the Exchange Hotel.

The speaker stood on an empty deal packing-case. A man in a cart was listening with a lackluster eye to the address. Some three or four others, in a sort of vehicle which might either be a hearse or a piano van, had also drawn up for the benefit of the address. Five or six men in long black coats and high hats, some whittling sticks, and chewing tobacco, and discharging streams of discolored saliva, completed the group.

"N-ine h-hun-nerd and fifty dollars! Only nine h-hun-nerd and fifty dollars offered for him," explained the man in the tone of injured dignity, remonstrance, and surprise. . . . A man near me opened his mouth, spat, and said, "Twenty-five." "Only nine hunnerd and seventy-five dollars offered for him. Why, at's radakolous— only nine hunnerd and seventy-five dollars offered for him."

Beside the orator auctioneer stood a stout young man of five-and-twenty years of age, with a bundle in his hand. He was a muscular fellow, broad-shouldered, narrow-flanked, but rather short in stature. He had on a broad, greasy, old wideawake [a hat with a low crown and wide brim], a blue jacket, a coarse cotton shirt, and rather ragged trousers and broken shoes. The expression on his face was heavy and sad, but it was by no means disagreeable, in spite of his thick lips, and high cheek-bones.

I am neither sentimentalist, nor Black Republican, nor negro worshipper, but I confess the sight caused a strange thrill through my heart. I tried in vain to make myself familiar with the fact that I could, for the sum of $975, become as absolutely the owner of that mass of blood, bones, sinew, flesh, and brains as of the horse which stood by my side. There was no sophistry which could persuade me that the man was not a man—he was, indeed, by no means my brother, but assuredly he was a fellow-creature.

Later in the day, returning to his hotel, Russell encountered another slave auction. This time, the auctioneer, "a fat, flabby, perspiring, puffy man," was trying to sell a Negro girl. "She, too, had a little bundle in her hand and she looked out at the buyers from a pair of large, sad eyes."

The asking price was $610—"niggers were going cheap," Russell was told. But no one would bid. "Not sold today, Sally, you may get down," the auctioneer said.

Curiously, the story that appeared in the *Times* on May 30 is much more compelling than the account he wrote later in his book. Either way, it was—and still is—powerful stuff. When Southerners read it weeks later, they felt Russell had betrayed their hospitality.

The next day, Russell called on Jefferson Davis, the new president of the Confederate States of America. "He did not impress me as favorably as I had expected," Russell wrote, "though he is certainly a very different man from Mr. Lincoln. He is like a gentleman—has a slight, light figure, little exceeding middle height, and holds himself erect and straight. . . . His manner is plain, and rather reserved and drastic . . . The expression of his face is anxious, he has a very haggard, care-worn, and pain-drawn look." (Mrs. Davis, on the other hand, was "a comely, sprightly woman, verging on matronhood, of good figure and manners, well-dressed, lady-like, and clever. . . . Some of her friends call her 'Queen Varina.'")

Davis urged Russell to remember that Southerners "are not less military because we have no great standing armies. But perhaps we are the only people in the world where gentlemen go to a military academy, who do not intend to follow the profession of arms."

During his stay in Montgomery, Russell was befriended by an extraordinary Southern figure, "Colonel" Louis T. Wigfall, formerly a U.S. senator from Texas. During the bombardment of Fort Sumter, Wigfall and a Negro oarsman made their way to the fort in a small rowboat. Wigfall actually landed on the quay, a white handkerchief flying from the end of his sword, and demanded Sumter's surrender. Wigfall, having paid his respects "to Bacchus or Bourbon, for he was decidedly unsteady in his gait and in his speech," cornered Russell to make sure he knew all the details about his exploit.

A day or two later, when he appeared to be sober, Wigfall tried to explain to Russell the true meaning of the South:

> We are a peculiar people, sir! We are an agriculture people; we are a primitive but a civilised people. We have no cities—we don't want them. We have no literature—we don't need any yet. We have no press—we are glad of it. We have no commercial marine—no navy—we don't want them. We are better without them. Your ships carry our produce and you can protect your own vessels. We want no manufactures; we desire no trading, no mechanical or manufacturing classes. As long as we have our cotton, our rice, our sugar, our tobacco, we can command wealth to purchase all we want from those nations with which we are in amity.

It was a common belief, with Wigfall and many prominent Confederates, that Britain would be forced to come to the aid of the Confederacy simply to keep her textile mills running.

Punch put it this way on March 30, 1861:

> Though with the North we sympathize
>   It must not be forgotten
> That with the South we've stronger ties
>   Which are composed of cotton.

A month later, on April 29, a *Times* leader warned "that civil war in the United States means destitution in Lancashire."

In a letter to Lord Lyons, head of the British delegation in Washington, dated May 21, Russell predicted that Britain and France would allow the Union to go ahead with a blockade of Southern seaports, thus depriving those Lancashire mills of their cotton as well as depriving the Confederacy of the means to wage a protracted war. He said Southern ideas of "political economy are enough to drive the venerable A. Smith out of his quiet resting place with a fresh ed(ition) of the Wealth of Nations in his claw!"

Russell enjoyed good food, fine wine, lively companions, and a comfortable bed. The Mills House in Charleston had been passable, but he was not happy with his accommodations in either Portsmouth or Montgomery. "If the South secedes," he wrote, "they ought certainly to take over with them some Yankee hotel keepers. This 'Exchange' is in a frightful state—nothing but noise, dirt, drinking, wrangling." He was delighted to leave the Confederate capital (soon to be moved to Richmond) on May 10.

His means of conveyance was a steamer called the *Southern Republic*. Russell was not without a sense of humor, and this giant steamship struck him as wonderfully amusing. She was "three towering stories high . . . a colossal ark," owned and skippered by a rogue Irishman named Meagher. In departing, Russell said, "the short puff of the engine is enlivened by the wild strains of a steam-organ called a calliope, which gladdens us with the assurance that we are in the incomparable 'land of Dixie.'"

Negroes, he said, were restricted to "the lower floor, a Hades consecrated to machinery and freight." First-class passengers lounged on a roofed balcony "from which a party of excited secessionists are discharging revolvers at the dippers on the surface and the cranes on the bank of the [Alabama] river."

The voyage from Montgomery to Mobile, Alabama, covered more than four hundred miles, and the *Southern Republic*, the most amazing ship Russell had ever seen, made it in thirty-five hours.

In Mobile, Russell hired a small schooner and paid a visit to a blockading Federal warship, the *Powhatan*. Here, for the first time, he saw professional fighting men, the sailors from the regular U.S. Navy, whose role in winning the war for the Union is often undervalued. "Her crew," he wrote in a letter to the *Times* dated May 18, "are as fine a set of men as ever I have seen of late days on board a man of war. They are healthy, well fed, regularly paid, and can be relied on to do their duty to a man."

He saw more Confederate troops, too, and, waking up one morning, thought he was back in the Crimea. "For close at hand . . . came the well-known *reveille* of the Zouaves, and then French clangours, rolls, ruffles, and calls ran along the line." Breakfast one morning was impressive—"fried onions, ham, eggs, biscuit, with accompaniments of iced water, Bordeaux, and coffee."

Russell had arrived now on the Gulf Coast, and these cities—Mobile, Pensacola, Florida, and especially New Orleans—were extraordinarily cosmopolitan. According to the 1860 census, Mobile's foreign-born population was 7,061, out of a total of 29,258. The same census showed that New Orleans, by far the South's largest city, had an immigrant population of 64,621, mostly Irish, German, and French, out of a total population of 168,675. Russell was one of a handful of commentators on the Civil War to take note of the diversity among the urban white population in the Confederacy.

Russell arrived in New Orleans on May 21, early in the morning. "There is an air of French civilization about New Orleans," he wrote in a letter dated the day of his arrival. "The shops are 'magasins;' cafes abound. The pavements are crowded with men in uniform, in which the taste of France is generally followed."

He visited slave quarters whenever he had a chance, and by now he was in a perfect rage about what he was observing. In his published diary, he said many of the gentlemen he had met "indulge in ingenious hypotheses to comfort the(ir) consciences. . . ." And then he became bitterly sarcastic:

The negro skull won't hold as many ounces of shot as a white man's. Potent proof that the white man has a right to sell and to own the creature! He is plantigrade [walking on the soles of his feet], and curved as to the tibia! . . . Surely he cannot have a soul of the same colour as that of an Italian or a Spaniard, far less of a flaxen-haired Saxon! See these peculiarities in the frontal sinus—in sinciput or occiput! Can you doubt that the being with a head of that shape was made only to till, hoe, and dig for another race?

Russell was now certain how he felt about slavery—he despised it—but he was never quite sure what to make of American troops, North or South. Beauregard had told him that it was still early days and that he shouldn't expect the soldiers or their fortifications to measure up to European standards. Just wait, Beauregard had suggested, for these soldiers one day will be the wonder of the world. Russell was still not convinced. In the letter from New Orleans dated May 21, he said he had not yet seen Confederate troops "moving together with regard to their capacity for organized movements such as regular troops in Europe are expected to perform." Russell was surprised that the tents put up by the Confederate troops sometimes follow "individual or company caprice."

What, after all, was a veteran war correspondent to make of the "Perret Guards"? "Here," Russell said, in astonishment, after visiting their encampment, "was a company of *professional* gamblers, 112 strong, recruited for the war in a moment of banter by one of the patriarchs of the fraternity."

It was now early June and Russell was beginning to run out of steam. From New Orleans he traveled up the Mississippi, stopping to visit a plantation owned by former Louisiana governor Alfred Roman. Once again he visited the slave quarters, and this time he expressed his distaste for what he saw at great length in a letter to the *Times* dated June 14. By now, he was beginning to repeat himself.

"I have at last got out of the land of Dixie & whiskey, & am speeding on towards Washington," he wrote his colleague, Bancroft Davis, from Cairo, Illinois, on June 22. He had finally begun to realize the impact his letters were making, North and South. "I am told I am very unpopular with the North & in New York. I can't help it. I must write as I feel & see & I believe I may have the consolation accorded to the impartial of finding myself still more unpopular in the South. I would not retract a line or word of my first letters on the cross."

2

Bull Run from the Rear

RUSSELL LEFT CAIRO for Chicago aboard the passenger cars of the Central Illinois Railroad on June 23. "The latest information which I received today is of a nature to hasten my departure for Washington; it can no longer be doubted that a battle between the two armies assembled in the neighborhood of the capital is imminent," he wrote in his diary.

It wasn't until July 3, though—the first great battle, Bull Run, was only eighteen days away—that he finally arrived in the capital. "Nearly four months since I went by this road to Washington," he wrote in his published diary. "The change which has since occurred is beyond belief. Men were then speaking of place [a job] under government, of compromises between North and South, and of peace; now they only talk of war and battle."

During his train journey through the North, Russell had seen for the first time Union volunteers, and he was struck by how different they seemed from the Confederate volunteers he had observed in his swing through the South. "These [Union] volunteers have none of the swashbuckler bravado, gallant-swaggering air of the Southern men," he noted. "They are staid, quiet men, and the Pennsylvanians, who are on their way to join their regiment in Baltimore, are very inferior in size and strength to the Tennesseans and Carolinians."

On July 5, Russell dropped by the unfinished Capitol, noting that the stairways were slippery with tobacco juice. He said the messengers

19

and the doormen wore "no distinctive badge or dress" the way they did at Westminster and the senators looked like "bakers or millers" in their slop coats and wideawake caps. Members of the House of Representatives were even less impressive.

On the thirteenth, he toured the camps of the gathering Union army, and blanched at what he saw. "In the first place," he wrote in his published diary,

> there are not, I should think, 30,000 men of all sorts available for the campaign. . . . In the next place, their artillery is miserably deficient . . . and provided with the worst set of gunners and drivers which I, who have seen the Turkish field guns, ever beheld. They have no cavalry, only a few scarecrow-men . . . and some few regulars from the frontiers, who may be good for Indians, but who would go over like tenpins at a charge from Punjaubee regulars.

This was a grumpy and dyspeptic Russell. Why he would have expected anything else from these raw troops, most of them recruited for just ninety days' service, is hard to fathom. At the outbreak of the war, the Regular U.S. Army numbered 1,000 officers and 16,000 men, and most of them were posted at forts in Indian territory. By the time the war was over, almost 3 million men would have answered the call to arms—850,000 in Confederate gray and more than 2 million in Union blue. And that little cadre of regular officers would have produced the likes of Lee, Jackson, and Stuart on one side and Grant, Sheridan, and Sherman on the other. July of 1861 was the beginning, and of course it was amateur war making for both armies.

By the sixteenth—battle was now just five days away—Russell was still trying to find transportation to the front. He needed a horse. "Something over 15 hands not *white*—strong forelegs particularly up to 15 ½ stone, a good walker."

In a letter to Delane, also dated July 16, Russell said he was anticipating a return to the field—for anything would be better "than the infernal pandemonium . . . of excitement" in the capital. Russell was showing signs of serious stress.

Nothing angered him more than U.S. newspapers; he believed they were partly responsible for the chaos. "The Indian press is really respectable journalism compared to the section of the New York papers which are generally quoted in England, & I find that no one of any note in society attaches the least importance to the opinions or leaders of such a paper as the N.Y. Herald, for example, tho' they read it for the news."

Tho' they read it for the news. What an extraordinary throwaway line. That's precisely why Americans did read James Gordon Bennett's newspaper, for he was the first editor anywhere who cared only for delivering the news as fast as he could print it (and making a fat profit in the process).

Early on the morning of the seventeenth, Russell dropped by the quarters of the Union generalissimo, the aging three-hundred-pound hero of the Mexican War, Winfield Scott, and learned that Scott's field commander, Brigadier General Irvin McDowell, would move his 35,000-man Army of Northeastern Virginia, ready or not, against General Beauregard's 21,600-man Army of the Potomac, dug in near a railroad junction called Manassas, near a stream called Bull Run, the next day.

Russell was disappointed in the Union headquarters.

> I look around me for a staff, and look in vain. There are a few plod-
> ding old pedants, with map and rules and compasses, who sit in
> small rooms and write memoranda; and there are some ignorant and
> not very active young men, who loiter about the headquarters' halls,
> and strut up the street with brass spurs on their heels and kepis
> raked over their eyes as if they were soldiers, but I see no system,
> no order, no knowledge, no dash!

But Russell's criticism of the Union command could also be made of himself; he had no system, no knowledge, and no dash in making his own preparations for covering the battle. He still hadn't bought a horse—or a tent or a blanket. To top things off, his watch wasn't working. Late on the seventeenth, a local citizen offered him a dark bay, "spavined and ringboned," for $1,000. He tried again the next day, the eighteenth, without success.

> Every carriage, gig, wagon, and hack has been engaged by people
> going out to see the fight. The price is enhanced by mysterious
> communications respecting the horrible slaughter in the skirmishes

at Bull's Run. The French cooks and hotel-keepers, by some occult process of reasoning, have arrived at the conclusion that they must treble the prices of their wines and of the hampers of provisions which the Washington people are ordering to comfort themselves at their bloody Derby.

Late on the twentieth, the day before the battle, Russell finally secured the services of what he called a "hooded gig, or tilbury," drawn by two horses. The carriage was followed by a single "charger" on which a young Negro boy sat with difficulty. Accompanying Russell in the gig was the second secretary at the British legation, Frederick Richard Warre, a languorous gentleman who was two hours late in meeting the dawn deadline for their departure to the front.

The delay meant that Russell, the most experienced war correspondent in the field that day, would miss all of the fighting.

He told the story of what he did see in a long dispatch that appeared in the *Times* on August 6. When copies of that day's paper made their way back by steamer to the North, Union patriots exploded in indignation. No dispatch written by anyone during the Civil War ever caused such an unholy ruckus.

There was no question of Russell pulling his punches. He began his story this way:

> I sit down to give an account . . . of what I saw with my own eyes, hitherto not often deceived, and of what I heard with my own ears, which in this country are not so much to be trusted. Let me, however, express an opinion as to the affair of yesterday. In the first place, the repulse of the Federalists, decided as it was, might have had no serious effects whatever beyond the mere failure—which politically was of greater consequence than it was in the military sense—but for the disgraceful conduct of the troops. The retreat on their lines at Centreville seems to have ended in a cowardly route— a miserable, causeless panic. Such scandalous behaviour on the part of soldiers I should have considered impossible, as with some experience of camps and armies I have never even in alarms among camp followers seen the like of it.

Russell had talked at some length to General Scott, and he must have known about the old man's reluctance to attack Beauregard's army in northern Virginia. Scott knew—just as Russell knew—that the Union army wasn't ready to fight. But politics demanded it, fed in no small degree by an hysterical standing headline in Horace Greeley's *New York Tribune.*

FORWARD TO RICHMOND! FORWARD TO RICHMOND!

The Rebel Congress Must Not be
Allowed to Meet There on the
20th of July

By That Date the Place Must Be Held
By the National Army

Russell liked the Union field commander; they had become friends. But nowhere in his dispatch does Russell indicate what McDowell was trying to accomplish at Manassas. Simply put, McDowell planned an attack against Beauregard's left flank. The flanking Union column, two divisions numbering about 10,000 men commanded by Colonels David Hunter and Samuel P. Heintzelman, was supposed to cross Bull Run at Sudley Springs Ford while the rest of the army, under Brigadier General Daniel Tyler, made a diversionary attack at the Stone Bridge, where the Warrenton Pike crossed Bull Run.

McDowell's design presumed that sixty-nine-year-old Brigadier General Robert Patterson (like Scott, a veteran of the War of 1812) with his 18,000-man Army of Pennsylvania could keep General Joseph Johnston's 11,700-man Army of the Shenandoah pinned down near Harper's Ferry, Virginia. Johnston, however, eluded Patterson's feeble efforts and brought his troops to Manassas in railway cars in time to join Beauregard and even the odds.

Russell wasn't there to see any of it, but the Federal attack—signaled by the firing of a Parrott 30-pounder rifle at 5:30 A.M.—got off to a surprisingly good start. After crossing Bull Run, in a move that surprised the Confederate commanders, the Yankees chased forty-five hundred Confederate troops up Matthews Hill. Like the Union troops later in the day, thousands of green Confederates fled in panic. But help was on the way. Tyler's diversionary attack near the Stone Bridge hadn't fooled Confederate colonel Nathan G. Evans. He posted a small guard at the bridge and moved the rest of his

THE BULL'S RUN BATTLEFIELD.

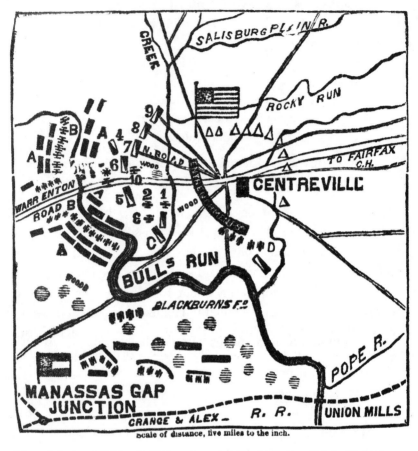

Map of the battlefield at Bull Run, from the *New York Herald*, July 25, 1861. (Clements Library, University of Michigan)

undermanned brigade to meet the advancing Union troops. Brigades commanded by Brigadier General Barnard Bee and Colonel Francis Bartow rushed to Matthews Hill, too, but it still wasn't enough. The Union line, reinforced by brigades under Colonels William T. Sherman and Erasmus Keyes, rolled back the Confederate line. A little-known Virginia commander named Thomas Jonathan Jackson held firm. Bee shouted to his retreating troops: "There is Jackson standing like a stone wall! Rally behind the Virginians!" Or maybe, some say, he was upset that Jackson wasn't moving out to help him and said, "Look at Jackson standing there like a damned stone wall!" It doesn't make much difference. Bee was mortally wounded and Jackson went on to glory, known forever as Stonewall.

It was now almost noon, and there were about two dozen reporters representing Northern newspapers scattered over the battlefield, including Charles Carleton Coffin, Henry Villard, and Uriah Painter, who would make their mark in the months and years ahead. A handful of reporters, maybe only half a dozen, represented Southern papers on the battlefield, but they included Peter W. Alexander of the *Savannah Republican* and Felix Gregory de Fontaine, working for both the *Charleston Courier* and the *Richmond Enquirer.*

Russell, in his ridiculous gig, was struggling to get to the scene of the fighting. He first heard the sound of the guns about 9:30 A.M., though he couldn't be sure of the time because his watch still wasn't working. "It [the gunfire] never ceased all day," he wrote in his infamous dispatch. Sometimes, he said, it was hard to hear the guns over the "the rattle of the gig."

In his published diary, which often elaborates on his August 6 story, Russell described the reactions of the black boy on the charger to the sounds of gunfire. "With eyes starting out of his head, [he] cried, 'I hear them, Massa; I hear them, sure enough, like de gun in de Navy Yard.' " Russell was not alone among Civil War correspondents in using dialect, and much of the time the quotations have a manufactured look about them. Russell, at least, was eclectic; he quoted Americans with German and Irish roots in questionable dialect, too.

Russell's companion, the lethargic Frederick Richard Warre from the British delegation, also stirred at the sound of the guns. "Are we really seeing a battle now?" he asked. "Are they supposed to be fighting where all that smoke is going on? This is rather interesting, you know."

A few minutes after hearing the first sounds of gunfire, Russell observed a large body of men moving toward him, away from the battlefield.

> It soon appeared that there was no less than an entire regiment marching away, singly or in small knots of two or three, extending for some three or four miles along the road. . . . I asked an officer,

"Where are your men going, Sir?" "Well, we're going home, Sir, I reckon, to Pennsylvania." It was the 4th Pennsylvania Regiment. . . . "We're going home . . . because the men's time is up. We have had three months of this work." I proceeded on my way, ruminating on the feelings of a General who sees half a brigade walk quietly away on the very morning of an action . . . because the letter of their engagement allowed them to go no further.

Russell and his companions had traveled some twenty-six or twenty-seven miles, and Russell figured it was time to stop for a rest. "In the midst of our little reconnaissance," another Englishman, Frank Vizetelly, an artist-correspondent for the *Illustrated London News* (we will meet him later, covering the Confederates), came thundering up on his horse to report that the action "had been commenced in splendid style by the Federalists." Vizetelly joined Russell and Warre for a sandwich feast in the shade of the buggy.

After polishing off his share of the sandwiches, Russell abandoned the buggy and mounted his black charger. With Vizetelly at his side, he galloped toward the sound of the guns.

Suddenly up rode an officer, with a crowd of soldiers after him . . . "We've whipped them on all points," he shouted. "We've taken their batteries, and they're all retreating!" . . . Such an uproar as followed. The spectators and the men cheered again and again, amid cries of "Bravo!" "Bully for us!" "Didn't I tell you so?" and gutteral "hochs" from the Deutschland folk and "hurroos" from the Irish.

This, of course, was the noontime high point of the day for the Union army. Russell didn't know it—he would never actually know firsthand any of the details of the battle—but as he was taking time for his sandwiches the Union commanders were ordering an hour's pause to reorganize their troops. That was enough to allow the Confederates, now personally commanded by both Beauregard and Johnston, to pull themselves together. The Confederates reformed their lines on Henry Hill, and fighting resumed there at 1 P.M.—both sides weaving back and forth—and lasted until about 4 P.M., when the exhausted Union troops gave way and began what was at first an organized withdrawal, stiffened temporarily by the disciplined behavior of

1,200 Union regulars and a detachment of 350 marines from the Washington Navy Yard.

Russell saw a new set of wagons and horses coming away from the battlefield, "endeavouring to force their way against the stream of vehicles setting in the opposite direction," he wrote in his dispatch. It was the beginning of the panic-stricken retreat. He continued:

> They looked excited and alarmed, and were running by the side of the horses—in front the dust quite obscured the view. At the bridge the currents met in wild disorder. "Turn back!" "Retreat!" shouted the men from the front. "We're whipped! we're whipped!" They cursed and tugged at the horses' heads, and struggled with frenzy to get past. Running by me on foot was a man with the shoulder-straps of an officer. "Pray, what is the matter, Sir?" "It means we're pretty badly whipped, and that's a fact," he blurted out in puffs, and continued his career. I observed that he carried no sword.
>
> The teamsters of the advancing wagons now caught up the cry. "Turn back—turn your horses" was the shout up the whole line, and, backing, plunging, rearing, and kicking, the horses which had been proceeding down the road reversed front and went off towards Centreville. . . . Still, there was no flight of troops, no retreat of an army, no reason for this precipitation.

But as Russell got closer to the front, the full dimensions of the rout became more and more evident.

> Soon I met soldiers who were coming through the corn, mostly without arms, and presently I saw firelocks, knapsacks, and great-coats on the ground, and observed that the confusion and speed of the baggage-carts became greater, and that many of them were crowded with men, or were followed by others, who clung to them. The ambulances were crowded with soldiers, but it did not look as if there were many wounded. Negro servants on led horses dashed frantically past; men in uniform, whom it were a disgrace to the profession of arms to call "soldiers," swarmed by on mules, chargers, and even draught horses. . . . Men literally screamed with fright when their way was blocked up . . .

But Russell, the old veteran, remained cool. "But where was the fiend? I looked in vain . . . [for] the firing was comparatively distant."

It was now late in the day on Sunday, and Russell began worrying about meeting his deadline. He needed to get his dispatch aboard a steamer that left Washington at 2:30 Monday to meet a transatlantic steamer that sailed from Boston on Wednesday. So he turned his horse around and headed back to join his companions and their trusty gig. But there was nothing to be seen of any of them. They had already begun the journey home. Russell took the same path.

Carts were rattling past him, and contents were spilling out of them on the road. "'Stop,' cried I to the driver of one of the carts, 'everything is falling out.' '— you,' shouted a fellow inside, 'if you stop him [the driver], I'll blow your brains out'. . . . My attempts to save Uncle Sam's property were then and there discontinued."

The stampede, Russell wrote, now became general.

"'What are you afraid of?' said I to a man who was running beside me. 'I'm not afraid of you,' replied the ruffian, levelling his piece at me and pulling the trigger. It was not loaded or the cap was not on, and I did go off as fast as I could, resolved to keep my own counsel."

In his diary (but not in his story), Russell said he observed a body of men charging down the road crying out that they were being chased by Confederate cavalry. "I came up with two officers who were riding more leisurely; and touching my hat said, 'I venture to suggest that these men should be stopped, sir. If not, they will alarm the whole of the post and the pickets on to Washington.'" The two officers nodded to Russell, and continued on their way. Watching the scene, Russell said in his diary, were a number of gentlemen in a private carriage, including Henry J. Raymond, founder and editor of the *New York Times*. Russell said they were looking "by no means happy."

Russell joined the retreating mass until he came to some pickets guarding the road leading to the Long Bridge over the Potomac into Washington itself. He described the scene:

A musket was levelled at my head. . . . "Stop, or I'll fire." At the same time the officers were shouting out, "Don't let a soul past." I addressed one of them and said, "Sir, I am a British subject. I am not, I assure you, running away. I have done my best to stop this disgraceful rout (as I had) and have been telling them there are no cavalry within miles of them."

Russell eventually talked his way past the pickets, crossed the bridge, and returned to his quarters (now located in shabby rooms above a wine store run by an unfriendly Swiss couple). There, he wrote his dispatch in time to make the steamer to Boston. He had hoped his story of the retreat would be accompanied by a story about the battle itself (which, of course, he hadn't seen). But Delane ran Russell's story alone. The next day, the *Times* ran an editorial—a leader—mocking the Union army for its incompetence. Russell didn't mean to—for he supported the Union cause—but his Bull Run dispatch encouraged the *Times'* editors in their precipitous switch to the Southern side.

It was more than two weeks later when copies of the *Times* containing Russell's story began arriving in the North. Dozens of newspapers reprinted it, or large sections of it, and the reaction was instantaneous and overwhelming. Readers hated every word. Newspapers nicknamed him, derisively, "Bull-Run Russell," and it stuck. "The terrible epistle has been read with quite as much avidity as an average President's message," the *New York Times* said. "I hear I am the best abused man in America," Russell told a friend.

One day, touring one of the Federal fortifications ringing the capital, a Union soldier with German roots spotted the now-famous correspondent. "Pull-Run Russell!" he shouted. "You shall never write Pull-Runs again." He cocked his rifle and threatened to pull the trigger. The sergeant of the guard intervened, and the soldier with the German accent said it was just a joke.

Russell described his hate mail in a diary entry dated August 23:

> The torrent is swollen to-day by anonymous letters threatening me with bowie-knife and revolver, or simply abusive, frantic with hate, and full of obscure warnings. Some bear the Washington postmark, others come from New York; the greater number—for I have had nine—come from Philadelphia. Perhaps they may come from that "gallant" 4th Pennsylvania Regiment.

Reporters for Northern newspapers wrote stories about the disgraceful retreat (we will hear from them in chapter 3), but only Russell was singled out for such ferocious criticism. Russell never understood why. The likely answer is the tone of the story—the tone, in fact, of many of his stories, North and South. He was patronizing, and thin-skinned Americans on both sides of the dispute resented it.

Russell never comprehended that he was writing for two readerships—one in Britain and one in America—and that words that might be acceptable in London would be resented in New York. Russell's friend, Massachusetts senator Charles Sumner, a leader of the antislavery forces, got it just right. He told Russell: "They [Yankee readers] feel that this is not friendly, that it is *dehaut en bas*, that you write down upon us—and this you can imagine is not pleasant."

Martin Crawford, in his introduction to Russell's private diary and letters, noted that Russell was a

> vain, pompous, even on occasions absurd figure, [but] he was also an affectionate and generous companion, who abhorred the pretensions of others, whether individuals, classes, or nations. In calmer circumstances, perhaps, such independent qualities might have been regarded with some admiration; but in the turbulent atmosphere of civil war America, they were bound to arouse the deepest suspicion.

Russell was no longer welcome, and the leaders in the government and the army who had been so keen to befriend him in March of 1861 had no use for him now. Unable to get a pass to join any of the Union armies, badgered by his editors over his expenses, attacked in the Union newspapers for what appeared to be an ethical lapse (he supposedly gave inside information to a market speculator), he boarded the new Cunard liner, *China*, and sailed for home on April 9, 1862.

3

Bull Run from the Front

MAYBE ONE OF THE REASONS newspaper readers in the North were so unhappy with Russell's patronizing depiction of the panic-stricken retreat at Bull Run was that initially they had been led to believe they had won the battle.

This was the headline in an early edition of the *New York Herald* on Monday, July 22:

A GREAT BATTLE
BRILLIANT UNION VICTORY!

Capture of Bull Run's
Batteries

The Rebels Routed and Driven
Back to Manassas

The Most Sanguinary Battle Ever
Fought in America

One Hundred and Twenty-five
Thousand Men Engaged

The *Boston Journal* ran this headline:

BY TELEGRAPH.
GREAT BATTLE

Near Manassas Junction!

The Enemy Forced to Retire

Three Masked
Batteries
Taken

Desperate Conflict of
Nine Hours

Bravery of the Federal Troops

THE REBELS COMPLETELY ROUTED

How could American newspapers get it so wrong? The key, of course, is that line on top of the *Boston Journal*'s story: "By Telegraph."

"Dot, dash-dash-space-dot-dot-dot-dot-space-dot-dash-space-dash."

"What hath God wrought!"

This was the first message by telegraph on a regular line, sent by Samuel F. B. Morse on May 24, 1844, from the Supreme Court chamber in Washington across forty miles of wire to a railroad depot in Baltimore. It changed communications forever. And it made the American Civil War the first instant-news war in history.

Telegrams in the North during the war moved almost all of the time across the lines of either the Western Union Telegraph Company or the U.S. Military Telegraph. Sometimes it was difficult to tell one from the other, for a very clever man named Anson Stager headed both. By the end of the war, the Union was operating fifteen thousand miles of telegraph lines; the Confederacy, one thousand.

For the reporters, the trick was getting their messages sent by what they all called "the lightning." The army hadn't taken charge of the telegraph lines at the time of the first battle at Bull Run, so it was relatively easy for the reporters to slip their dispatches through. As the war progressed, getting a story on the lightning became tougher and tougher. Reporters frequently were forced to do the next best thing—jump on a train and take the story back to the newsroom in person. Steam engines pulling railway cars was, of course, another technological advance in the Civil War. It allowed both troops—Johnston's Army of the Shenandoah at Bull Run, for example—and journalists to move around in ways no army and no reporter had ever done before.

Because these reporters were so highly competitive, the temptation was to dash off messages before the battle had been fairly won or lost. Bull Run was particularly embarrassing, because at noon on Sunday, July 21, it did appear that the Union army was on its way to a significant victory.

Thus this lead in the *New York Herald* in an unsigned story in an early edition on Monday:

I am en route to Washington with details of a great battle.
We have carried the day.

The same newspaper began its story the next day this way: "Our troops, after taking three batteries and gaining a great victory at Bull's Run, were eventually repulsed, and commenced a retreat on Washington. After the latest information was received from Centreville at half-past seven o'clock last night, a series of unfortunate events took place . . ."

But it was not just that most of the reporters were wrong about the outcome, they were often wrong about the details. One of the headlines screamed about "masked batteries." Masked batteries, indeed. Again and again in these early dispatches, the correspondents quivered with fear of masked—or camouflaged—Confederate batteries, ready to rain fire down on defenseless soldiers and journalists. There were no masked batteries at Bull Run, or anywhere else for that matter. Another headline talked about 125,000 men being engaged. The true number was 68,800, and a third of them never saw action. Other headlines talked of terrible bloodshed—"the most sanguinary battle ever fought in America." In fact, by Civil War standards, the casualties were modest—482 killed and 1,126 wounded on the Union side, 382 killed and 1,565 wounded on the Confederate side.

Long after the war, the man who wrote the best and fullest account of the Bull Run battle, the *New York World*'s Edmund Clarence Stedman, said:

The early correspondents, of whom I was one, knew nothing of military life, tactics, modern warfare. . . . We pioneers were creating the profession of the War Correspondent in America, and this . . . was prentice work. But for synthetic [meaning empirical, or verifiable] quality, topographical comprehension, and as a bit of effective

English narrative, [my story] is not so bad for a greenhorn of twenty-seven.

Reporters on the Confederate side were no better, and probably a little bit worse. They always had a tougher time with censorship and military discipline than their colleagues on the Northern side; they had the added disadvantage of seeing their cities, and presses, overrun by Union armies. Even before Bull Run, all the telegraph lines in the Confederacy had been taken over by the government. And Beauregard, three days before the battle, issued an order that said in effect that reporters couldn't approach the battlefield. Some of them— de Fontaine of the *Charleston Courier*, Alexander of the *Savannah Republican*, Leonidas Spratt of the *Charleston Mercury*, William G. Shepardson of the *Montgomery Advertiser*, and David Grieve Duncan of the *Richmond Dispatch*—managed to sidestep the order and watch the battle from a position on a hill above Mitchell's Ford.

They were allowed by the authorities to use "the lightning," and they did so with the same unfortunate results. One of them, probably Duncan, reported that Jefferson Davis himself had taken command of the rebel center.

But they caused the biggest furor by suggesting that Brigadier General Richard S. Ewell, who was posted on the far right of the rebel line with his brigade of Alabama and Louisiana troops, had bungled badly. Alexander said he failed to carry out an order from Beauregard to attack the enemy on the other side of Bull Run. One paper even charged Ewell with treason (withdrawing the charge a few days later). Ewell's brigade did spend most of the day marching back and forth, without coming to grips with the Yankees. Part of the problem was Beauregard's orders; hardly anyone understood them. But Ewell was a strange fellow, racked by heartburn and subsisting on cracked wheat; later in the war he would break down under stress.

Civil War reporters were not recognized by either side as noncombatants trying to do their jobs under difficult circumstances. When they were captured, they were sent off to prisoner-of-war camps just like anyone else. J. P. Pryor of the *Memphis Daily Appeal* found himself in the wrong place during Bull Run and was captured by Federal troops, the first reporter to fall into enemy hands.

Stedman, easily the best reporter on the field that day, grew up in rural Connecticut and always thought of himself as a literary fellow. He edited small newspapers in Norwich and Winsted before moving to New York with his young bride, Laura. He wrote for various newspapers and published a few poems in the *Tribune*. His first book, *Poems Lyrical and Idyllic*, was published in 1860. The only explanation for his decision to become a war correspondent was his keen interest in the war itself.

He arrived in Washington on April 15 and wrote his first piece for the *World* the next day. He was one of the first reporters to join McDowell's army as it moved into northern Virginia on July 17. "We had a perfectly magnificent time today," he wrote Laura. "I never enjoyed a day so much in my life. Was in the van throughout, at the head of the army, and it was exciting and dramatic beyond measure." He witnessed the skirmishing at Blackburn's Ford the next day. "Under fire from beginning to end," he wrote in his diary. "Helped to right the first gun. Came out safe. My telegraphic dispatch beat the other papers."

Stedman became a stockbroker when the war was over, but poetry always came first. He wrote a poem, "Cavalry Song," after his first skirmish.

> Our good steeds snuff the evening air,
>   Our pulses with their purpose tingle;
> The foeman's fires are twinkling there;
>   He leaps to hear our sabres jingle!
>   HALT!
> Each carbine sends its whizzing ball:
> Now, cling! clang! forward all,
>   Into the fight!

Stedman's story in the *World*, a second-tier New York newspaper, is less fanciful. "And now in what order shall I describe the events of yesterday?" he asks in the second paragraph.

> Even now, how shall one pretend to give a synthetic [again, meaning empirical or verifiable] narration of the whole battle, based on the heterogenous statements of a thousand men; a battle whose

arena was a tract miles in breadth and length, interspersed with hills and forests, when contending forces were divided into a dozen minor armies, continually interchanging their positions. . . . Even the general commanding the federal forces was ignorant, at the close, of the positions of his several corps; was ignorant, at the beginning, of the topography of the dangerous territory on which he attacked an overpowering foe.

That's both accurate and perceptive. McDowell, in fact, didn't know the territory. He marched against a strongly held position without any useful maps. And when the pell-mell retreat was under way, he had no idea of the whereabouts of the various units of his army. As Stedman suggested, this would be a war in which the front lines stretched for miles. Once, generals and observers might have occupied a prominent position and observed the entire battlefield. But this would be the first modern war, with very large armies constantly on the move.

Stedman recognized the Union army had suffered a grievous and humiliating defeat, and he said so in no uncertain terms: "I know that a grand army, retreating before superior numbers, was never more disgracefully or needlessly disrupted and blotted, as it were, out of existence in a single day. That is the truth, and why should it not be recorded?"

Stedman apologized for not knowing more of the details—"I acknowledge my inadequacy," he wrote—but, in fact, he saw quite a bit of the action, and described it generously. Most of the day, he was in the company of a number of other correspondents. It was the first deployment of what the correspondents themselves would sometimes call their "Bohemian Brigade." They flocked together—reporters still do it today—for companionship and comfort, and in order to exchange information. They also figured—and this, too, is just as true today as it was then—that it is always a good idea to keep an eye on the competition.

Stedman rode out to battle with Henry Villard of the *New York Herald* and Edward Howard House of the *New York Tribune,* and for at least some of the time was in the company of Mr. Raymond of the *New York Times.* A number of these Civil War correspondents were extraordinary men, and none was more extraordinary than Villard. His real name was Ferdinand Heinrich Gustav Hilgard, and he was born in Rhenish Bavaria in 1835. He came to the United States in 1853 without any money and unable to speak a word of English. He was taken in by members of the German community in New York, Milwaukee, and elsewhere, and eventually began writing articles for a number of German-language newspapers. When he became fluent in English, he switched to English-language newspapers and ultimately caught the eye of James Gordon Bennett, proprietor of the *New York Herald*. He married Fanny Garrison, daughter of the famous abolitionist, William Lloyd Garrison. After the war, he became a multimillionaire, eventually assuming control of the Northern Pacific Railroad Company. The mansion he built on Madison Avenue is now a part of the Palace Hotel and the home of one of New York City's finest restaurants, Le Cirque 2000.

Recalling Bull Run in his memoirs, Villard remembered the time, early on the day of battle, when he and his two hungry friends, Stedman and House, spotted an empty cabin shaded by a large cherry tree. Villard climbed the tree

> to supply myself and friends with the fruit. . . .
>
> I had just got on a branch when suddenly a terrific roar burst out from the woods seemingly within a few steps of us, followed by a mighty whizzing and clattering all around us. The rebel infantry in the woods had fired a volley against the [Federal] skirmishers. In less than a minute another volley followed, accompanied by the same great roar and the small noises all around us. It then flashed upon us that the latter were caused by thousands of bullets whistling by us and striking the farm buildings, fences, and trees round about. We were, indeed, right in the line of fire of the whole rebel brigade. With the second volley there came also the deep detonations of artillery fire. Then there was a deafening crash, and I found myself thrown from the tree to the ground. Stedman and House shouted, "Are you hurt?" from their shelter behind the farm house, to which they had rushed after the second volley. Fortunately, no harm had befallen me. . . . As for myself, I had certainly had a strong foretaste of actual war. Though not a combatant, I had undergone the formal baptism of fire, and a fire as hot as I was ever

under in my varied adventures as a war correspondent. I can truly say that the music of "bullet, ball and grapeshot" never had much terror for me thereafter.

Later in the day, Villard was separated from his friends and rode on to join Tyler's column preparing to make that feint that fooled no one at the Stone Bridge. "My accompanying Tyler," Villard wrote, "was a fatal mistake . . . we were kept in entire ignorance of events on the field."

RAYMOND WAS THE ONLY EDITOR on the battlefield that day; his reporter, Lorenzo Livingston Crounse, shared his carriage. They first came under fire during skirmishing on the nineteenth. Crounse wrote the story in the next day's paper, when going to war was still something of a lark. A cannonball soared over their heads "and lodged in the woods to the east, far, far from the gentlemen for whose special benefit it had been projected." Standing in the cannonball's range were Raymond, Crounse, Stedman, Villard, House, and Richard Cunningham McCormick of the *New York Evening Post*. Who would have written about the first battle of the war, Crounse asked, "had that initial ball of the second flight been aimed a littler lower?" But, Crounse insisted, none of the reporters even flinched. "Some, at least, of that group, I venture to say, quailed more at the baptismal fount than they did at this flying missile."

Raymond stepped in and took over the story on the day of the battle. It's a familiar ploy, known to modern correspondents as "bigfooting." J. Cutler Andrews, the most painstaking of all the historians who have written about the press in the Civil War, said Raymond wired his paper from Centreville at two o'clock Sunday afternoon that a Union victory was in the making "and that all that remained was for McDowell to march on to Richmond." But Raymond's brief 2 P.M. dispatch was, in fact, a model of restraint.

Bull's Run Bridge, Sunday, July 21—2 p.m.

The great battle occurred to-day, and the result is not certain at the moment I write. Both sides have fought with terrible tenacity. The battle has been hot and steady for three hours, and the loss must be very heavy—certainly not under one thousand on each side.

Raymond managed to describe McDowell's strategy fairly accurately. "The attack [by Tyler's column] was intended mainly as a feint. The real attack was by Hunter, who took a narrow road two miles out leading to the right. . . . His orders were to proceed high up the stream, cut himself a path through the woods, cross over, and turn the position of the rebels on the north."

Stedman probably had the best vantage point to watch the battle. Now accompanied by Uriah Painter, a young reporter for the *Philadelphia Inquirer,* he rode up on a hill from which he could actually see rebel reinforcements arriving in cars on the Manassas Gap Railroad. They "formed a solid square and moved swiftly forward to join in the contest. The whistle of the locomotive was plainly audible to those in our advance."

He watched, too, as elements of Tyler's division finally crossed Bull Run and joined the action. They were led up Henry Hill by the famous Irish regiment—the Sixty-ninth New York, part of Sherman's brigade.

> It was a brave sight—that rush of the 69th into death-struggle. . . . Coats and knapsacks were thrown to either side, that nothing might impede their work, but we knew that no guns would slip from the brave hands of those fellows, even if dying agonies were needed to close them with a firmer grip. As the line swept along, Thomas Meagher [their commander] galloped towards the head, shouting, "Come on, boys! You've got your chance at last!"

But, in fact, the charge by the "Fighting Sixty-ninth" failed just as an earlier charge by the Seventy-ninth New York, the Highlanders (they sometimes wore kilts), had failed. The survivors from both regiments fell back in confusion. Exhausted, Stedman wrote, they were compelled "to resign the completion of their work to the Connecticut regiments which had just come up."

Stedman thought that this was the critical moment, with the Connecticut regiments advancing in line with the Zouaves and the Rhode Islanders. But their commander, Colonel Keyes, hesitated, and the chance was lost. Stedman—already a military expert—argued in his story that McDowell bungled by failing to place reserves in position to commit to the seesaw battle when they were desperately needed. Stedman watched as the Union lines broke and the troops began their disastrous retreat. "It was difficult to believe in the reality of our sudden retreat," he wrote.

> "What does it all mean?" I asked Alexander [a captain attached to a sappers unit from Ohio]. "It means defeat," was his reply. "We are beaten. It is shameful, a cowardly retreat. 'Hold up, men,' he shouted, 'don't be such infernal cowards!'"

Stedman apparently was too modest to mention in his dispatch that he picked up the colors of the Fifth Massachusetts Regiment and tried to rally the troops. His friend, Painter, writing in the *Inquirer*, mentioned Stedman's bravery: "The enemy appeared in sight, firing their guns, the balls raining on us thick. Emerging from the valley we saw the reporter of the World, with the standard of the Massachusetts Fifth, waving it over him and pleading for the men to rally around him, but it was in vain. They heeded him not."

Before the battle, a number of the reporters had used a farmhouse in Centreville as a sort of rustic headquarters. They met there again, by pure happenstance, during the retreat—Villard, Stedman, Painter, Joseph Glenn of the *Cincinnati Daily Gazette*, and one or two more. Villard discovered late in the day that McDowell had abandoned any idea of making a stand in Virginia and ordered the entire army—or what was left of it—to fall back upon Washington. He wrote:

> I hurried back to our quarters and did my duty to my friends by waking them and telling them the news and urging them to lose no time in starting back. Two acted promptly and got away, but the other two—Glenn and Painter—could not rouse themselves and fell asleep again. They woke late in the morning [the Monday after the battle], and, when they had leisurely dressed and come down for breakfast, found several officers in rebel uniforms sitting on the veranda. Fortunately, they were taken by these to belong to the family owning the house, and politely asked whether breakfast could be had. They had presence of mind enough to answer, "Oh,

yes, with pleasure"; and, pretending to go in search of the servants, managed to make their escape from the rear of the house by climbing over a fence into an adjacent corn-field, and so safely reaching the woods to which it extended. They arrived in Washington very much elated, of course, at their adventure.

Another correspondent roaming the Bull Run battlefield was thirty-eight-year-old Charles Carleton Coffin of the *Boston Morning Journal*, perhaps the toughest, and eventually one of the most skilled, of all Civil War correspondents. He had been reared on a farm in New Hampshire and had studied surveying and engineering. A bit of a prude, and sometimes pretty smug about it, he didn't drink or smoke, and never took the Lord's name in vain. (The only time he ever took a spirituous drink, his devoted biographer wrote, was a sip from an officer's flask at a very "dark moment" during the Battle of the Wilderness.) He probably saw more action than any other correspondent, North or South. At Bull Run, he observed the battle from his position with a New York artillery unit, probably the one serving with the Seventy-first New York militia.

But his story—it filled less than a column in the *Boston Journal*—was a disappointment. Coffin didn't even mention the fact that the Union had been badly defeated until the thirteenth paragraph. Coffin was nothing if not dedicated; he would write better stories in the future.

Reporters, even the best of them, never got all the details right. Stedman wrote the best account of Bull Run, but he made mistakes. In explaining the defeat—the section appears at the very end of his story—Stedman was wrong when he said the Confederates outnumbered the Federals two to one. He exaggerated when he said the rebel position was impregnable. But he was right when he said "many of our leaders displayed a lamentable lack of military knowledge. There was no real generalship in the field. They [the commanding officers] exhibited personal bravery but advantages gained were not secured." It really was a pretty good day's work for a twenty-seven-year-old poet.

Villard probably won the race to be the first reporter to send news to New York stating flatly that the Union army had been badly defeated (making up for the *Herald*'s earlier report about a great Union

Charles Carleton Coffin of the *Boston Morning Journal*.
(Author's collection)

victory). His dispatch was only six hundred words long; he explained
in his memoirs that he needed special permission from his editor in
chief to send anything longer. Still, it was long enough for the *Herald*
to publish an extra. He then sat down and wrote a detailed account,
and this time he received permission to send all of it by wire. "Alas!
when it reached me in print, I discovered, to my great disgust, that
so much of it had been stricken out or altered that I could no longer
feel any pride in the mutilated remnant as my own work." The problem was that Villard had been critical of the performance of most of
the New York regiments, and his editors "did not dare to print my
fulminations on my word alone."

Poor Villard was summoned to headquarters in New York and
told that his next assignment would be in Kentucky.

4

The Three Graces: Greeley, Bennett, and Raymond

SUNDAY, THE DAY OF THE BATTLE, had been fiercely hot and sunny. Monday, the day after the battle, was appropriately gray and wet. In the White House, Lincoln accepted the defeat with sorrow, and then began making plans to build a better army led by better generals.

In New York, Horace Greeley, the famous editor, had a nervous breakdown.

It was, after all, his newspaper that had urged, day after day, "Forward to Richmond!" And that Monday morning, it was his newspaper that carried a report from its man on the scene, Stedman's friend Edward Howard House, that the rebels had been routed, leaving "the National troops undisputed victors."

It was only when Greeley picked up the *Herald,* containing Villard's six-hundred-word account of a terrible Union defeat, that he learned the truth.

Where should the blame be placed? In Tuesday's paper, in a lead editorial written by Greeley's right-hand man, Charles A. Dana, the *Tribune* called for the replacement of Lincoln's entire cabinet! Other New York editors reacted gleefully. Bull Run, they all said, was Greeley's fault, not the cabinet's. Bennett's *Herald* said that Greeley and his "ferocious Jacobins" had brought it on. Stung by the criticism, Greeley wrote his own editorial on Wednesday, the twenty-third, a disgraceful attempt to shift the blame to his own employees. "The watchword, Forward to Richmond!," he said, "is not mine. . . . So with the late article urging a change in the Cabinet." Anyway, he rambled on, he had never "imagined such strategy as the launching of barely thirty thousand . . . against ninety thousand rebels enveloped in a labyrinth of strong entrenchments and unreconnoitered masked batteries."

Torn by conflicting emotions—war to save the Union and destroy slavery was moral, but sacrificing thousands of young men to win it was not—he retired to bed, suffering from what his friends called "brain fever."

It was late at night on July 29, eight days after the battle, that he scrawled a half-crazed letter to the president of the United States. It would be difficult to find anything else quite like it.

> Dear Sir: This is my seventh sleepless night—yours, too, doubtless—yet I think I shall not die, because I have no right to die. I must struggle to live, however bitterly. But to business. You are now considered a great man, and I am a hopelessly broken one. . . . Can the rebels be beaten after all that has occurred, and in view of the actual state of feeling caused by our late awful disaster? If they can—and it is your business to ascertain and decide—write me that such is your judgment, so that I may know and do my duty. And if they can not be beaten—if our recent disaster is fatal—do not fear to sacrifice yourself to your country. . . .
>
> If the Union is irrevocably gone, an armistice of thirty, sixty, ninety, one hundred and twenty days—better still for a year— ought at once to be proposed with a view to a peaceful adjustment. . . . But do nothing timidly or by halves. Send me word what to do. I will live till I can hear at, at all events . . .
>
> Yours, in the depths of bitterness,
> HORACE GREELEY

Lincoln never replied to the letter; what, after all, could he have said? But he was overheard to call it "pusillanimous."

New York City was the nation's newspaper capital in 1860, and Greeley was one of its three principal editors (the others being Raymond of the *Times* and Bennett of the *Herald*). *Harper's Illustrated*

Weekly called the three editors, in jest, "the Three Graces." They all despised one another.

The three men, keenly competitive, would cover the war with more passion than good sense. Relying heavily on the telegraph, they would often rush news into print without any background checking. Being first was what mattered most.

Greeley was an American original. He was born in Amherst, New Hampshire, on February 3, 1811, went to school irregularly (and for the rest of his life resented those with college degrees), worked on a weekly newspaper in Vermont, and moved to New York City in 1831, when he was twenty years old. He was a Whig at first (and a Republican later), and his sponsors included such Whig bosses as Thurlow Weed and William H. Seward. He published the first issue of his newspaper, the *Tribune*, on April 10, 1841.

No one else in New York (or anywhere else, for that matter) looked even remotely like him. His biographer, Jeter Allen Isely, offered this view:

> He was of average height and weight, but his shoulders drooped, his large head jutted forward, and his nearsighted eyes peered from behind thick lenses. A white duster or a baggy overcoat, its pockets stuffed with documents ready for the typesetter and the morning edition, draped sack-like over his upper body. His suits were poorly fitted, with one or both trouser legs caught carelessly along the top of muddy boots, but his linen was scrupulously clean. A flaxen throat beard, reinforced by whisps of pale yellow hair from beneath a white hat, partially hid his collar. His complexion was clear, and his round face normally wore a pleasant, almost absent-minded expression.

Isely said his third-floor office overlooking Washington Square was cluttered with "piles of pamphlets, papers, books, and manuscripts" that "lay in confusion about his desk. Seated with his nose close to a screeching quill, he scribbled at a furious speed."

He was a devout Universalist (akin to a Unitarian), and he neither smoked nor drank. He followed the teachings of Sylvester Graham—the graham cracker man—and kept his body pure on cambric tea, crackers, and vegetables. He was a sucker, in fact, for all kinds of

Horace Greeley of the *New York Tribune*. (Library of Congress)

prophets and social experiments. Along with Arthur Brisbane, he was the leading exponent in the United States of the French socialist Charles Fourier, who believed that society should be broken down into "phalanxes," in each of which sixteen hundred men would work five thousand acres of land. Greeley actually helped to develop three phalanxes, all of which failed. After the Civil War was over, he helped organize a colony in Colorado—it failed, too—but out of it grew the city that bears his name.

He did find time to marry a Connecticut schoolmistress, Mary Cheney, and they had seven children, five of whom died at an early age. Mrs. Greeley drifted away into her own cranky world of spiritualism. Greeley's only real love was his newspaper, and the causes he could promote in its pages.

He published a daily newspaper, aimed at a metropolitan audience, and semiweekly and weekly editions. Circulation of the weekly edition in 1860 was two hundred thousand, spread throughout all of the free states. His presses also rolled out *Tribune* almanacs and thousands of highly opinionated pamphlets. Every winter, the great editor toured his far-flung empire on a lecture tour, speaking excitedly to thousands of his loyal readers. Even though it never caught on in the deep South, where his views on slavery were unpopular, the *Tribune* really was the nation's first national newspaper.

Greeley's readers refused to accept all his radical views, but they were mesmerized by his extravagant personality and his extraordinary writing (and lecturing) skills. In the middle of the nineteenth century, America was chockablock with eccentrics, and Greeley stood head and shoulders above them all.

He was "experimental, self-contradictory, explosive, irascible, and often downright wrongheaded," wrote another of his biographers, William Harlan Hale. "He preached thrift and could not practice it himself. He promoted conservative Whiggism and became a socialist immediately thereafter. He talked pacifism, but turned into one of the foremost fomentors of the Civil War. He helped found the Republican Party, only to run against it himself as an insurgent backed by Democrats [in 1872]."

The biographer James Parton wrote in April of 1866 that "there never lived a man capable of working more hours in a year" than Greeley. But, said Parton, in one of the finest essays on journalism ever written, Greeley was never "a great journalist. . . . He has regarded journalism rather as a disagreeable necessity of his vocation, and uniformly abandoned the care of it to others."

Greeley was only interested in ideas, the more impractical the better. For more than two years, from its founding in 1841 until 1843,

Early photo of the staff of the *New York Tribune*. Seated, left to right: George M. Snow, financial editor; Bayard Taylor; Horace Greeley; George Ripley, literary editor. Standing, left to right: William Henry Fry, music editor; Charles A. Dana; Henry J. Raymond. (Library of Congress)

Greeley's editor for news was that very same Henry Jarvis Raymond who reported Bull Run for his own newspaper, the *New York Times*. "If Mr. Raymond had been ten years older, and had founded and conducted the paper, with Mr. Greeley as his chief writer of editorials," that would have given the *Tribune* top prize among American newspapers, Parton said.

But Raymond defected from the Tribune in 1843 to the *Courier and Enquirer*, and founded his own newspaper, the *New York Times*, in 1851. Greeley called him the "little villain," a nickname that stuck with him for the rest of his life. Raymond's successor, Charles A. Dana, was another skilled journalist, but he and Greeley disagreed on a number of points in the days leading up to Bull Run. Dana said—a little too simplistically—he was fired in April of 1862 because Greeley was for peace "and I was for war." Dana accepted a job in the War

Department, working for Secretary Stanton, where he was no friend to members of his old fraternity.

NOT VERY MANY PEOPLE liked James Gordon Bennett. Yet he was quite probably the greatest journalist the United States has ever produced. He created the modern English-language newspaper—warts, lots of them, and all. He was a genius.

He was born on September 1, 1795, in a tiny, isolated farming community near Keith, fifty-five miles north of Aberdeen, in Scotland. His family were Catholics. By local standards, they were reasonably prosperous farmers, and James and his brother, Cosmo, were taught to read the Bible and all the Latin poets. When James was fifteen, he was packed off to a small Catholic seminary called Blair's College in Aberdeen to study for the priesthood. He spent four years there, and mastered, among other things, French and logic and science and even bookkeeping. In middle age, he may have published America's most vulgar newspaper—that's what his critics said—but he was, in fact, the best-educated of all the Civil War–era editors.

He first began thinking about emigrating to America after reading Benjamin Franklin's autobiography. He sailed to Halifax, Nova Scotia, in 1819, and worked his way south to Boston the next year, taking a job as a proofreader in a printing shop. Moving steadily south, he stopped for a few months in New York, where he met Aaron Smith Willington, owner of the *Charleston Courier*, perhaps in 1823 the best newspaper in the South. Willington offered him a job, and Bennett took it. He spent ten months in South Carolina, causing him "to look forever afterwards with feelings of friendliness and sympathy upon the southern cause," according to Oliver Carlson, his biographer. The great man in South Carolina in those days was John C. Calhoun, and young Bennett, a man without much principle or ideological commitment, became as attached to Senator Calhoun's views as he ever became attached to views of any kind.

Charleston was one of the liveliest cities in the South, but Bennett refused to take any part in the fun. Carlson wrote:

> He knew that his figure was ungainly, his face ugly (he was cross-eyed), his speech harsh and queer-sounding, his manners brusque,

James Gordon Bennett of the *New York Herald*. (Library of Congress)

and his tongue sharp. Knowing these facts, instead of trying to correct or modify them, he scoffed at those who wasted their time with such tomfoolery as dancing, flirting, drinking, or playing cards. He turned all his energy into his work. . . . "I eat and drink to live," he declared . . . "not live to eat and drink. Social glasses of wine are my abomination; all species of gormandizing, my utter scorn and contempt. When I am hungry, I eat; when thirsty, drink. Wine or viands taken for society, or to stimulate conversation, tend only to dissipation, indolence, poverty, contempt, and death."

He left Charleston after ten months—no one has ever explained why—and returned to New York City. There, he went to work, first, for the *Enquirer*, and later, for the *Courier and Enquirer*, at the time the best paper in the city. He was sent to cover Washington; his dispatches—the sort of journalism you might see these days in the *Washington Post*'s gossipy "Style" section—actually suggested he had a sense of humor. He roamed all over the city, to salons and saloons, to the halls of Congress and to the White House itself. He wrote an amusing piece about why Americans shake hands all the time. He wrote about a party in Carusi's Assembly Rooms, where "it was most delightful to see the pretty little wretches selling dolls most wickedly to the bachelors, and the bachelors, looking most woefully up in their faces, like an old fox at a bunch of grapes elevated on the architrave of an ionic column." Readers, just as curious then as they are now about the private lives of famous people, lapped it up.

Back in New York, with $500 in his pocket, he published the first number of his own newspaper, the *Herald*, on May 6, 1835. The price: one cent. Essayist Parton wrote:

> It was born in a cellar in Wall Street,—not a basement, but a veritable cellar. Some people are still doing business in that region who remember going down into its subterranean office, and buying copies of the new paper from its editor, who used to sit at a desk composed of two flour barrels and a piece of board, and who occupied the only chair in the establishment. For a considerable time his office contained nothing but his flour-barrel desk, one wooden chair, and a file of Heralds.

The paper was small, four pages of four columns each, printed at a nearby shop, but it was well written. "Everything *drew*, as the sailors say," Parton wrote. What intrigued readers was Bennett's lack of party ties and moral principles. He mocked everything, including religion.

He is credited with inventing the "money article," stating on June 13, 1835, that "stocks yesterday maintained their prices during the session of the Board, several going up." His coverage of the great Wall Street fire was exceptional, including a drawing of the flaming Exchange and a map showing other buildings that had been destroyed or damaged.

Parton attributed Bennett's success to "immense expenditure and vigilance in getting news, and a reckless disregard of principle, truth, and decency in [the *Herald*'s] editorials." Parton wrote those words in 1866; it is now 2000, and critics might say the very same thing about the *Wall Street Journal*. Bennett was always ahead of everyone else.

He became controversial from the start because of his audacity. Though a Roman Catholic himself, he called upon the "Catholic bishop and clergy of New York to come forth from the darkness, folly, and superstition of the tenth century." He called the pope a "decrepit, licentious, stupid, Italian blockhead" and said he should be replaced by an American.

In 1836, Bennett said he was sick and tired of the "eternal turmoil and confusion" of democratic politics and that it would be better to elect somebody—he didn't care whom—"emperor of this great republic for life."

But it was his enthusiastic and explicit coverage of crime news that really caused fierce controversy. It all began on April 10, 1836, with the hatchet murder of twenty-two-year-old Helen Jewett, "a finely formed and most beautiful girl," and the attempt by her killer to burn down the bawdy house in which she worked. The next day, Bennett visited the scene of the crime at 41 Thomas Street and viewed the body in an upstairs bedroom. The story made journalistic history.

> What a sight burst upon me! There stood an elegant double mahogany bed, all covered with burnt pieces of linen, blankets, pillows, black as cinders. I looked around for the object of my curiosity. On the carpet, I saw a piece of linen sheet covering something as if carefully flung over it.
>
> "Here," said the police officer, "here is the poor creature."
>
> He half uncovered the ghastly corpse. I could scarcely look at it for a second or two. Slowly I began to discover the lineaments of the corpse as one would the beauties of a statue of marble. It was the most remarkable sight I ever beheld—I never have, and never expect to see such another. "My God," exclaimed I, "how like a statue. I can scarcely conceive that form to be a corpse." Not a vein was to be seen. The body looked as white, as full, as polished as the purest Parian marble. The perfect figure, the exquisite limbs, the

fine face, the full arms, the beautiful bust, all surpassed in every aspect the Venus de Medici according to the casts generally given of her.

"See," said the police officer, "she has assumed that appearance within the hour."

The perfection of the picture, Bennett conceded later in his story, was marred by "dreadful bloody gashes on the right temple."

Perhaps the most embarrassing of all of Bennett's stories was the announcement on page 1 of his paper on June 1, 1840, that he was going to be married in a few days "to one of the most splendid women in intellect, in heart, in soul, in property, in person, in manner, that I have yet seen in the course of my pilgrimage through human life." Her name was Henrietta Cream, and some of Bennett's journalistic rivals invited libel suits by hinting in print that she wasn't any better than she should have been. Their only child, James Gordon Bennett Jr., was born on May 10, 1841.

It was this kind of reporting—neither Hearst nor today's "Channels Five Alive" could do it better—that gave the *Herald* its reputation for vulgar indecency.

The *Herald* stories about the murder of the beautiful prostitute caused a sensation, and the circulation of Bennett's newspaper surged. It was during this period, from 1836 to 1841, that Bennett joyfully wallowed in the journalistic sewer. His biographer, Carlson, said it was a calculated effort to boost circulation. Then, his goals having been reached, Carlson argued, he pulled back and began to put out a somewhat more respectable sheet. By the time the Civil War began, Bennett was a rich man and the *Herald* the most widely read daily in New York City.

Bennett's best reporter, Henry Villard, was a man of common sense and principle. He had made his mark covering Lincoln's presidential campaign vigorously and fairly for a paper that was lambasting the Republican candidate in its editorial columns. As war loomed, Villard wasn't so sure he wanted to remain on Bennett's payroll. He must have been especially outraged by Bennett's editorial on April 10 attacking Lincoln for plunging the nation into "an abyss of ruin." The *Herald* called for the overthrow of Lincoln and the Republican Party.

Four days later, the *Herald* plant was surrounded by a screaming mob and Bennett's frightened employees barricaded the doors and windows. Greeley's *Tribune* thundered that the least Bennett could do was display an American flag. A nervous Bennett began backing down and soon his plant was blazing with dozens of American flags. The next day, the fifteenth, the same day Lincoln issued his call for seventy-five thousand volunteers, Bennett's *Herald* pledged its support to Lincoln and the Union. It was almost a complete turnaround, but well within the Bennett guideline that neither he nor his paper would ever be the member of a minority. The next day, the sixteenth, he ordered Villard to come to New York at once. Villard wrote:

> I obeyed the summons by the night train. On reaching the Herald office, I found an invitation to accompany him in the afternoon to his residence at Washington Heights and to spend the night there. As was my host's regular custom, we drove from the office up Broadway and Fifth Avenue and through Central Park to the Heights.
>
> I had seen Bennett only twice before, and then but for a few minutes each time, and the opportunity to learn more of this notorious character was therefore not unwelcome to me. I must say his shameful record as a journalist and particularly the sneaking sympathy of his paper for the Rebellion, and its vile abuse of the Republicans for their antislavery sentiments, made me share the general prejudice against him to such an extent that I had been thinking for some time of severing my connection with the Herald. . . .
>
> With his fine tall and slender figure, large intellectual head covered with an abundance of light curly hair, and strong regular features, his exterior would have been impressive but for the strabismus [the cross-eyed squint], which gave him a sinister, forbidding look. Intercourse with him, indeed, quickly revealed his hard, cold, utterly selfish nature and incapacity to appreciate high and noble aims.

Villard joined Bennett and his son, James Jr., for dinner, after which the editor came to the point. He wanted Villard to do two things:

First: carry a personal message to Lincoln stating that the *Herald* would support any "war measures" by the government to suppress the rebellion, and the sooner it was put down the better.

Second: offer to the government young Bennett's 160-ton yacht, the *Rebecca,* for the Federal revenue service, and to secure in consideration of that generous gift the appointment of the twenty-year-old lad as a lieutenant in the revenue service.

Upon his return to Washington, Villard delivered the message to a grateful Lincoln, in person, and Treasury Secretary Salmon P. Chase accepted both the yacht and young Bennett—Third Lieutenant Bennett, if you please—for a comfortable and nonviolent service in what would eventually become the Coast Guard.

THE THIRD OF THE GREAT New York editors was Raymond of the *Times.* He and Greeley truly despised one another, for both of them lusted for elected office (sometimes the same office). In that contest, Raymond was an easy winner. At one time or another he was speaker of the state assembly, lieutenant governor, chairman of both the state and national Republican parties, and a member of Congress.

John Russell Young, a war correspondent for the *Philadelphia Press* (he was at Bull Run, too), knew and admired Raymond.

> He was the kindliest of men; he had an open, ox-like eye, neat, dapper person, which seemed made for an overcoat, a low, placid, decisive voice, argued with you in a Socratic method by asking questions and summing up your answers against you as evidence. . . . He was never in a hurry, and yet there was no busier person in journalism. Raymond had the Rochefoucauld sense of observation, and in conversation you found yourself in presence of a thinker in a constant state of inquiry and doubt. He was a journalist in everything but his ambitions, and those tended to public life. . . . He was conservative. He could not endure a caucus. There was nothing in this world entirely right or entirely wrong,—no peach that did not have a sunny side.

Raymond was born on January 24, 1820, on an eighty-acre farm near Lima, a small village in the Genesee valley in upstate New York.

It was a warm, caring family, and Raymond's parents saved up $1,000 to send him off to what is now the University of Vermont. He, too, fancied himself as a poet, and some of his work was published in an early Horace Greeley publication called the *New-Yorker.*

I've been roaming—been roaming
Far from the haunts of men,
Where sylvan cascades foaming
Awake the shaded glen.

After graduation, he joined Greeley in New York at the *New-Yorker,* and when Greeley began the *Tribune* in 1841 he signed on as assistant editor. But, as we have already noted, Raymond was a cautious man and a conservative one, and he was never comfortable with Greeley's radical and sometimes crackpot ideas. When the *Courier and Enquirer* offered him $25 a week, a $5 pay hike, he took it.

With $80,000 in pledges from his partners, Raymond brought out the first number of his own paper, the *Times,* on September 18, 1851. Frederic Hudson, for many years Bennett's second in command at the *Herald,* said Raymond aimed to publish a "modestly model newspaper," and so he did.

The editor was a good journalist and the newspaper was a good newspaper, but together they never quite clicked. One of the problems was Raymond's ambitions for public office; they interfered with his duties at the paper. The other problem, and probably a bigger one, was his dithering; he always had trouble making tough decisions. Maybe it was all part of the fact he was such a political animal.

He was the kind of man his rivals loved to poke fun at. They had a field day when Raymond set out to cover the war at Bull Run in person. The *Herald* ridiculed Raymond's brief exposure to the war between Austria and Italy and France (including the bloody battle at Solferino) in 1859 and took to calling him "the Hon. Jefferson Brick," a literary allusion to a dim-witted editorial assistant in one of the American chapters of Charles Dickens's book *The Life and Adventures of Martin Chuzzlewit.*

Henry J. Raymond of the *New York Times*. (Library of Congress)

It didn't help that Raymond's own dispatch recounting the defeat at Bull Run, filed for Monday morning's edition of the *Times*, was held up in Washington and didn't see the light of day until Wednesday. The *Herald* published a poem, "Ye Plaintive Ballad of Jefferson Brick," to commemorate Raymond's battlefield performance.

It was a July morning when Mr. Jefferson Brick,
All thought of danger, scorning, marched in the double quick.
Quoth he, "I am a soldier who has at running drilled!
I drilled at Solferino—my boots with fame are filled—
So come along McDowell and limber out each gun
'Tis you must do the fighting and I will do the run."

And so the three great newspapers went to war, sometimes with the South, sometimes with each other—Greeley and the *Tribune* wringing their hands over what to make of it, Bennett and the *Herald* wishing the South could somehow be accommodated, and Raymond and the *Times* firmly pledged, as good Republicans, to support Lincoln and the Union.

5

Out West

THE CIVIL WAR occupied two stages—the eastern theater, centering in Virginia, and the sprawling western theater, running up and down the Mississippi River and extending from the Alleghenies to New Mexico.

The fighting in the East was more thoroughly covered by the press for a number of obvious reasons—the arena was compact, geographically; it was close to major newspaper offices, especially those which maintained bureaus in Washington; and, not least of all, it was the more crucial of the two. But the war in the West was serious business, too, even though it has often been downplayed by eastern-oriented historians.

The soldiers in the western armies, observers said, tended to be bigger and stronger, more independent and less disciplined than soldiers in the East. Reporters covering the western armies were special, too—hard-drinking, hard-riding, sometimes hardworking. The best of them were very good indeed; the rest were devious, dishonest, sophomoric, undisciplined. Sherman made no differentiation; he rejoiced when two of them were captured by the rebels and seethed when another escaped the harshest penalties of a court-martial.

They were the real rough-and-tough Bohemian Brigade, and they took a certain pride in their cantankerousness.

One of them, Franc Bangs Wilkie, came close to epitomizing everything good and bad about the western correspondent.

He grew up on a farm in Saratoga County, in upstate New York. Many of these war correspondents attended small liberal arts colleges—Vermont, Trinity, Amherst, Antioch, Hamilton, Beloit, Williams. Wilkie was typical; he arrived at Union College, in Schenectady, then in full flower under its celebrated president, Eliphalet Nott, in 1854, "with hayseed still in my hair and with the aroma of the barnyard scarcely removed from my boots."

Wilkie had saved enough money to pay for his first semester at Union by teaching school, working as a blacksmith, and building a barn for one of his neighbors. "I was distressingly poor," he said. To pay the rest of his costs, he began contributing to the *Evening Star*, a local daily, for a salary of $4 a week. In a month, he was the literary editor and making $8 a week. It was enough to see him through (though the college didn't actually give him a degree until several years later).

Sometime after leaving Union, Wilkie moved to Davenport, Iowa, to edit a weekly Democratic Party newspaper supporting Stephen A. Douglas for president. He had married Nellie Morse in 1857 (they had two children the next few years, a boy and a girl) and settled in Dubuque. He said in his memoirs, "I began business as a war correspondent in May, 1861, as the representative of the Dubuque, Iowa, Herald, on the promise of the munificent salary of $10 a week."

Wilkie may have had no choice, but the *Dubuque Herald* was a curious paper to work for as a war correspondent. The paper was owned and edited by sixty-year-old Dennis Mahoney, a riproaring copperhead who believed the war was a terrible mistake. His friends called him "Old Dogmatism." A Federal marshal and a squad of soldiers pulled the old man from his bed in August of 1860 and whisked him out of the city. He was tossed into the Old Capitol Prison in Washington. Wilkie said Mahoney was arrested (but never charged with anything) to prevent him running for Congress. He was released after the election was over.

Wilkie worked for the *Herald* for just three months, during which time he was never paid a penny. He described how he got by:

It may puzzle many people to know how a correspondent could live, travel, write, and all that without any cash capital. I managed it for a time; I railroaded all over the west, lived in fairly good style, had a mule for my transportation in the field, and during the three months I am certain that I was not the possessor in all of ten dollars.

The secret is a simple one in its explanation. The soldiers and officers were all new to the service, as a matter of course. They were about to leave home for the first time in their lives on what promised to be a mission of danger; they were ambitious, and they were anxious that they should be heard from by the people at home. Hence the correspondent of the home paper was a person of consequence. He had passkeys to every tent in the regiment, was a welcome guest at every mess, was on terms of perfect equality with every officer and private, calling many of them by their first names.

Wilkie's western army was commanded by the gaudy "Pathfinder," John C. Frémont, as absurd a figure as either side produced during the entire war. But Frémont was a general to be reckoned with, if for no other reason than he was married to the highly ambitious Jessie Benton Frémont, the daughter of Missouri's most famous son, Senator Thomas Hart Benton (who had died in 1858). Serving under Frémont was a brigadier general named Nathaniel Lyon. One of Lincoln's highest priorities was the preservation of Missouri on the Union side, and he counted on Frémont and Lyon to do the job by finding and then destroying a ragtag Confederate army commanded by Sterling Price operating in the southwest corner of the state.

Wilkie had attached himself to the First Iowa Regiment. Hardly any of these young soldiers—not more than one in a hundred—really believed serious fighting awaited them, Wilkie said.

They were clerks on small salaries; they were lawyers with insufficient business; they were young men with no occupation and anxious for employment; they were farmers' boys disgusted with the drudgery of the soil. . . . To these were added husbands tired of the bickerings of domestic life. . . . It was a picnic, a pleasure-trip, a triumphal jaunt through Dixie, with flying banners and beating drums.

Wilkie and the boys from the First Iowa arrived in Macon, in northeastern Missouri, early in June. The citizens had fled and abandoned almost everything, including a newspaper plant that had published the *Missouri Valley Register*. "My journalistic instincts were aroused by a sight of the deserted office," Wilkie wrote. So, securing a detail of soldiers with printing experience from the regiment, he published on June 15, 1861, the first and last number of *Our Whole Union*.

The issue was a single page, printed on white paper with blue ink. In his lead article, Wilkie had this to say: "A printing-office has no more right to remain idle than a pretty woman has to remain un-married."

The regiment was ordered to move out the next day and so that should have been the end of it. But a copy of the one-day wonder was picked up by a representative of the *New York Times* in Saint Louis and forwarded to Henry Raymond in New York. The editor, desperate for reporters to cover the war, invited Wilkie to become a part-time contributor, offering him $7.50 for every column of type he wrote, plus limited expenses. Wilkie switched employers, quickly and enthusiastically. He never met Raymond, but the association was always a happy one. Raymond, he said, "surely was the most appreciative, kindliest, and most courteous of journalists."

Wilkie had been a reporter for a local newspaper; he was now in the big time, working with the national press. It is a distinction reporters made then, just as they do now. The first national journalist Wilkie met was an important one, Thomas W. Knox of Bennett's *New York Herald*, the man who would be court-martialed by Sherman for revealing secrets to the enemy. "He was a large, heavy man, rather clumsy in movement and ungainly in form," Wilkie wrote. "He was dark, with small, keen brown eyes, a large head, and had an expression of great sagacity, with an intermingling of a trace of the sardonic." Wilkie remembered clearly his performance at a place called Forsyth, where Union and Confederate troops were exchanging fire across a stream.

> I noticed two men in citizens' clothes in the front rank of the cavalry, who were shooting across the river as fast as they could cock their revolvers. One of them I recognized as the bulky Knox, and the other as a correspondent of a St. Louis newspaper, a young fellow named Fish. . . . As their revolvers were of the vest-pocket pat-

tern, not over three inches in length, and the distance of the enemy not less than a hundred yards, and as the foes were well-screened by timber, it is not likely that either Knox or Fish were responsible for the shedding of much Southern blood.

Wilkie's letters began appearing in the *Times* under a standing headline, THE REBELLION IN MISSOURI or SITUATION IN MISSOURI. Papers then didn't use bylines for reporters. Stories written by reporters in the field usually carried a tag line, "From Our Special Correspondent." Then, at the end, the reporter's pen name would sometimes appear, usually in capital letters. Wilkie's pen name was GALWAY, recalling his old homestead in upstate New York.

Wilkie's first story, dated August 3, 1861, was written in Curran, Stone County, Missouri. It was fairly typical of thousands of "letters" written by correspondents throughout the war. "Last Thursday night," it began, "orders came to the camp . . . to strike our tents and prepare for a march." Nothing much actually happens in these stories; in this one, a Union 12-pounder cannon is unlimbered and a shrapnel shell is fired at a log cabin containing what appeared to be some Southern cavalrymen. The shot missed.

The first real battle in the West—and Wilkie's first great opportunity—was at Wilson's Creek, ten miles south of Springfield, on August 10, less than three weeks following Bull Run. Though outnumbered almost two to one, "Daddy" Lyon decided to attack "Old Pap" Price and his deputy, Ben McCulloch, the Texas Ranger hero from the Mexican War, before they could attack him. It wasn't quite as foolish as it sounded, because Price's Missouri militiamen were equipped with shotguns and old flintlock muskets—when they were equipped with anything at all—and had collected round stones to fire from rusty cannon.

The result was a surprisingly bloody battle—almost as many were killed and wounded at Wilson's Creek, about 1,200 on each side, as at Bull Run—and the Union cause suffered a terrible blow with Lyon's death.

Knox had taken part in some skirmishing, but this was his first real battle, and what surprised him most was the question of distances. "Distances," he wrote, "seemed much greater than they really were." Knox stood by the side of a Captain Totten as his battery opened the conflict.

"How far are you firing?" Knox asked.

"About 800 yards; not over that," the captain responded.

"I should have called it 1600, had I been called for an estimate."

Knox also thought he could begin to tell the difference between a minié ball—a deadly conical bullet fired from a rifled musket—and a common round ball fired from an old smoothbore musket. They made different "whistling" sounds, he thought.

The battle ended once again in a Union rout, with the Federal troops running panic-stricken from the field, first to Springfield and then to Rolla, halfway to Saint Louis. Like Bull Run, too, the Confederates failed to organize a pursuit of their shattered enemy.

There had now been two major battles, Bull Run and Wilson's Creek, and in each of them the Federals had skedaddled. The Confederates said it just proved what they had always known—one rebel was worth five Yankees.

Wilkie and Knox roamed the battlefield, coming under heavy fire for the first time in their lives. They spent a lot of time collecting the names of the dead and the wounded, an important newspaper service throughout the war because neither army had any procedure for publishing casualty lists. And then it was time for them to skedaddle—in search of a place to file their stories.

Wilkie hadn't heard from Raymond or anyone else at the *Times*, and didn't know the paper had begun publishing his stories, and so he jumped to the conclusion they were no longer interested in hearing from him. When he reached Rolla, an important rail junction, he talked a telegraph operator into sending a list of the Iowa killed and wounded to the *Herald* in Dubuque. He then boarded the cars—an Illinois Central train—and set out to deliver his account of the battle in person.

He arrived in Dubuque about ten o'clock in the evening. He was tired and wanted nothing more than to get home without being seen.

I had not gone a hundred yards when I heard a rush of feet and a clamor of voices approaching me on the levee. In a moment or two, three or four people met me, clasped my hands, congratulating me on my safe return, and began asking for news of the "boys." Meanwhile, other rushing feet were heard; and almost in less time than I can tell it, the levee was swarming with an eager, tumultuous crowd. As we advanced toward the main street the throng increased, and by the time we entered on the gas-lighted region the mass of people crowded the street from curb to curb in a crush that was terrific.

Two of the companies in the First Iowa—the Governor's Grays and the Jackson Guards—were from Dubuque, and it was Wilkie's sad task to repeat to the anxious crowd what he had said in his telegram: some of the boys weren't coming home.

Raymond must have been seriously chagrined that Wilkie had failed to send an account of Wilson's Creek to New York; it was, after all, big news, and he had no one else to tell the story. When he heard Wilkie's explanation—that he hadn't heard a word from the *Times*, even though he had mailed them several "letters"—Raymond sent him a telegram. RETAIN PLACE, BY ALL MEANS, it said.

The confusion cleared up, Wilkie packed his bags and took the cars to Saint Louis and General Frémont's headquarters. He hadn't been there more than a day or two when he met Brigadier General Sam Sturgis on the street, "who told me he was going to lead a column" to relieve twenty-eight hundred men from Colonel James A. Mulligan's Irish Guard penned up in Lexington, near Kansas City, by Price's troops. Sturgis invited Wilkie to join him, and he agreed to tag along. When Sturgis saw the strength of the Confederate position, he decided to call it a day. He turned around and headed back to camp.

But Wilkie, fortified with a bottle or two of Catawba wine "opened by a wealthy resident of the vicinity," decided he would saddle up "and go down the river and enter the rebel lines."

General Sturgis tried to talk him out of it. But Wilkie was obstinate, and Sturgis bid him a fond good-bye, with this closing remark: "You're a damned fool anyhow, and will be hanged, as you deserve to be!"

Price at first thought Wilkie was a Union spy, "and gave me in charge of the provost-marshal with orders to treat me as a gentleman." It helped when one of General Price's aides recalled reading Wilkie's dispatch to the *Dubuque Herald* about Wilson's Creek that had been reprinted by the *Saint Louis Republican*. The aide told Price it was a fair and accurate account, and that led, in Wilkie's words, "to a favorable change of opinion in regard to myself in the estimation of the Confederate leader."

As soon as Mulligan and the Irish Guard surrendered, kindly Old Pap Price told Wilkie he could go about his business. He eventually boarded the cars and made his way back to Saint Louis without a penny to his name and without his overcoat, "borrowed" by one of Price's officers.

On his first visit to Saint Louis, Wilkie had fraternized with Knox. He also had met another national correspondent, Albert D. Richardson of the *New York Tribune*, one of the Bohemians who would soon give great joy to Sherman by falling into rebel hands.

Wilkie liked Knox; he took an immediate dislike to Richardson. "He was prim, formal, precise, and had none of the openness and good-fellowship to which I was accustomed in the West. I fancied that he looked on me as a fresh country specimen, toward whom he, consciously or unconsciously, assumed an air of superiority."

When he arrived in Saint Louis the second time, after his experience at Lexington, he was in a fine fix. He had no money and no change of clothing. The only two people he knew in Saint Louis were Knox and Richardson, both of them comfortably ensconced at Barnum's Hotel. Wilkie made his way to the hotel, hoping to borrow some cash to tide him over from one or the other of the two men.

I called on them . . . and found only Richardson. I explained where I had been, and delicately hinted at my impecuniosity. Of course my visit to Lexington and my having the sole account of the events there, interested him. We were both representing New York newspapers, and it was at once a "scoop" and a humiliation to be beaten by a country reporter. He asked to see my letter, under promise that he would make no use of it to which I would not consent. He read the letter and, then, without any reply to my intimation that I would like to negotiate a small loan, he said,—

"I'll tell you what I'll do."

"Well, what is that?"

"This isn't a bad letter," he answered in an indifferent manner, "and I don't mind offering you one hundred and twenty-five dollars in gold for it for the use of the Tribune."

Wilkie ran some fast arithmetic through his head. His story would run about five columns in the *Times*, at a rate of $7.50 per column. Five times $7.50 came to only $37.50. "It was skillfully baited, this hook; it would be a couple of weeks before I could get returns from the office, and meanwhile I needed money. . . . My thoughts ran rapidly all over these things, and then I declined his offer." He sent the story to New York, and Raymond loved it.

"Mr. Raymond sent a draft for a handsome sum to my wife; he wrote me a very complimentary letter; [and] he published a half-column editorial on my feat, pronouncing it [in a fit of hyperbole] 'unparalleled in the history of journalism.'" He then made Wilkie a full-time correspondent, gave him a nice weekly salary, and promised to cover all his expenses. Knox showed up, too, and "guaranteed my responsibility to the proprietors of the hotel until I could get some funds. In a few days I had reclothed myself, had received Raymond's letters and assurances, and from that moment for many a day thereafter the world held no prouder, happier or more satisfied young man than myself."

Brimming with confidence, Wilkie announced to Knox and Richardson, "Well, boys, I believe I'll go around and call on Fremont." Yes, yes, Knox and Richardson agreed. "You ought to have done that before," one of them, barely concealing his glee, said. "Fremont will not like it when he learns that you have been in town for several days without calling on him," the other chimed in.

And so an innocent Wilkie set off to pay a call on the commanding general of Mr. Lincoln's western army.

I went over to his headquarters. There was a large yard in front, in which there were innumerable orderlies in gay uniform, a gorgeous barouche, on whose seat was a driver in livery . . . Cavalrymen with drawn swords guarded the entrance to the house, while scattered around were waiting officers, members of Congress, colonels, generals, privates, orderlies with messages, all trying to secure an audience with the Federal leader.

I gave my card to a non-commissioned officer on guard, who looked me over curiously and somewhat superciliously, and, at length, with some reluctance, disappeared within. He returned in a few moments, and introduced me into an anteroom filled with a dense mass of soldiers and civilians.

That anteroom led to another anteroom, which led to still one more anteroom, all filled with people trying to talk to Frémont. Knox and Richardson knew all about it, of course; they had already been there and done that. They never got past the third anteroom, either.

In his stories—they were now getting better play in the *Times*—Wilkie dealt fairly and accurately with the Pathfinder. On October 1, he wrote that the time had arrived for Frémont "to demonstrate to an anxious public his fitness or unfitness for the tremendous responsibilities he has assumed." The "fate of Missouri," he said, was in the general's hands.

He worried about Frémont's headquarters, with its "magnificent trappings and caparisons," its "beautiful music," its "admirable evolutions." Wilkie had been with Lyon, "with his old white hat, his stern countenance, his common everyday soldiers," at Wilson's Creek. Those soldiers feared the old man in life and revered him in death. And soldiers who had faced the enemy knew "our Secession friend is an unkempt blackguard . . . clad in a shirt innocent of soap and water" who shows no appreciation at all for "the gilded trappings of our gallant army." And then he went on to make this observation: "I believe that Gen. Fremont is a hard worker; he labors incessantly to promote the cause in which he is engaged; he leaves nothing undone that can be done by personal effort, or advanced by personal sacrifice; yet, in spite of all this, things seem to advance with supernatural slowness."

That was superior analysis, for 1861 or any other time.

Frémont already was in trouble with Lincoln for issuing a proclamation on August 30 in which he announced he would shoot all guerrillas caught inside Union lines and that he would confiscate the property and free all the slaves belonging to Confederate supporters in Missouri. Lincoln remonstrated that if Frémont killed all the Confederate guerrillas inside Federal lines, the Confederates would kill all the armed supporters of the Union inside their lines. Lincoln also worried that Frémont's order to free the Missouri slaves was not wise at a time when the president was desperate to placate Missouri and Kentucky and keep them in the Union. Lincoln asked, and then ordered, Frémont to rescind it.

Frémont was in such deep trouble that he decided only strong measures would do: he would take the field against General Price's army (fast fading away as the militiamen went home to bring in their crops). Headquarters for the Frémont advance, Wilkie learned, would be little Jefferson City, the capital, in central Missouri.

It was here that the Bohemian Brigade made its first formal appearance. Assembled at Jefferson City, in addition to Wilkie, were the ubiquitous couple, Knox and Richardson, along with Richard T. Colburn of the *New York World*, George W. Beaman of the *Saint Louis Democrat*, Joseph B. "Mack" McCullagh of the *Cincinnati Daily Gazette*, and two war artists, Henri Lovie from *Frank Leslie's Illustrated Newspaper* and Alexander Simplot (another Union College alumnus) from *Harper's Weekly*.

Add one more—the reporter who impressed Wilkie the most. He was Junius Henri Browne, representing Horace Greeley's *New York Tribune*.

> He was under-sized, slender as a woman, with a pale, effeminate face, hands and feet as diminutive as a child, sensitive mouth, and with an expression of helplessness which was intensified by a baldness. . . . There was nothing in his appearance to indicate that he would hold together for a journey over a country of a half a mile in length.

And yet he was tough as nails; he would prove that during the long months he spent in Confederate prisons and in the dramatic escape he and Richardson made from Salisbury Prison in 1863. He was also the most celebrated womanizer in the press corps; he would enhance that reputation by finding time during his escape to dally with a farmer's daughter in the proverbial hayloft.

Richardson recalled that as many as twenty correspondents converged upon Jefferson City and took up residence in a "wretched little tavern" with first-class prices. "The landlord, who was aged, rheumatic, and half blind, labored under the delusion that he kept the house; but an intelligent and middle aged slave, yclept John, was the real brain of the establishment."

While they waited for Frémont to take the field, the correspondents "discussed politics, art, society, and metaphysics, and would soon kindle into singing, reciting, 'sky-larking,' wrestling, flinging saddles, valises, and pillows."

"J.G.," almost surely Joe Glenn, dropped in on a session at the tavern and wrote an account of it in the *Cincinnati Daily Gazette.*

> I found the representatives of the Missouri Republican, the Cincinnati Commercial, the New York World, and the [New York] Tribune engaged in a hot discussion of matrimony, which finally ran into metaphysics. The Republican having plumply disputed an abstruse proposition of the Tribune, the latter seized an immense bolster, and brought it down with emphasis upon the glossy pate of his antagonist. This instantly broke up the debate, and a general *melee* commenced. The Republican grabbed a damp towel and aimed a stunning blow at his assailant, which missed him and brought up against the nasal protuberance of Frank Leslie. Then the Missouri Democrat sent a coverlet which lit upon and enveloped the knowledge-box of the Herald.

Frémont took the field with thirty-eight thousand men, marched to Springfield, and then marched back. "The entire expedition," Wilkie said, "was without any incident of consequence . . . the greatest humbug and farce in history." Frémont was replaced, and the army set off for Saint Louis.

By the time they reached Saint Louis, a city with strong secessionist sentiments, the Bohemians were swaggering. One of the correspondents, Wilkie recalled, attended the theater one evening, "ensconsed himself in a front seat in the first gallery above the parquet, and, leaning back comfortably, . . . thrust his legs, incased in a pair of huge cavalry boots, over the railing in front, where they projected in full view of the audience." Boots! Boots! people cried.

Remove the boots! An usher pounded on the Bohemian's boots with a rod used for lighting the gas lamps. No response. Other ushers came along with more poles, and pounded harder on the correspondent's boots. All to no avail. Finally, a group of ushers tried to remove the arrogant Bohemian from his seat. Colonel Ed Joslyn, commanding officer of the Thirty-sixth Illinois, was seated nearby, and he ordered the ushers to cease and desist. Thereafter, said Wilkie, the Bohemian with the cavalry boots "drew in his leathers, and calmly sauntered around to the stairway, then down and into the street."

Drink had something to do with it. The Bohemians were bored; they didn't like Saint Louis, and they took to hard liquor. Even Junius Henri Browne, usually the gentlest of all the Bohemians, took too much on board one evening and announced he was setting off into the streets of Saint Louis "to mop the boulevards with anybody and everybody in the hateful city." He never got past the front door.

Cairo, a small city at the southernmost tip of Illinois, where the Ohio River meets the Mississippi, was a key to western strategy. From Cairo, the Union army—and navy—could move downriver all the way to New Orleans and cut the Confederacy in half, or move down the northward-flowing Tennessee and Cumberland Rivers and overrun Tennessee and Kentucky. By December 1861, little Cairo was the new rallying point for the western army, and the place was humming. Wilkie wrote: "Every other civilian one met was a correspondent, or claimed to be; and one heard for the first time of the existence of journals by the hundred in every part of the northwest. Each regiment had its special representative from the home paper, and quite often each company had a 'war correspondent' in its mess."

And the only hotel of any consequence in what Wilkie called "this mud hole of a town" was the Saint Charles. "It was always jammed to repletion by officers, contractors, speculators, Hebrew dealers, river men, Northern visitors, correspondents, and scores of other classes."

In Jefferson City, the Bohemians shared six rooms. In Cairo, with vastly increased numbers, they were all assigned to Room Number 45.

Wilkie, now the wily old veteran, told what would happen when a rookie journalist pulled into town:

"I am the correspondent of the Pecatonica Horn" would be announced by the newcomer, with an eye on Knickerbocker, the clerk, to observe the expression of awe that would pass over his modest face at finding himself in the presence of a dignitary of such grandeur. "I want a first-class room. Can I get one on the front next to the levee, and not too high up?"

"Certainly," would be the suave and deferential answer. And then, after a study of checks, as if undecided whether to give the applicant the front parlor or a suite of rooms on the floor above, the clerk would continue, "Yes, there's Room No. 45; just what you want. Here, boy, show the gentleman to No. 45. Any baggage? No? All right. The boy will show you up. The key is in the door."

The "boy" was mythical and Number 45 was on the third floor, back, "overlooking a yard full of refuse and a section of country mostly under water." Wilkie continued:

Entering the room, his bucolic nature would experience a paralytic shock. There were two beds in the room, on each of which there would be likely to be a man on the outside, having on all his clothes, including his boots, with a flushed face, stertorous breathing, and exhaling a stifling alcoholic aroma. All about the room were indescribable dirt and confusion. Saddles, bridles, and horse-blankets were scattered in every direction; pieces of clipped crockery on a tumble-down washstand, with a broken-nosed pitcher, furnished the appliances for ablution, minus the water, towels, and soap.

There was a broken chair or two, a looking-glass that broadened his horrified face till it appeared as distorted as the vision of a nightmare or the worst phases of a freak in a museum of monstrosities. The bed-clothing was streaked and daubed with the pigments of dirty boots; the pillows were under the bed or under the feet of the occupant; there was a vile atmosphere, impregnated with whiskey, stale tobacco-smoke, unwashed stockings, and perspiring feet.

Such, said Wilkie, was the sight that greeted the poor young man from the *Pecatonica Horn*. "Remonstrance was useless; it was Room 45 or nothing." The smart reporter learned to cope with it. "He became crafty, and watched for opportunity to capture a bed, into which, if disposed to be swinish, he crawled, placing himself squarely in the middle and holding it against all comers."

For all the dirt and chaos, this was a glorious time for these young correspondents. Some of them had seen action—a few had seen men dying—but for most of them this was a time of expectations, and innocence. Wilkie, a congenial soul, admired almost all of his fellow Bohemians, except Charles Carleton Coffin of the *Boston Morning Journal*, the Bull Run veteran, who had turned up in Cairo to see what the war in the West was all about. His "patronymic," Wilkie thought, was "ominous," and he "moved about with all the solemnity of an undertaker."

By now Frémont was long gone, and the new man in the West was Ulysses S. Grant. Wilkie noticed that before Grant arrived in Cairo, there was a shortage of whiskey; after his arrival, the place was flooded with it.

The Union's great western leaders were slowly filing into place— Grant, William Tecumseh Sherman, and Flag Officer Andrew H. Foote among them. For the Bohemians, it was time to say good-bye to Knickerbocker at the front desk of the Saint Charles Hotel and join the Union's first real western army in the field.

The Confederate commander, Albert Sidney Johnston, had established a line of defense that ran from little Columbus, Kentucky, on the Mississippi River, across southern Kentucky to Bowling Green and beyond. Fort Henry, on the Tennessee River, and Fort Donelson, on the Cumberland River, were both major defensive positions on that line. If those two forts fell, the Confederate commanders knew, the way would be open for Union armies to seize some of the most productive and valuable territory in the South. Grant believed Fort Henry was the weakest point in Johnston's line of defense and he asked his commanding officer, Major General Henry "Old Brains" Halleck, for permission to take the troops and Foote's gunboats down the Tennessee River and capture Fort Henry. Halleck dithered, but eventually gave Grant permission to make the attack.

Most of the correspondents chose to accompany the army. Wilkie, getting savvier day by day, saw the difficulties ahead, and made arrangements to join the navy.

This was no deep-sea navy. This was a riverboat navy in which ugly gunboats designed by James B. Eads, a Saint Louis engineer, were the dreadnoughts. They had the same boxy look as the *Merrimac,* and they were protected by armored casemates. The big ones were 175 feet long and drew only 6 feet of water. They carried thirteen guns, three of them monster 9- and 10-inchers.

Fort Henry, built on low-lying ground at a bend in the Tennessee River, was a simple earthwork, with a number of bastions containing about twenty guns, ranging from 12-pounders to a 10-inch Columbiad. On February 5, 1862, the transports began their run to a point about six miles below the fort to land the fifteen thousand troops they carried. Wilkie's Fort Henry story was dated February 7 and ran in the *Times*—on the front page—on February 12. He set the scene with these somewhat overwrought words:

> It was nearly midnight before the boats took their departure, and prior to that hour everything seemed ominous of evil. The sky was hung with gloom like a hearse. Not a single kindly star witnessed our departure. . . . External indications were all against us—heavy volumes of thick black smoke rushed away like mounting streamers upon a strong South wind.

Grant's idea was to attack Fort Henry with his troops at the same time the navy flotilla was opening fire with its big guns. The gunboats opened fire at 10 A.M., but the soldiers were delayed by muddy ground.

The flotilla was led by four of the Eads gunboats: *Cincinnati,* Foote's flagship, and *Carondelet, Saint Louis,* and *Essex.* Wilkie rode along on a dispatch boat, perhaps the *W.H.B.,* which he described in one of his stories as a "gallant little craft." If so, his companions were General Grant and his staff.

The overland distance between Fort Henry on the Tennessee and Fort Donelson on the Cumberland was only about a dozen miles. When Fort Henry's commander, Brigadier General Lloyd Tilghman, saw what was steaming in his direction, he ordered the twelve hundred soldiers in the fort to march on over to Donelson to fight another day. But he kept most of his gunners in the fort, and they put on a very decent show.

Grant had been right about Fort Henry. It was bad place to locate a fort, because it was subject to flooding. Flooding was occurring on February 6, which meant that only nine of the fort's twenty big guns could be brought to bear. From his comfortable perch on the dispatch boat, Wilkie watched as the gunboats and the fort's nine cannon exchanged fire. The Union gunboats were struck more than fifty times by rebel shells, and one of them punctured *Essex*'s boilers and put her out of action; in all, a dozen Union sailors were killed.

Wilkie could actually see Richardson, who had accompanied the troops, climb a tree on the riverbank to get a better view of the action. In his memoirs, Richardson said he was one of a number of correspondents in that same tree. But because of heavy smoke they couldn't see the Confederate fort.

It was all over in less than two hours. Richardson climbed down from his tree and went inside to take a look at what was now Union property. "In the barracks," he wrote,

> we found camp-fires blazing, dinners boiling, and half-made biscuits still in the pan. Pistols, muskets, bowie-knives, books, tables partially set for dinner, half-written letters, playing-cards, blankets, and carpet-sacks were scattered about.
>
> Our soldiers ransacked trunks, arrayed themselves in Rebel coats, hats, and shirts, armed themselves with Rebel revolvers, stuffed their pockets with Rebel books, and miniatures, and some were soon staggering under heavy loads of Rebel whisky.

Richardson himself collected "a package of elegantly written letters, full of a sister's affection." A year later, he returned the letters to the young woman in Jackson, Mississippi, who had written them.

Wilkie pawed through the rebels' personal effects, too, and said in another story filed the same day that he couldn't believe the number of "love epistles" left behind by the fort's defenders.

> Could some of the haughty "chivalry" see a lot of Yankee privates gathered around some individual who had made a capture of some amiable Southern *dulcinea* encased in *papier mache*, and hear the remarks passed . . . their aristocratic noses would curl to the very roots of the eyebrows in utter scorn—nor would they be less powerfully affected, could they see some Yankee pull a *billet-doux* from his

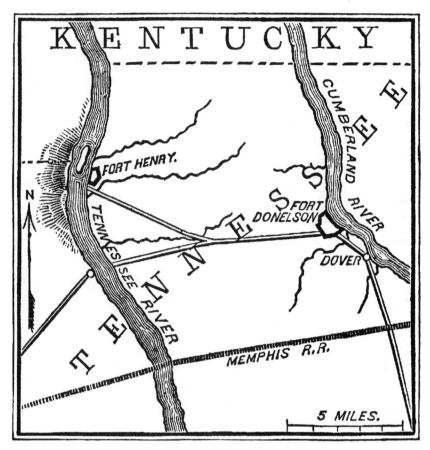

Map of Forts Henry and Donelson in February of 1862. (Author's collection)

greasy pocket, and proceed to read it aloud to a crowd of jeering comrades. Every Southern soldier seems to have fanned into a flame the affections of some Patsy or Jemima at home. Southern skies must be conducive to a flourishing growth of love.

Grant was always an enigma to Wilkie. Though he campaigned with Grant for two years, and met him many times, the general never actually spoke to Wilkie. Richardson, on the other hand, got along famously with Grant. A few days after the fall of Fort Henry, Richardson stopped by Grant's headquarters to bid him good-bye and say he was returning to New York City.

"You had better wait a day or two," Grant said.

"Why?"

"Because I am going over to capture Fort Donelson tomorrow."

"How strong is it?"

"We have not been able to ascertain exactly, but I think we can take it. At all events, we will try."

The march from Fort Henry to Fort Donelson looked easy enough on the map, just a dozen or so miles. But the weather had turned cold and nasty with sleet and snow, and neither the troops nor the corre-spondents had warm clothing or tents to endure it. Browne was in trouble even before the march began; he had been almost blinded when a box of ammunition exploded at Fort Henry, damaging one eye and inflaming the other. He wrote, "Well I remember how we of the Press wandered about . . . half-starved and half-frozen, having left our blankets and india-rubbers behind, and brought no rations with us, supposing, as did everyone else in the army, that the capture of Donelson would be a simple before-breakfast recreation."

Browne and a companion from the *New York World* were so hun-gry that they began tagging along behind army wagons, hoping to pick up a stray biscuit or piece of hard bread that sometimes fell out on the rough road.

Wilkie endured no such hardship. He was still on the dispatch boat "and found myself, in due season, without any discomfort, on the Cumberland River within striking distance of Fort Donelson."

Fort Donelson wasn't really a fort at all, but rather a sprawling, well-defended military camp high on a bluff on the west side of the river. The Confederates' big guns—one of them firing 128-pound round shot—were placed along the cliffs, at three different levels. Foote brought his big gunboats into action on the fourteenth the same way he had done a few days earlier at Fort Henry, but this time he came in so close he exposed his warships to plunging fire from the Confederate batteries. *Saint Louis* and *Louisville* were knocked out first, drifting downstream without power. The rebels then turned their fire on *Carondelet* and *Pittsburgh*. *Carondelet* was hit by one of those gigantic 128-pound cannonballs; it pierced a casement and bounced around inside the gunboat "like a wild beast pursuing its prey." Both *Carondelet* and *Pittsburgh* were forced to withdraw to make repairs.

One of the Bohemians, Frank G. Chapman of the *New York Herald*, was aboard *Louisville* when the rebel shells began flying. "A monstrous shot passed through [the gunboat], killing a lot of seamen, dismounting a gun, and doing other damage," Wilkie wrote. "The correspondent was found down below, and thus escaped all damage. The Bohemians rallied him freely about his queer choice of a location to see the attack, which he met by asserting that he had gone down there to light his cigar." (Chapman, in fact, must have been a huge disappointment to Bennett and the *Herald*. His stories came in late and failed to give an adequate picture of the action.)

The Confederate commander inside Fort Donelson was John B. Floyd, who had been President Buchanan's secretary of war from 1857 to 1860 and who had been run out of the government in disgrace after it was found he had been up to his ears in payroll padding and other forms of graft. Next in line of command was Gideon Pillow, a Tennessee politician with a considerable reputation for mendacity and opportunism. The third member of the Confederate command was Simon Bolivar Buckner, who had picked up a distaste for Pillow when the two served together in the Mexican War. This was in no way the Confederates' first team. (But the fort's cavalry commander was none other than Nathan Bedford Forrest, a first-teamer always.)

The big problem for Donelson's Confederate defenders was Grant's army and navy, boxing them in on all sides. Junius Browne was out there with a reporter from the *Saint Louis Republican*, somewhat rested and refreshed now that the long march was over. He watched as Union sharpshooters tried to pick off a rebel gunner, "whom we could not see, though we could determine, by the puff of the smoke from the vent, about where he stood."

One of the sharpshooters asked Browne if he was a good shot. "If you are, here is as good a rifle as ever killed a Rebel; and if you'll pepper that fellow over there at that gun, I'll give you anything I've got." Browne reported that he took the sharpshooter's Enfield

> with the air of Leather Stocking, and, waiting until the gun went off again, . . . I fired at the very moment the blue smoke puffed above the earthworks.

For some reason or other, the [rebel's] gun was not fired for nearly five minutes.

The sharpshooter looked at me with wonder and admiration, and saying, "I think you fixed him that time."

Browne returned the rifle to the sharpshooter, and walked away "while my laurels were still green."

"That sharpshooter," he wrote, "will believe to his last hour I killed that Rebel gunner."

Wilkie came ashore, joined some sharpshooters, and squeezed off a few rounds at the fort's defenders, too.

Hand-wringing was the order of the day among the Confederate commanders. They finally decided they would attempt a breakout from the fort along a river road leading south, after which they would march to Nashville, more than seventy miles away. The attack began the morning of the fifteenth against the Union right flank commanded by Brigadier General John A. McClernand. Grant, typically, wasn't there; he was a few miles above Donelson visiting Flag Officer Foote (who had been slightly wounded by a splinter during the bombardment). It was 1 P.M. when Grant reached the battlefield to discover the rebels had driven McClernand back almost a mile and had come perilously close to making their escape. He ordered fifty-four-year-old C. F. Smith, a Regular Army man if there ever was one, to lead what turned out to be a successful countercharge. Before the day was over, the Confederates abandoned their attempt at a breakout.

Floyd didn't want to surrender to the Yankees; he worried they would reopen those corruption charges against him, and Pillow had made a well-publicized boast that he would never surrender to the enemy. Floyd escaped in a steamboat and Pillow sneaked away in an old scow. Forrest, disgusted with the entire affair, rode out of the fort with his cavalrymen and made a dignified escape. That left Buckner to negotiate a surrender of the thirteen thousand men under his command. He sent a letter to Grant urging the appointment of commissioners to negotiate the terms of the surrender. Grant, with old C. F. Smith at his side, cheering him on, rejected the notion of commissioners. Grant replied, in words that made him a national hero, "No terms except an unconditional and immediate surrender can be accepted. I propose to move immediately upon your works."

After the surrender, Wilkie wandered around the battlefield, inside and outside the fort's perimeter, and encountered that most curious of all these war correspondents, Charles Carleton Coffin of the *Boston Morning Journal.*

> A man passed me on a lively trot who carried paper and pencil, and who halted a moment here and there to jot down a sentence. A glimpse of a jaundiced face and a solemn countenance revealed the identity of Coffin, the Boston correspondent, who was doing the fortifications on the run. As far as I could see him he kept up the pace, up hill and down, over breastworks, parapets, rifle-pits, rocks, fallen trees, and all other obstacles. He ran with his head down, like an animal which trails by scent.

Wilkie's story on the surrender of Fort Donelson ran in the *Times* on February 22, a week after the battle. It was a big spread on page 1, complete with a rough map of the action. "The whole operation was exceedingly brilliant," Wilkie said, "and reflects high credit upon Gen. Smith, who personally superintended the operation, exposed himself precisely as if he had been a private soldier, and was among the first to mount the breastwork."

All the Union regiments fought gallantly, Wilkie noted, except perhaps the Forty-fifth Illinois, which is "accused of having made a precipitate and unwarranted retreat, but probably they have sufficient reasons to satisfy themselves at least, and possibly the public."

Coffin's story appeared in the *Boston Morning Journal* on the twenty-fourth, two days after Wilkie's story turned up in the *Times*. The *Journal* was a very small paper—usually just four pages—and Coffin's story filled four columns; it was a vast improvement on his Bull Run story, which had filled less than a column. He may not have been a lot of fun to be around, but he would become one of the Civil War's finest battlefield correspondents. He was beginning to show why in his Fort Donelson story.

Fort Donelson, Tennessee.
Feb. 16, 1862.

Fort Donelson is ours, and the second gateway is opened to the heart of the Southern Confederacy.

Not bad, even by modern standards. The fact is, these correspondents—the good ones, at least—were capable of writing solid, readable battle stories when they had time to put them together. Coffin noted in his story that he had "deferred writing each day's proceeding that I might give a connected and intelligible account." Connected and intelligible it was.

Wilkie had chided Coffin for running around the battlefield like an animal on the trail of a scent. But Coffin had a good eye, and what made his story so effective was the descriptive detail. Consider this description of the captured Confederate soldiers:

> Hogarth never saw such a sight . . . They wore all kinds of uniforms, brown colored predominantly, as if they were in the snuff business and had been rolled in tobacco dust. There was sheep gray, iron gray, dirty gray, with bed blankets, quilts, buffalo robes, pieces of carpetry of all colors and figures, for blankets.
>
> Judging by the garments, one would have thought that the last scraps, odds and ends of humanity, had been brought together. . . . I do not write this as imputing at all their bravery, but to show the straitened conditions of the Southern Confederacy.

Wilkie's friend, Knox of the *Herald*, missed the capture of Forts Henry and Donelson. He had broken away from the rest of the Bohemian Brigade to join Brigadier General Samuel R. Curtis, a serious, pedantic man, who had just succeeded in driving Price's army out of Missouri. But the Confederates now had a new commander, the dashing Earl Van Dorn, who vowed to drive the Yankees back up the Mississippi all the way to Saint Louis.

He commanded "as motley an army as ever the sun shone on," Shelby Foote wrote. Part of Van Dorn's command was an Indian contingent—two thousand Creeks, Seminoles, Choctaws, Chickasaws, and Cherokees—commanded by Albert Pike, dressed in the full regalia of a Sioux warrior. The Indians brought their scalping knives with them, and showed every intention of using them. Another part was commanded by the old Texas Ranger and hero of the war with Mexico, Ben McCulloch, leading his eight thousand leathery veterans from Texas and Arkansas. The third part was the three-hundred-pound Sterling Price and his seven thousand Missourians.

"Soldiers! Behold your leader!" Van Dorn proclaimed to his seventeen-thousand-man army. "He comes to show you the way to glory and immortal renown." And then they set off to drive Curtis back to Saint Louis, Van Dorn somewhat humiliated by the necessity of traveling in a carriage; he had hurt himself falling off a horse.

Union scouts, including Wild Bill Hickok himself, rode into Curtis's camp and told him a rebel army led by a full major general was on its way. Curtis fell back to Pea Ridge, Arkansas, where he was soon joined by Brigadier General Franz Sigel's four regiments, and dug in. Sigel and most of his soldiers were German-Americans, and spoke in broken English, when they spoke English at all.

Van Dorn's initial assault on the Union lines gave every indication of a sweeping success. The Indians, whooping and hollering, forced one of the Yankee commanders, Peter Osterhaus, into an embarrassing retreat. But when the Union guns turned on them, they decided they had seen enough. In the brief time they were engaged, they did manage to take a few Yankee scalps. Then—terrible tragedy for the rebels—the fiery Ben McCulloch was killed. The next day, Sigel led his Germans in a bold attack that broke the back of Van Dorn's army. His soldiers simply ran away from the battlefield, disappeared, and weren't seen together again for a week or more. It was that rare instance of a smaller Union army defeating a larger Confederate one. It was an important and significant victory, for it secured what Lincoln had wanted so badly—Missouri safe in the bosom of the Union.

Knox and William Fayel of the *Saint Louis Missouri Democrat* were the only correspondents on the field, for either side. When the battle was over, they climbed on their horses and rode two hundred miles to Rolla, Missouri, where they boarded the cars for Saint Louis.

Knox managed to draw two rough maps and write a brief account of the battle and send them off to his editors in New York. The little package ran in the *Herald* on Friday, March 21, under the headline:

THE HARD FOUGHT BATTLE OF PEA RIDGE

The Battle Fields of March 7 and 8, 1862, at Pea Ridge,
Arkansas—the Flight and the Pursuit.

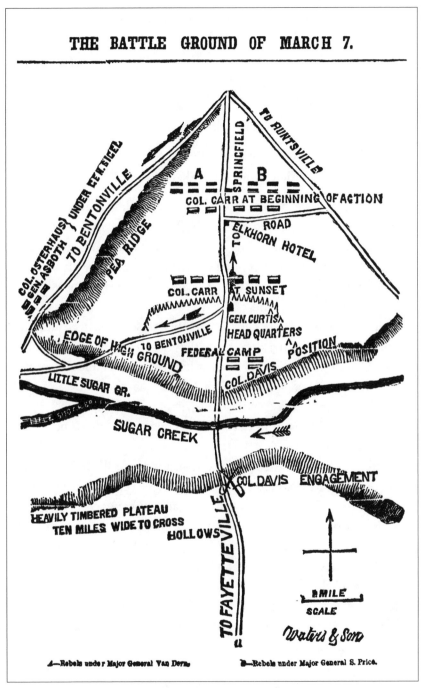

THE BATTLE GROUND OF MARCH 7.

A

B

COL. CARR AT BEGINNING OF ACTION

COL. OSTERHAUS} UNDER GEN. SIGEL
GEN. ASBOTH

TO BENTONVILLE

PEA RIDGE

TO SPRINGFIELD

TO HUNTSVILLE

TO ELKHORN HOTEL ROAD

COL. CARR AT SUNSET

GEN. CURTIS
HEAD QUARTERS

EDGE OF HIGH GROUND

TO BENTONVILLE

FEDERAL CAMP

POSITION

COL. DAVIS

LITTLE SUGAR CR.

LITTLE SUGAR CR.

SUGAR CREEK

COL. DAVIS ENGAGEMENT

HEAVILY TIMBERED PLATEAU
TEN MILES WIDE TO CROSS

HOLLOWS

TO FAYETTEVILLE

A MILE
SCALE

Waters & Son

A—Rebels under Major General Van Dorn.   B—Rebels under Major General S. Price.

Thomas Knox's map of Pea Ridge, from the *New York Herald*, March 21, 1862.
(Clements Library, University of Michigan)

But the story of this important Union victory was only ten paragraphs long, offering little in the way of graphic detail.

The day before, though, March 20, the *New York Tribune* turned over all of page 6 to a full and seemingly detailed first-person account of the battle. It began:

From our special correspondent.

BATTLE FIELD ON SUGAR CREEK, BENTON CO., ARKANSAS.
Monday morning, March 10, 1862.

The special correspondent was the enterprising Junius Browne, who wrote the story in his hotel room in Rolla, the rail depot two hundred miles from the battlefield. He even drew a map to accompany the story that captured the general outlines of the battle. "It was the cruellest event of the war, so far as it related to the experiences of the correspondents," Wilkie said.

In his memoirs, the *Tribune*'s Albert Richardson said his colleague, Browne, and another reporter from the *New York World*—possibly Richard Colburn—repaired to Rolla when they heard about the battle and wrote "elaborate accounts of the two days' conflict . . . [by] perusing the very meager official dispatches, knowing what troops were engaged, and learning from an old countryman the topography of the field."

It's too bad we aren't sure of the identity of the *World*'s reporter, for his dispatch was particularly outrageous. "Even now," he wrote, "while I attempt to collect my blurred and disconnected thoughts, the sound of booming cannon and the crack of rifle rings in my ear, while visions of carnage and the flame of battle hover before my sight. Three days of constant watching, without food or sleep, and the excitements of the struggle, have quite unstrung my nerves."

Richardson insisted it wasn't until months later that Browne's editors learned his first-person Pea Ridge story was fraudulent. That's hard to credit. But, either way, they must have loved it, for the story created what every modern editor craves—a buzz. Browne's story was widely reprinted, and the *Times* of London called it the best battle account published in a U.S. newspaper during the war.

But what made Browne's story really hum was the way he described the behavior of the Indians during the battle; dozens of newspapers in the North picked up the theme. They were all outraged at the scenes so vividly portrayed by Browne.

> The savages indeed seemed demonized, and it is said the Rebels did everything in their power to excite them to frenzy, giving them large quantities of whiskey and gunpowder. . . . The appearance of some of the savages was fearful. . . . With bloody hands and garments, with glittering eyes and horrid scowls, they raced about the field with terrible yells. . . .
>
> The Indians in many instances could not refrain from scalping their enemies, and it is said that as many as a hundred of our brave men were thus barbarously treated. They frequently scalped the dead they found on the field, and in ten or twelve cases so served soldiers who were merely wounded. . . . Friend and foe were entirely alike to them; they fired at the nearest mark, and used their long knives indiscriminately upon all within their reach. For more than twelve hours they continued this impartial warfare, killing and wounding more of the Missouri and Arkansas troops than they did of ours.

The Indians did take a few scalps, much to the regret of the Confederate commanders. But they played almost no role in the outcome of the battle, and they never appeared again in such large numbers, fighting on either side, for the rest of the war.

Wilkie, meanwhile, had made his way back to Cairo, at the mercy once again of the Saint Charles Hotel and its front-desk clerk, the infamous Knickerbocker. It was there Wilkie met Henri Lovie, the artist for *Frank Leslie's Illustrated Newspaper*. Wilkie gave Lovie what modern journalists call "a fill" on the action at Fort Donelson. Lovie then worked up a nice drawing; his published sketch was labeled "our correspondent on the spot."

6

Afloat

WHEN LINCOLN TOOK OFFICE, fifty of the U.S. Navy's ninety warships were sailing ships—beautiful, but in the words of one historian, "as obsolete as the galleys of Themistocles" in 480 B.C. Of these ninety ships, forty-two were in service, ready for war. Most of these active-duty ships were powered by steam (though still carrying sails), and they were scattered all over the world—*San Jacinto* on the African coast, *Iroquois* in the Mediterranean, *John Adams* in the East Indies.

Union strategists knew that from this nucleus they would need to build a very large oceangoing navy to blockade thirty-five hundred miles of Confederate coastline, from the Rio Grande to Chesapeake Bay, and run down Confederate raiders on the high seas. They would also need to build from scratch small gunboats to support amphibious operations along the Atlantic coastline and a riverboat fleet to support the armies in the West.

Secretary Gideon Welles's Navy Department bought more than four hundred merchant vessels, including New York City ferryboats, and did the best it could to equip them for war (a little like trying to make a shirt out of a vest, one navy officer said). The real job was building serious warships, and for months that was a puzzle. Should they be wood or iron? As late as October of 1861, navy commanders were still arguing in an official report that ironclad warships were useful only for harbor or coastal defense. With some reluctance, conceding the faint possibility they might be wrong, these old sailors agreed to proceed with the construction of three ironclad ships. One of them was designed by a Swede, John Ericsson; he named his low-lying, turreted ship *Monitor;* she looked, one critic said, like a plate with a Christmas pudding on top. Ericsson built her in a New York shipyard in record time.

As soon as the war began, a quarter of the navy's regular officers—260 in all—defected to the Southern side. But not a single warship switched sides. Thus, for the Confederacy, with no warships of its own, no shipyards of any consequence, no machine shops, no rope yards, no big naval guns, the challenge was even greater. But the South's imaginative secretary of the navy, Stephen Russell Mallory, understood better than anyone else the significance of ironclads. "I regard the possession of an iron-armored ship as a matter of the first necessity," he wrote on May 8, 1861. "Such a vessel at this time could traverse the entire coast of the United States, prevent all blockade, and encounter, with a fair prospect of success, their entire navy." Using what was left of a scuttled Union steam frigate called the *Merrimac,* he built a superweapon, christened it the *Virginia,* and gave the Union its greatest single scare of the war. One ship—Ericsson's *Monitor*—took on *Merrimac* (*Virginia,* to the Confederate navy) early in March of 1862 and saved the Union's wooden navy. Light now dawned at the Navy Department, and it began building monitors at a prodigious pace—thirty-five in 1862 and twenty-five more in 1863. By late 1864, the U.S. Navy was the world's most powerful.

For editors, North and South, covering fighting on land was a lot easier than covering fighting on water. Reporters on land could use the telegraph; they could jump on the railroad cars and ride to their newsrooms; they could even use the mail. Reporters afloat had none of those newsgathering advantages. And so most newspapers simply finessed the idea of creating specialists to write about naval warfare.

But there was one outstanding exception—and, no surprise, it was James Gordon Bennett and the *New York Herald.* Bennett hired a real sailor, Bradley Sillick Osbon, away from the *New York World* and made him his chief naval correspondent. Except for the fact he missed the epoch-making battle between the *Merrimac* and the *Monitor*—no small miss—Osbon earned his keep.

Everything about Osbon was special—even his name. He said his great-grandfather's name was Osborne. He sold corn brooms and when a new shipment came in with his name misspelled "Osbon" on the handles, he figured it was cheaper to change his name than send the brooms back.

Osbon was another poor boy from upstate New York. His father was a Methodist minister and, because the family moved so often, young Osbon was sent to a boarding school in Sheffield, Massachusetts. He ran away when he was eleven years old and enlisted as part of a crew of a canal boat bound upstream from Hudson, New York. He got off at Troy and signed on to drive horses on the towpath. Faced with a bill of fare of salt pork and potatoes twenty-one times a week, he resigned at Schenectady and came back down the river to New York City. "I was captured in the metropolis, taken home, cleaned up, and endowed with a new suit of clothes," he said in his memoirs. "Then I ran away again."

Altogether, Osbon said, "I spent about three years in running away and being dragged home. I was once taken in Fulton Market, sleeping in a fish wagon." Osbon's father finally decided enough was enough and asked a friend, Francis M. French, captain of a transatlantic sailing ship, *Cornelia*, to take the unruly lad to sea. "I was between 13 and 14 years of age."

From then on Osbon was a real sailor. While serving in the whaler *Maxwell* he touched shore in the South Seas at Tongatabu, in the Friendly Islands, "and fell in love with the dusky little daughter of a king, who wanted me to remain on the island. Here was one of my great lost opportunities, for I might have succeeded to the throne and become father to a race of monarchs. But I was young then and the world seemed waiting to be conquered."

He moved on to Hong Kong, where he joined an international coast guard organized to suppress Chinese pirates. He described it in his memoirs:

I enlisted on a flotilla that made pirate hunting its daily occupation. This Navy was composed of a number of open boats maintained largely by the British government, seconded by the Chinese authorities. The boats were about forty feet long, carried each a small howitzer and a crew of about thirty-five men—mainly Europeans. The pay was good, and there was prospective prize money, though, as usual, I was attracted chiefly by the desire for adventure.

Osbon joined the crew of boat Number 23, part of what he called the "lucky division," and in the six months he served with the little flotilla "we engaged eleven junks, which we destroyed, and five with which we had running fights but lost them, owing chiefly to fogs." One of the pirate junks put up a spirited resistance, and Osbon barely escaped with his life. He recalled:

> The odds were terribly against us, as the pirates had been prepared, while we had been surprised and had lost valuable men. All told there were about sixty of us . . . to do the work. We lost several men boarding the pirate, but we were desperate and went in with our cutlasses at once, keeping our firearms in reserve. I have been in many hand to hand fights, both in that service and in the Argentine navy, but I never saw worse slaughter than I witnessed that morning on the pirate junk. The pirates were like devils, but we were all good swordsmen, and we cut them down almost as fast as we could get at them. In the midst of it I suddenly found myself cornered by three of the enemy, who were giving me the tussle of my life with their crooked swords. I could do nothing but parry, and I felt that I could not keep that up for very long. In fact, I was on the point of exhaustion when a young English boy ran up behind one of my opponents, and putting a pistol to his head scattered his brains over the deck. The suddenness of it startled the others, and an instant later I had cleft one of the pirates across the jaw and borne down upon the other with the point—thus, with Bob's help, finishing the three of them.

That put an end to it. The deck, Osbon said, was littered with the bodies of ninety dead and wounded pirates; twenty more had jumped overboard. The junk was carrying $60,000 in specie, a very large sum, and it was divided among the members of Osbon's little flotilla by a prize court in Hong Kong.

Not only did Osbon fight Chinese pirates, but he also participated in a naval battle in Argentina. It was late in 1853, he wrote, that he arrived in Buenos Aires as second mate of the sailing ship *Margaret*

Eliza, out of New York. Much to Osbon's delight, the country was in the midst of a revolution, the details of which he never quite fathomed. For the record, an arrival in Buenos Aires in late 1853 would suggest he was witnessing an attempt by revolutionary forces to overthrow the government.

The revolutionary fleet was commanded by an American sailor of fortune, Commodore Juan Halsted Coe, and Osbon sought his permission to accompany the flagship, a little English-built steamer called *El Correo*, against the government fleet. It turned out to be a fierce battle in which nine out of eleven of *El Correo*'s officers were killed or seriously wounded. "When the first officer was stricken down I volunteered to take his place and did the best I could to fill it. When the fight was over we had captured seven prizes, though with a heavy loss of life on both sides," he wrote in his memoirs. Coe was so impressed with Osbon's performance—at least Osbon said he was—that he offered him command of any of the captured prizes. Osbon picked out the *Veinte-cinco de Mayo* ("in honor of some anniversary") and became a commander in the revolutionary navy.

His service in that navy came to a shabby end when Commodore Coe delivered his fleet to the government for $250,000 in gold, and set sail for England. Coe gave Osbon advance warning of his treachery, and entrusted him with half the gold to take to his wife in New York. Osbon rejoined his own ship, the *Margaret Eliza*, and delivered the gold safely to an appreciative Mrs. Coe. The commodore, Osbon concluded, "was a professional revolutionist. I was simply a sailor of fortune, fighting for the joy of adventure."

Wonderful stories, these, but are they true? The suspicion is that the basic outline is accurate—we do know, after all, that there was an international squadron tracking down Chinese pirates and that Commodore Coe did command a flotilla in Argentina. Still, it is fairly obvious Osbon embellished some of these tales. He was still doing it when he was a spry 80 years old. One of his friends, T. W. Sheridan, recalled in a letter to the Proceedings of the U.S. Naval Institute in May 1937 that he had talked to Osbon about those Chinese pirates in 1906. Sheridan said Osbon told him that when he and his victorious shipmates sailed into Hong Kong harbor, "gantlines were rigged from each yardarm and the gurgling captives were swung aloft to gurgle their last gasps to the roar of applause that greeted the triumphant Osbon's return. There was only one fly in the ointment; there were not enough pirates to go around and the lee main topsail yard was barren of any swinging ornament."

Osbon, Sheridan wrote, possessed an orderly mind, and that empty topsail yard offended him. So when he was told the Chinese cook had burned the pea soup he took action. "Swiftly, the fat, useless, and cunning scoundrel was rushed to the rigging, noosed by the neck, and swung aloft to fill the vacant place."

Sheridan admitted Osbon never furnished any documentary proof of this alarming episode, "and it may be that he just told it for the moral effect of inculcating a spirit of order and symmetry."

When he finally arrived back in New York from Argentina, Osbon, now "Captain" Osbon, discovered he had a gift for telling stories—who could question that?—and began delivering a series of popular lectures about his sailing career. His stage performances caught the attention of the editors of the *New York World*, and they hired Osbon in the spring of 1860 as the paper's first marine reporter.

Osbon had a flair for secret missions, and his first breakthrough as a reporter was his description of the Union navy's mystery ship, the Stevens Bomb-proof Floating Battery, under construction since 1842 in a dry dock in a Hoboken, New Jersey, hillside. The Stevens Battery was designed to be a real warship, and if it had been completed in a timely manner—it was never completed at all—it would have been the first seagoing ironclad in history (beating out the French *Gloire*, launched in 1859).

As war approached, interest in the Stevens Battery became fairly intense. Reporters for the *Herald* made several unsuccessful efforts to get close enough to the dry dock to see the mystery ship. Osbon said his editors promised him $20 if he could "get the eagerly sought description . . . a large sum in those days, but I cared more for the glory." Osbon recalled:

> One morning I went over there to reconnoitre. I found that the stories of watchmen, guns, etc., had been exaggerated, and presently

discovered a hole in the fence, through which I crawled, taking such risk as seemed necessary to the work in hand. Fairly inside the excavation [in the hillside], I found no ladder by which I could get into the vessel, but there were open rivet holes, and sharpening some sticks I put those through as I climbed and presently was inside, pacing off the dimensions, and estimating the depth. I came out unobserved, went to the machine shop and saw parts of her engine. With my knowledge of steamships, I constructed the battery in my mind with fair accuracy, then went to the office and asked permission to go aboard, but was peremptorily refused and ordered off the premises. Next morning Commodore Stevens [the ship's designer] read a description of his vessel, which created a profound sensation among naval men as well as newspaper editors, and everybody wanted to know who had been smart enough to get to the windward of the commodore.

Not long thereafter, Osbon managed to make certain he was the only reporter to accompany the expedition sent by Lincoln to relieve Major Robert Anderson and his garrison at Fort Sumter. Osbon simply asked an old friend commanding one of the ships, the revenue cutter *Harriet Lane*, if he could come aboard. The ship's skipper said he could, but only if he signed on as a member of the crew. Osbon sailed for Charleston as the ship's clerk and signal officer. More than any other Civil War journalist, Osbon led this amazing double life—both naval officer and journalist, switching from one role to the other as circumstances dictated.

In his story published April 19—really a day-by-day diary—Osbon listed in small type all the officers aboard the *Harriet Lane*, including, ninth down the list, Captain's Clerk B. S. Osbon.

Osbon and the *Harriet Lane*—now officially a navy ship, an unhappy surprise for many members of her Revenue Service crew—arrived off the Charleston bar on April 11, with most of the other ships in the expedition still missing. In his story, Osbon wrote:

> We are now in five fathoms of water, and the Baltic "rounds to," and Captain Gustavus Fox [soon to be Welles's deputy at the Navy Department and a malignant figure in Osbon's career] hails us and says, " . . . they are firing on Fort Sumter." We can plainly see the

smoke of the guns at Moultrie and Sumter. The war has commenced. Our bow and stern ports are taken out, pumps rigged, hose screwed on, and all hands seem in fine spirits; some of the boys have taken off their shirts, and seem as anxious as willing to fight. At twenty minutes past 11 o'clock, the drum beats to "quarters," guns are manned, officers put on their side arms, magazine and shell room is opened, and we are ready to do active duty.

The Union ships moved closer until they were about four miles from Fort Sumter.

From this position we could see the flash of the guns from Sumter, Moultrie, and Cummings Point battery, and on Sumter the good old stars and stripes waved over the devoted band who were returning the fire of the forts with rapidity, and, evidently, some precision, for occasionally the firing at Moultrie and Cummings Point slackened. The shells from the Point battery did not seem to burst as well as they could have wished, for many of them passed clear over Sumter, and exploded between it and Moultrie. Clouds of white smoke rolled along the surface of the water, and boom after boom of the heavy guns constantly saluted our ears. The most extensive excitement prevailed on board of our squadron. The *Baltic* was swarming with soldiers, who were watching the firing with no ordinary interest. . . .

By 2 o'clock the men were getting excited, and if the order had been given to go in, I really believe that every man would have given three hearty cheers for the Union and Major Anderson, and been ready to lay down his life for the reinforcement of Fort Sumter.

Osbon told a different story in his memoirs:

I shall never forget the scene on board the *Harriet Lane* that memorable morning. The first shot had brought every man to the deck, and, standing on the wheelhouse or any high point for a better view, the men who but a day or two before had been ready to mutiny rather than go into action, now screamed and swore and raved and demanded that they be led against these assailants of the old flag. . . . [But] we knew that we could do no good—that with the heavy sea and unmarked channels, and with the accuracy of the Confederate gun fire, vessels such as ours could never reach Sumter.

On Sunday, the fourteenth, after the fort surrendered, Anderson and his troops were taken aboard the flotilla's flagship, the *Baltic*. Clever Osbon wangled a transfer to the flagship and spent most of the return trip to New York interviewing Anderson. On the face of it, the expedition was a failure, and in his memoirs Osbon wrote that the man who had directed it and who would become the navy's assistant secretary, Gustavus Fox, sidled up to him with a request: leave my name out of the story. Osbon said he agreed, and in his story he praised Anderson and almost everyone else involved in the fort's surrender, without mentioning Fox. But, of course, as we have seen, Fox's name did appear fleetingly in the story.

The ships arrived off Sandy Hook, New Jersey, on the eighteenth, and Anderson's brief report—edited by Osbon—was sent by telegraph to Washington. Osbon took his story to the *World*'s office, and it caused a sensation the next day. He said—he was never a modest man—that he and his paper were "triumphant" in their "great beat."

To almost everyone's surprise, Anderson and his garrison and the sailors involved in the expedition that failed to relieve him became the heroes of the hour. No one was more surprised than Gustavus Fox, who publicly complained that Osbon had downplayed his role in the expedition on purpose. Osbon replied—also publicly—that he had done so only because Fox had asked him to write the story that way. The likely explanation is that Fox was angry in the knowledge that he could have been a hero, and blamed Osbon, and not himself, for the lost opportunity. All we do know is that for the rest of the war, Osbon's most persistent critic and enemy was Gustavus Fox, and in 1864 he finally got even by arresting Osbon for giving information to the enemy.

While James Gordon Bennett and his deputy, managing editor Frederic Hudson, liked Osbon's story about the Stevens Battery, they were truly impressed by his story on Fort Sumter. They offered Osbon $25 a week to come over to the *Herald* as its naval editor—three times what he had been making at the *World*—and he accepted.

The Civil War took place just as the world's major navies were making the difficult transition from sail to steam. The U.S. Navy still possessed some of its old sailing ships—the *Constitution*, the greatest fighting frigate of them all, was on the list, for example—but the new navy being built by Welles and Fox and a brilliant engineer, Benjamin Franklin Isherwood, would be powered by steam. And steam meant coal, and coal meant coaling stations. To enforce its blockade, the Union navy needed coaling stations up and down the Atlantic coast and in the Gulf of Mexico so that its ships could be coaled without making long trips back to Northern ports.

Port Royal, South Carolina—we know the area better today as Hilton Head—was chosen as the site for the Union navy's first big anchorage and coaling station on the Southern coast, and a grand fleet was assembled to capture it. Transports would accompany the fleet with thirteen thousand soldiers and marines commanded by Brigadier General Thomas W. Sherman, the "other Sherman." The Union navy that sailed from Hampton Roads, Virginia, on October 29, 1861, included four of Isherwood's brand-new gunboats, all of them built in an astonishingly short time and known throughout the navy as the "90-day gunboats."

The destination was supposed to be secret, but the *New York Times* infuriated navy officials by announcing the fleet's departure—prematurely, as it turned out—and its destination and even listing the ships and army units that were a part of it. The fleet's commanding officer, Flag Officer Samuel F. Du Pont, complained to the Navy Department that the *Times*' story could mean the loss of four or five thousand Union lives. "But what does the Times care for that if it can be in advance of rival sheets?" Du Pont asked.

Osbon knew the fleet's destination but he kept his mouth shut and found a berth on the powerful forty-eight-gun steam frigate *Wabash*, Du Pont's flagship, as the correspondent of the *New York Herald* with a pass signed by Navy Secretary Welles. But before the fleet weighed anchor, the skipper of one of the transports, *Matanzas*, came aboard the *Wabash*, announced that one of his officers was very ill, and asked Du Pont if he could borrow a substitute from the flagship. Du Pont said he had no one to spare. The commander of the transport then spotted Osbon seated at a table near Du Pont. "Hello, Osbon," he said, "why can't you come along with me?" Du Pont agreed, and Osbon once again became an officer in the navy, even before the fleet had sailed.

The *Matanzas* carried the Forty-eighth New York Volunteers, an outfit filled with somber, God-fearing Methodists, whose trust in Providence was tested severely when the fleet ran into a gale off Cape Hatteras. *Governor* was lost, but only seven of the six hundred marines aboard perished; another transport, *Peerless*, loaded with stores, also sank but without any loss of life. The fleet, minus *Governor* and *Peerless*, assembled off the Port Royal bar on November 4, and the canny Osbon quickly shifted his base to the flagship, *Wabash*, where the reporter/naval officer even sat in on the decisive council of war. (Several other reporters sailed with the fleet, but none of them arranged to watch the fight from the deck of a real warship, least of all the commanding officer's flagship.)

Port Royal, it appeared, would be a tougher nut to crack than the Union commanders had anticipated. It was defended by two forts, Walker at Hilton Head and Beauregard on the other side of the channel at Bay Point, and both of them bristled with powerful guns, some of them rifled. The forts were commanded by Thomas F. Drayton. One of the Union ships, the *Pocahontas*, was commanded by his only brother, Percival Drayton. Both of them were South Carolinians and some navy officers wondered about Percival Drayton's loyalties. The Confederates had also assembled a mosquito fleet—three side-wheel steamers, each carrying two 32-pound field artillery guns.

The plan was to send the Federal fleet, led by *Wabash* and *Susquehanna*, its two most powerful ships, straight up the channel, so that their port broadsides pummeled Walker and their starboard guns, Beauregard. Two miles above the forts, they planned to turn around and come down the channel to finish the job.

Osbon had a splendid view of the action.

> We had . . . spectators. As the residents of Washington had driven out to behold the spectacle of Bull Run, so now from Beaufort, Charleston, Savannah, and all the country around, a crowd of excursionists had gathered to witness the destruction of the Yankee fleet.

Seven large steamers crowded with sightseers appeared around the headlands, one of them flying the English, and another the French flag, showing that consuls of these nations were aboard.

Wabash opened fire with her 10-inch bow guns, and let go five minutes later with her heavy broadsides. "Our sightseers," Osbon said, "were beholding as grand a spectacle as the world will ever produce." Osbon watched as Commodore Josiah Tattnall's little mosquito fleet

> began popping at us from his position at the mouth of Skulk [Scull] Creek, but the range was too long and the marksmanship too poor to cause much annoyance. In fact, I do not think Flag Officer DuPont even remembered his existence until I said, "Flag Officer, that fellow over there is firing at us; can't we do something about him?" [At the beginning of the Civil War, the navy had no admirals of any kind. Thus the infelicitous title, flag officer.]
>
> But Commodore Tattnall had already decided that his Mosquito Fleet did not belong in that battle, and before a vessel could be sent after him he had retired up Skulk [Scull] Creek to a place of safety.

Osbon took great pride in his red whiskers—"a beard whose glory had excited even the Prince of Wales [during his visit to the United States]," he noted, with a typical lack of modesty. At the height of the exchange between the forts and Du Pont's ships, Osbon peered at the action from a port shattered by enemy gunfire. The moment he stuck his head through the port, one of *Wabash*'s big guns opened fire, "and a wadding of rope yarn blew back into my long whiskers, and in an instant my face was in flames. . . . It took me but a second to extinguish the conflagration. . . . I hurried below, took a pair of shears and trimmed my whiskers a la Grant." Osbon came back on deck and announced, "I have been severely wounded—in the whiskers."

One of Fort Walker's guns—a 32-pounder—was hitting the Union warships with some regularity. Osbon said he marveled as Percival Drayton took the *Pocahontas* close inshore and opened fire on Thomas Drayton's fort in "a brilliant display of marksmanship" that wrecked the annoying gun and resolved any doubts of Percival Drayton's loyalty.

The battle lasted about three hours. When it was over, Osbon joined Commodore John Rodgers in the whaleboat that was sent ashore to demand Fort Walker's surrender. "As the boat touched the gravelly beach, the men jumped out, and taking Captain Rodgers and myself on their shoulders landed us dryshod on the soil of South Carolina. . . . In another minute the Stars and Stripes were flying above Fort Walker, and for miles around the air was rent with cheers of the soldiers and sailors from the combined fleets."

Osbon was a man of considerable parts. Somewhere, somehow, he had become a reasonably accomplished artist. He earned cash on the side by sending sketches from time to time to *Harper's Weekly*. His Port Royal sketches were published in the November 30 issue and give an impressively vivid picture of the expedition.

Osbon returned to Fortress Monroe and began thinking about the *Merrimac*. He knew the Confederates had raised her and were converting her into a powerful ironclad, their superweapon. He decided it would be worthwhile to see how they were coming along. He wrote Hudson, his managing editor, "asking him to send me down a sixteen-foot Hell Gate pilot boat such as was used for boarding vessels in Long Island Sound. Mr. Hudson was a man of prompt action. The boat came almost immediately, and one night when a light fog lay on the river I made up my mind to undertake the job planned." He described the foray:

> I prepared for the occasion by covering my thole-pins with sheepskin in order to make no noise with my oars. Then with a compass and a lead line in the boat I pulled softly across past the Sewell Point batteries, which would have given me a lively time had they seen me, up around Crainey [Craney] Island—on up the Elizabeth River to the Gosport yard, where the *Merrimack* lay. I expected to have to get very close to the vessel before I could get a good look at her, but the fog had lightened a good deal by the time I was in her neighborhood and the night was not dark. When within a hundred yards of her I had an excellent view of the monster which was soon to descend upon our fleet of wooden vessels then lying in Hampton Roads.

Bradley Osbon's sketches in *Harper's Weekly* of the fleet preparing to attack Port Royal, South Carolina, in November of 1861. (Library of Congress)

Osbon fixed her dimensions and proportions in his mind and returned to Fortress Monroe undetected. There, he wrote a description of the supership for the *Herald* and drew a sketch of her for *Harper's Weekly*. He also told Major General John E. Wool, the seventy-eight-year-old commander of the Federal troops at Fortress Monroe, what he had seen. Osbon liked the old general—he had known him for years—and suggested that he was prepared to lead a boarding expedition to capture and destroy the *Merrimac*. Wool was old, but he wasn't crazy; he declined Osbon's offer.

Osbon must have known it would be only a few weeks before *Merrimac* got under way to begin her attack on the Union's fleet of defenseless wooden warships. It didn't take a prophet to understand this duel would be epoch-making for naval warfare and highly significant for the progress of the Civil War itself. Osbon missed it all.

He decided he would rather join an expedition that was being organized to batter its way past Confederate forts below New Orleans and then land fifteen thousand soldiers under the command of the repellant Major General Benjamin F. Butler to occupy the largest city in the Confederacy.

He took a train to Philadelphia, and offered his services to the sixty-year-old veteran who would command the expedition, David G. Farragut. "Mr. Osbon," Farragut said, "I am glad to meet you and should be pleased to have you in the flagship. But I can tender you only the position of clerk, as I have already appointed my secretary. The clerkship pays a salary of fifty dollars a month."

Osbon never explained why he made this curious decision, or if he even talked to Hudson and the other editors in New York about it. A few weeks earlier, he had given some thought to serving with David Dixon Porter, another navy commander, with the stipulation that he would also continue to work as a newspaper correspondent. Nothing came of that, but it is likely the same stipulation applied to his service with Farragut. Newspaper reporters sometimes worry that they are voyeurs to history, and never historical figures in them. Perhaps Osbon just wanted to be inside the action. Knowing he had no chance at all of finding a berth aboard *Monitor*, he may have figured he could get inside the action best by serving with a fleet.

In his memoirs, Osbon argued that Farragut's successful passage of the forts below New Orleans on April 24, 1862, was the navy's greatest single achievement in the Civil War. And maybe it was. It was certainly Osbon's greatest moment in the war.

The navy report of October 1861 that had concluded ironclads were only useful for harbor and coastal defense also concluded that warships could never succeed in running past powerful masonry forts. Now, in the spring of 1862, Farragut's own colleague, Porter (Farragut had sailed with Porter's father as an eleven-year-old midshipman in the War of 1812), agreed; he told Farragut it couldn't be done. The Confederate defenses were formidable—Fort Jackson, with seventy-four guns, on the right bank and Fort Saint Philip, with fifty-two guns, a little farther up on the other side of the river, both made of solid brick, joined by a barrier of cypress logs and eight old schooner hulks tied to one another by iron chains. This time, too, the Confederates had something better than Commodore Tattnall's mosquito boats at Port Royal. Their fleet included the ironclad ram *Manassas*, the ironclad *Louisiana*, not quite ready to steam, but still useful as a floating battery; three other floating batteries, one of them the unfinished *Mississippi*, designed to be the fastest warship in the world (but still missing some of her vital machinery); and a number of smaller gunboats.

Farragut commanded a fleet of eight steam warships (*Hartford, Brooklyn, Richmond, Pensacola, Mississippi, Oneida, Iroquois,* and *Varuna*), along with nine big gunboats, several armed steamers, and Porter's flotilla of twenty schooners carrying huge 13-inch mortars. They were all made of wood.

Osbon was aboard *Hartford,* serving as Farragut's clerk. Only a few days before the battle, the two men sat down for the first time and had a long chat. Farragut learned then that Osbon had fought Chinese pirates and Argentine warships, something he hadn't known when he took him on as clerk. Osbon filled him in on his fighting record and Farragut was so impressed he asked Osbon to take charge of the signals as signal officer of the fleet. "I thankfully accepted the task, and from that day until we were safely at New Orleans, made every signal that controlled the . . . squadron."

Osbon was nothing if not adventurous. When Farragut sent the gunboats *Kennebec* and *Wissahickon* upriver to take a look at the rebel defenses, Osbon went along. Osbon and the *Kennebec* came under fire from both Confederate forts "and we realized that to pass between those two well-armed and ably manned works at a perfectly point-blank range was going to be a task to try men's souls."

Porter maneuvered his mortar schooners into position the morning of April 18. Osbon said they were a "pretty show as they filed by, [with] their masts and rigging covered with tree branches" as camouflage. They opened fire at 10 A.M., each schooner sending off a huge 13-inch shell once every ten minutes. Farragut hadn't thought much of the schooners and now his suspicions were vindicated; they made a lot of noise and did very little damage.

Farragut went ahead with his own preparations. Osbon thought some of them were ingenious.

Through the inspiration of Engineer Moore of the *Richmond,* our chain-cables were arranged on the outside of the vessels immediately over the engines and boilers, and made an excellent protection.

Another idea was to whitewash the decks, so that in the dark—for it had been decided that we would run the forts in the night—rammers and other dark objects could be more easily distinguished. A third plan was to paint the outside of the vessels with a mixture of oil and mud, so they would be harder to see.

The night of April 20, the gunboats *Itasca* and *Pinola,* "dismasted that they might be less conspicuous," were sent upriver to break the river chain between the two forts. *Itasca* slipped over the chain, ran upriver, turned around, worked her engines up to full steam, and came barreling down the river so hard and so fast her bow rose three feet in the air when she broke the chain and opened a gap wide enough for Farragut's big ships.

The Confederates began sending fire rafts down the river, loaded with pine knots and well-saturated with oil, "the whole burning fiercely like a prairie fire and making a rare show in the night on the water." At the same time, Confederate sharpshooters ranged up and down the shoreline "to carry information and to pick off our men."

Farragut didn't like any of this, Osbon observed, and was growing more impatient by the minute. "We are wasting ammunition and time," he told Porter. "Wait one more day, Flag Officer," Porter replied, "and I will cripple them so you can pass up with little or no loss of life." This, said Osbon, "was a strong appeal to Farragut's tender nature," and he gave Porter an extra day.

An extra day's shelling gave no evidence of silencing the Confederate forts, but Porter still pleaded with Farragut for more time.

"Look here, David, we'll demonstrate the practical value of mortar work. Mr. Osbon, get two small flags, a white one and a red one, and go to the mizzen topmasthead and watch where the mortar shells fall. If inside the fort, wave the red flag. If outside the fort, wave the white one."

Osbon took his position and the mortars opened fire with renewed vigor.

Up there at the masthead where I could see, it kept me busy waving the little flags and I had to watch very closely not to make mistakes. On the deck, 'way aft, Farragut sat, watching the waving flags and occasionally asking for the score. The roar became perfectly deafening, and the ship trembled like an aspen. Still I kept the flags going, while every man in the fleet was watching and trying to keep count. At last I was ordered from aloft and the tally sheet was footed up, showing that the "outs" had it, by a large majority.

"There, David," said Farragut, "there's the score. I guess we'll go up the river tonight."

Farragut gained more fame for his "Damn the torpedoes! Full steam ahead!" attack at Mobile Bay in August 1864, but New Orleans was riskier. For Osbon, it was the single most exciting three hours in his long life. At 2 A.M. on Thursday the twenty-fourth, Osbon hoisted two red lanterns to *Hartford*'s mizzen peak, and the first of the seventeen ships in Farragut's squadron began moving upriver in single file.

"What do you estimate our casualties will be?" Farragut asked Osbon.

"Flag Officer," Osbon said, "I have been thinking of that and I believe we will lose a hundred."

"No more than that?" Farragut responded. "How do you calculate on so small a number?"

"Well," Osbon answered, "most of us are pretty low in the water, and, being near, the enemy will shoot high. . . . I believe a hundred men will cover our loss."

"I wish I could think so. I wish I could be as sure of it as you are."

Farragut took a turn or two around the deck, and while he did so Osbon glanced up into the sky and insisted in his memoirs that he saw "a great bird—a bald eagle it proved—circling above the fleet."

"Look there, Flag Officer," he called, pointing up. "That is our national emblem. It is a sign of victory."

This story is much too good to be true. Osbon seems to have forgotten when he was writing his memoirs that it was 3 A.M. when this bird was supposedly sighted—and dark.

The first division was led by the gunboat *Cayuga*, followed by the old paddle-wheel frigate *Mississippi*, three steam sloops, and three gunboats. Farragut led the second division in his flagship, followed by two more steam sloops. The third division was mostly gunboats. Shelby Foote, in his masterful narrative history of the Civil War,

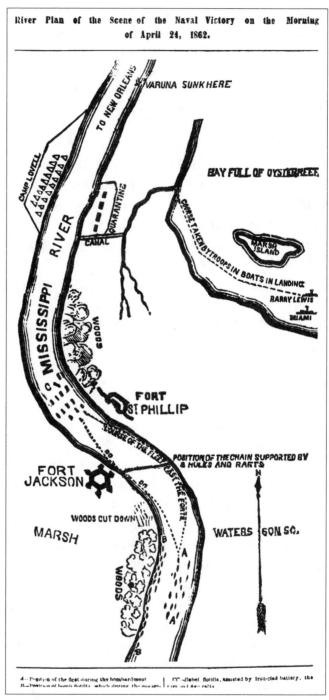

Bradley Osbon's map of New Orleans as it appeared in the *New York Herald*, May 14, 1862. (Clements Library, University of Michigan)

argued that the Union warships could throw ten tons of metal in one salvo against less than four tons for the Confederates. But the forts—Federal installations, originally—were made of bricks, and their gun platforms were stable; the ships were made of wood and the gun platforms were anything but stable. In fighting between ships and forts, the forts were supposed to hold the advantage.

It was 3:30 by the time *Hartford* got under way.

Carefully we felt our way through the opening in the chain, and then all at once the enemy's guns had found us, too, and solid shot was screaming overhead and fiery shells were bursting around us. At that moment, as if by inspiration, I hoisted our largest Star Spangled Banner at the peak, and hastening forward decked the fore and mainmasts each in the same way.

"Why do you do that?" called Farragut, for it was unusual to have the colors flying at night.

"Flag Officer," I shouted back, "I thought if we are to go down, it would look well to have our colors flying at night."

"All right," he returned, and presently behind us the *Brooklyn* and the *Richmond*, and the others had seen our flags above the smoke, and had their colors flying too.

By 4 A.M., *Hartford* was opposite Fort Jackson and coming under heavy fire. Farragut had climbed the port mizzen rigging to get a clearer view of the action. "With his feet on the ratlines and his back against the shrouds, he stood there as cool and undisturbed as if leaning against a mantel in his own home." Osbon worried he might be killed. "Flag Officer," he said, "we can't afford to lose you. They'll get you, up here, sure. . . . Come down!" Farragut had just made his descent when an exploding shell cut away rigging precisely where he had been standing.

"Death and destruction seemed everywhere," Osbon wrote.

A shell burst on our deck, the concussion stunning Lieutenant George Heisler of our marine corps. I ran forward to see what damage had been done, when the wind of another shell carried away my cap. For some reason it made me wildly furious. I swung my arms and vented futile rage into the battle smoke at the men over there behind the guns.

We were struck now on all sides. A shell entered our starboard beam, cut our cable, wrecked our armory and exploded at the main hatch, killing one man instantly and wounding several more. Another entered the muzzle of a gun, breaking the lip and killing the sponger who was in the act of "ramming home." A third entered the boatswain's room, destroying everything in its path and, exploding, killed a colored servant who was passing powder.

In the midst of all this appeared a Confederate steamer, her decks lined with troops, and they opened fire "with a volley of musketry." Marine Corps Lieutenant John Broome "trained two nine-inch guns on her and let go. We saw the shells strike. Then followed an explosion, horrified yells, a sudden career, and the waters of the Mississippi had covered her and all on board."

Osbon had a watch lashed to his sleeve and he noted it was 4:15 A.M. when the *Hartford* ran aground. "This," he said, "was indeed a crisis." Indeed it was. To make matters even worse, Osbon said the Confederate ram *Manassas* showed up and shoved a blazing fire raft under *Hartford*'s port quarter, "and in an instant our rigging and the side of our vessel had caught fire." (Most historians say the fire raft was shoved against *Hartford* by a steam tugboat; but Osbon was there and he was certain it was *Manassas;* he might be right.) He later recalled:

I realized that something had to be done about the fire raft instantly. Some 20-pound rifle shells were lying handy, and I rolled three of them to the waterways just above the blazing scow. It was fiercely hot there, and I threw a heavy coat over my head and, leaning down, began uncapping the shells. I had two of them ready when Farragut came over to see what I was at. As I was covered with the coat, he could only see that I was upon my knees, and he may have remembered that my father was a minister, for he said:

"Come on, Mr. Osbon, this is no time for prayer."

I got the cap off the third shell just then, but I paused long enough to say:

"Flag Officer, if you'll wait a second you'll get the quickest answer to prayer ever you heard of," and I rolled the three shells into the burning raft. Almost instantly they exploded with a great noise, tearing a wide hole into the fire raft and giving the little ironclad such a scare she backed off with her sinking charge, delivering a parting shot from her single gun.

In the next twenty minutes, Osbon said, the fire was extinguished and *Hartford*'s crew reversed engines and pulled her off the mud bar. She then moved upriver to take part in the final moments of the battle. All that was left of the Confederate fleet was *Manassas*. "Signal the *Mississippi* to sink that damn thing," Farragut told Osbon. A few minutes later, the old steam frigate that had carried Matthew Calbraith Perry to Japan in 1853 took after her, "and coming alongside plunged an entire broadside through her armor. Sinking rapidly, the ram made for shore, where thirty men men ran out of her gun port and escaped to the woods . . ."

It was 5 A.M. when *Hartford* came to anchor above the forts.

"Make the signal to report casualties, Mr. Osbon," Farragut ordered. The count, when it came in, was 24 killed and 86 wounded (37 killed and 147 wounded, according to most accounts of the battle). Osbon, his naval duties completed, now turned to his journalistic responsibilities. He was allowed to board little *Cayuga*, the gunboat given the honor of taking the official reports of the capture of New Orleans and the surrender of the forts back to Washington. As he left *Hartford*, the crew gave him three hearty cheers.

Osbon traveled all the way to Baltimore with *Cayuga* and then took the cars to New York with his story. It took up three pages in the *Herald* on May 10, far and away the most complete account of Farragut's great victory. But the *New York Times*' correspondent, Henry Jacob Winser, was first; he had sent his story by way of Havana and it ran a day earlier than Osbon's.

In Osbon's first big story—the one about the Sumter relief expedition—his editors at the *World* had simply let the narrative flow, starting at the beginning and moving chronologically and inexorably to the end. The *Herald* was a lot smarter. It topped his day-by-day account with a precede summarizing what the long story below would say. "We have further details of the brilliant victory at New Orleans," it began. "Our special correspondents"—Osbon, in truth—"came up in the *Cayuga*, and bring the graphic particulars of this splendid naval triumph. . . . The squadron under the command of Flag Officer D. G. Farragut has certainly accomplished one of the greatest achievements on record."

The story began with the description of an expedition upriver by Osbon's old revenue schooner, the *Harriet Lane,* on the thirteenth to determine if the rebels were building a new shore battery. Osbon, of course, was on board, and so was Farragut. As they drew near to the iron chain laid down by the Confederates to block their passage, "we were startled by a sharp report, and the whiz of a rifled musket ball which passed very close to the head of the Flag Officer. The scamps only fired a few [shots] before the guns of the *Harriet Lane* and several of the gunboats were throwing round shot, grape, and shrapnel into the woods in such rapidity as to make that particular place too hot for any riflemen to stand."

In his entry for April 16, Osbon gave the order of sailing for the squadron as it prepared to make the passage, naming all the ships and all their commanders.

The only thing missing from his dispatch is a detailed account of his own role in the battle. He left that entirely to his memoirs, making us wonder, once again, how much embellishment took place here. And the answer is, not nearly as much as occurred in those faraway campaigns in China and Argentina. His role at New Orleans was much too visible to too many people, and when the war was over Farragut himself liked to tell the story about discovering Osbon on his knees, apparently in prayer (but in reality uncapping those 20-pound rifle shells).

Readers today, when attention spans seem to be so much shorter, probably would recoil from stories without leads written at such length. But it would never have occurred to Civil War newspaper readers to complain about the pace of these dispatches. They were devoured, word for word, and handed from one eager hand to another; the more detail the better. The sad thing is, as the war went on, the three major New York newspapers ran fewer of them in their rush to beat the competition with brief stories filed almost every hour by telegraph. Osbon's story was a sensation.

Osbon resigned from the *Herald* late in 1864 to open a news bureau specializing in naval intelligence. In December, Union strategists began organizing a combined army and navy assault on Fort Fisher in North Carolina. David Dixon Porter, now an admiral, gave Osbon an advance peek at the order of battle and Osbon wrote a story based on that information. It was sent out to his clients—twenty newspapers in all—with the caution that the story shouldn't be run until the attack began. It's a standard journalistic procedure today, often labeled HFO, or "hold for orders."

Unfortunately, one of Osbon's clients broke the embargo—that happens these days, too—and ran the story before the attack was under way. All these years, Gustavus Fox had been seething over Osbon's famous Fort Sumter dispatch. Now Fox, the Navy's number two man, saw his opportunity; he ordered Osbon's arrest on New Year's Day, 1865, for violating the Fifty-ninth Article of War—furnishing information to the enemy. Osbon was remanded to the Old Capitol Prison in Washington, "where many a better man than I suffered long and ignominious imprisonment to satisfy the pique of some public official."

He languished in his jail cell for three months before he was brought to trial in New York City. "For several days," Osbon wrote, "I was a figure of national interest." President Lincoln, Osbon said, made it clear that he believed in Osbon's innocence. The trial was under way when Lincoln was assassinated at Ford's Theater; it ended a few days later with Osbon's acquittal.

One day soon after the completion of the trial, Osbon was called to the office of an old friend, one of New York's best-known shipbuilders, who handed him a small package.

"This is a little testimonial," he said, "from your friends in this city. Take it and go into the country to recuperate."

The package contained $5,000 in cash.

7

A Very Angry General

GENERAL WILLIAM T. SHERMAN INSANE

The painful intelligence reaches us in such form that we are not at liberty to discredit it that General W. T. Sherman, late commander of the Department of the Cumberland, is insane. It appears that he was at times, when commanding in Kentucky, stark mad.

T HOSE ARE THE two opening sentences of an astonishing six-hundred-word announcement that greeted the readers of Murat Halstead's *Cincinnati Commercial* the morning of December 11, 1861. When Sherman read the *Commercial*'s report the next day, he was not pleased.

It is no wonder that Sherman, more than any other general in the Civil War, North or South, *hated* reporters and the newspapers they worked for. He thought they were all liars and cowards and spies and troublemakers. "Buzzards," the whole lot of them. He was convinced he would win battles when they weren't around and lose them when they were. His obsession carried him to the point of arresting Thomas W. Knox of the *New York Herald* and court-martialing him for giving information to the enemy, being a spy, and disobedience of orders.

Ever since they started showing up on battlefields, reporters have been a trial and tribulation to flag officers. Reporters tend to be in-quisitive, argumentative, boisterous, undisciplined, and sloppy, precisely the attributes boot camps and officers' training schools try so hard to eliminate from their raw recruits.

British generals despised Billy Russell in the Crimea, but he was just a single voice. Now, in the American Civil War, there were dozens of Billy Russell imitators, many of them, probably most of them, incompetent and potentially troublesome to generals attempting to keep their reputations intact and their plans and movements secret from the enemy.

Add one more factor: generals, by the very nature of their calling, are totalitarian, which means they are completely unprepared for criticism by anyone from the lower ranks, especially *civilians*. Civil War generals deeply resented being second-guessed by men they viewed as amateurs.

Sherman was special only to the extent that he spent so much time complaining about reporters and thinking up ways to thwart them.

Sherman's father, Charles Sherman, a circuit-riding state Supreme Court judge from Lancaster, Ohio, was a great admirer of the valiant Indian fighter, Tecumseh, and named his son, born on February 8, 1820, for him: Tecumseh Sherman (the William was added later). He was one of Charles and Mary Sherman's eleven children, and his family called him Cump. His father died when Cump was nine years old, and he and the rest of the children were parceled out to friends and relatives. Cump moved two houses up the block to become the foster son of Thomas and Maria Boyle Ewing. Ewing was a politician destined to serve as secretary of the interior and as a member of the U.S. Senate. Without even talking to young Sherman, Ewing secured an appointment to West Point for the sixteen-year-old boy. Sherman enjoyed his four years at West Point and his nights at Benny Haven's tavern; he graduated in 1840, sixth in a class of forty-one (he would have ranked fourth if he hadn't racked up so many demerits for personal appearance). He was married in Washington in 1850 to Ewing's daughter, his own foster sister, Ellen. Among the guests: President Zachary Taylor, the entire cabinet, Henry Clay and Daniel Webster, and even the British ambassador.

The Ewings were a powerful, close-knit family and Sherman never felt he was quite a part of it. He chafed under the family's constant lectures about what he should make of himself; he resisted Ellen's lifelong effort to convert him to Roman Catholicism. One thing he surely didn't want to do was accept Thomas Ewing's advice and resign from the army to run the family saltworks. Working in a bank, especially one far away in California, was a more tempting idea. In 1853, he resigned his commission, and opened a branch of a Saint Louis bank in San Francisco. During the Panic of 1857, Sherman and other bankers did their best to stay open in the face of a run on their assets. According to historian John F. Marszalek, Sherman was upset by a misleading story in a local paper, the *Sunday Times*, that suggested his bank might fail. He cornered the editor in his third-floor office and told him he'd return and throw him out his own window the next time he indulged in such outrageous behavior. The editor moved the next day to ground-floor offices.

"Thus, in California," Marszalek wrote, "Sherman directly linked his failure to the activity of reporters. Newspapers had intervened to make a bad situation worse, to increase the strain he felt, and to help bring about his downfall. He learned to fear the press, to see newspapers as being capable of frustrating his deeply felt need for success. It was in California that the seeds of future press hatred were sown."

Sherman worried all the time about failure. And when things looked darkest, he tended to retreat into one of those awful bouts of clinical depression. From time to time, he did seem just a little bit crazy. The first setback we know about took place during the bad times in California.

After the bank failed, Sherman took a turn in a law office, didn't think much of that, and then accepted in 1859 a job as the founding superintendent of a military academy in Alexandria, Louisiana, which later moved to Baton Rouge and became Louisiana State University. When Louisiana seceded from the Union, Sherman packed up, headed north, and rejoined the Union army. With less than a week to train his troops, he led his brigade in the disastrous defeat at the first battle of Bull Run.

The trouble with the press began when he was sent to Kentucky in October of 1861 to succeed Robert Anderson, the hero of Fort Sumter but now in failing health, as commander of the Department of the Cumberland. Florus B. Plympton, a reporter for the *Cincinnati Commercial,* had no inkling of Sherman's hostility to the press when he showed up at headquarters with letters of introduction from his editor, Murat Halstead, a family friend, and Sherman's brother-in-law, Thomas Ewing Jr.

"It's eleven o'clock," Sherman said. "The next train to Louisville goes at half-past one. Take that train! Be sure you take it; don't let me see you around here after it's gone."

"But general," Plympton pleaded, "the people are anxious. I'm only after the truth."

"The truth!" Sherman bellowed. "That's what we don't want. Truth, eh? No, sir! We don't want the enemy any better informed than he is. Make no mistake about that train!"

Plympton, completely intimidated, took the train.

German-born Henry Villard, James Gordon Bennett's top reporter, was in Kentucky with Sherman, too. In his memoirs, Villard said it was obvious "that it was perfectly useless to approach General Sherman as a news-gatherer." But Villard knew that Sherman followed a regular pattern in which he would show up at precisely 9 o'clock every night at the Louisville offices of the New York Associated Press and remain there until 3 A.M. reading the wires, when he would return to his room at the Galt House. The man, everyone observed, never seemed to sleep.

Villard made it a practice to show up at the Associated Press office, too, "and as we met on neutral ground and I asked him no questions, we were soon on very good terms." Villard remembered:

> He was a great talker, and he liked nothing better than to express his mind upon the news as it came. There he sat, smoking a cigar (I hardly ever saw him without one), leaning back in his chair, with his thumbs in the armholes of his vest. Or he was pacing up and down the room, puffing away, with his head bent forward and his arms crossed behind his back. Every piece of military information drew some comment from him, and it was easy to lead him into a long talk if the subject interested him. He expressed himself without any reserve about men and matters, trusting entirely to the good faith of his hearers, who, as a rule, consisted only of Mr. Tyler (the

telegraph operator) and myself. As will be readily believed, we found the hours thus spent in his company a great treat, although we did not dream of the celebrity the General was to achieve.

Villard worried about Sherman's state of mind. The nervous general said, again and again, that he didn't have enough men under his command and if he were attacked he was certain he would lose. Villard continued:

> It was not really want of confidence in himself that brought him to this state of mind, but, as it seemed to me, his intense patriotism and despair of the preservation of the Union in view of the fanatical, bloodthirsty hostility to it throughout the South. This dread took such hold of him that, as I was informed by those who were in hourly intercourse with him, he literally brooded over it day and night. It made him lapse into long, silent moods even outside his headquarters. He lived at the Galt House, occupying rooms on the ground floor. He paced by the hour up and down the corridor leading to them, smoking and obviously absorbed in oppressive thoughts. He did this to such an extent that it was generally noticed and remarked upon by the guests and employees of the hotel. His strange ways led to gossip, and it was soon whispered he was suffering from mental depression.

In his memoirs, Villard conveniently forgot to mention that he wasn't the only reporter attending those late-night meetings in Louisville. Another reporter from the *Herald*, William G. Shanks, was there most nights, too.

Shanks remembered that Sherman would smoke as many as ten cigars in the course of these long visits to the telegraph office. The porter who cleaned the rooms called them "Sherman's Old Soldiers." Sherman's hands were in constant motion, "twitching his red whiskers—his coat buttons—playing a tattoo on the table—or running through his hair," Shanks said.

On October 17, Lincoln's disreputable secretary of war, Simon Cameron (soon to be replaced by the capable Edwin Stanton), came to town with a large personal entourage that included Samuel Wilkeson, then the chief Washington correspondent of Horace Greeley's *New York Tribune*.

In his memoirs, Sherman said he and Cameron and the rest of his party had lunch in his rooms at the Galt House, after which Cameron, not feeling well and stretched out on Sherman's bed, said, "Now, General Sherman, tell us of your troubles." Sherman said he was reluctant to be candid with so many strangers in the room. "They are all friends," Cameron said, "all members of my family, and you may speak your mind freely and without restraint." No mention was made that one member of Cameron's family was a newspaper reporter.

Sherman locked the doors and gave Cameron and his entourage a candid rundown of the problems facing his command in Kentucky. He voiced all his fears about his own precarious position and the growing strength of the enemy. To destroy the rebel power in the states watered by the Mississippi and its tributaries, he said, would take no less than two hundred thousand men. The desperate picture he painted, Villard wrote,

> was so contrary to, or rather in advance of, the then still prevailing ideas of the limited power of the Confederacy and the means necessary to overcome it, that it startled the secretary and excited doubts as to the state of the general's mind. Wilkeson told me, indeed, immediately after the conference, that Cameron thought the general was unbalanced by exaggerated fears as to the rebel strength, and that it would not do to leave him in command.

The situation turned nasty when Sam Wilkeson's *New York Tribune* ran a long story that claimed to be excerpts from an official report by the army's adjutant general, but there was hardly any doubt Wilkeson wrote key parts of it that gave details of Sherman's meeting with Cameron. The report was "accompanied by sarcastic criticisms of the timorousness of the General and his absurd demand for troops," Villard said.

The story set off the first wave of speculation about Sherman's mental health. In his memoirs, Sherman said the newspaper accounts of his "insane" request for two hundred thousand men is what did it. "Before I had the least conception of it, I was universally published throughout the country as 'insane, crazy, etc.'"

There's no question that Sherman was sinking deeper and deeper into the most serious of all his bouts with depression. In his letters to his wife, Ellen, he complained about headaches from smoking all those cigars; he admitted he wasn't sleeping or eating. He feared the enemy—he wildly inflated their numbers—was about to march on Louisville and overwhelm him. He said he just wanted to take Ellen and their children and "go hide in some quiet part of the world." He also said that "the idea of going down to History with a fame such as threatens me nearly makes me crazy—indeed I may be so now."

Ellen recognized the symptoms. Insanity was a part of the family history, she wrote Sherman's brother, John, and she rushed to Louisville to be at his side. She said she found him in "a morbid state of anxiety."

In mid November, Brigadier General Don Carlos Buell arrived in Louisville to relieve Sherman of his command. Sherman conceded in his memoirs that his superiors believed that

> the cares, perplexities, and anxiety of the situation had unbalanced my judgment and mind. It was, doubtless, an incident common to all civil wars, to which I could only submit with the best grace possible, trusting to the future for an opportunity to redeem my fortune and good name. . . . Indeed, it was not until the following April that the battle of Shiloh gave me personally the chance to redeem my good name.

Sherman took the cars to Saint Louis to report to Major General Halleck, who exercised extraordinary good judgment in dealing with his troubled subordinate. Halleck ordered Sherman to inspect the troops assembled at Sedalia, in Missouri, and report back to him on their general condition. Their general condition, he found, was simply terrible. They had been armed with muskets imported from Belgium that either wouldn't fire or blew up when they did. "I see no hope for them in their present raw and undisciplined condition, and some terrible disaster is inevitable," he wrote his brother, John, now a powerful member of the U.S. Senate. Sherman found that their commander, John Pope, had scattered them at various locations, making them, he thought, vulnerable to an attack by the Confederate commander, Sterling Price. So, on his own, he ordered them consolidated at Georgetown, on the La Mine River. Pope was perplexed; as far as he knew, Price was in no condition to make an advance. There was nothing to fear, he wrote Halleck.

Halleck, sensing something was seriously wrong with Sherman, contacted Ellen and told her to come to Saint Louis. Sherman was already there when she arrived.

Sherman's biographer, Lloyd Lewis, said they had this conversation:

Sherman: "Ellen, what are you doing here?"

Ellen: "I've come to bring you home."

Sherman: "I wouldn't think of going."

When reporters picked up word of Sherman's performance at Sedalia, they began a second round of speculation about his mental health. "The newspapers kept harping on my insanity and paralyzed my efforts," Sherman wrote in his memoirs. "In spite of myself, they tortured from me some words and acts of imprudence."

Halleck insisted that Ellen take Sherman home for twenty days to pull himself together. It was one of the smartest things Old Brains ever did for his country. "For the first ten days in Lancaster," Michael Fellman wrote in his psychological examination of Sherman, "he began to eat, sleep, and relax. Ellen read aloud to him from Scott and Shakespeare, and tried to provide a kind of embracing atmosphere."

Then, on December 12, the Shermans received their copy of the December 11 issue of the *Cincinnati Commercial,* edited by Sherman's alleged friend, Murat Halstead.

GENERAL WILLIAM T. SHERMAN INSANE

Villard admitted it was all his fault, though the chronology of these events in his memoirs is badly jumbled, probably intentionally. Villard said the trouble began back in October during Cameron's visit with Sherman in Louisville, when he first heard from Sam Wilkeson that Sherman was unbalanced. That, he said, "was a great bit of news, but in the public interest I did not feel free to use it." Instead, he said, he wrote a private letter to his friend, Halstead, because he was "very much attached to the Sherman family." But, said Villard,

"Halstead could not resist the temptation of utilizing the sensational information for his paper." Villard was shocked.

> To my painful surprise and great indignation, he printed, in the first issue after receiving my letter, an editorial paragraph saying in substance that "the country would learn with surprise and regret that Brigadier General Sherman had become insane." Thus I was the innocent cause of the publication of this cruel misstatement, which resulted in so much annoyance and distress to the General and his friends.

Villard's account doesn't make sense. The conference in Louisville took place in October. The "cruel misstatement" appeared in the *Commercial* on December 11. Editor Halstead probably got it right. He said Villard came to Saint Louis personally in December with word that Sherman was insane and that Halstead must print the story because no one else would. Lewis, in his Sherman biography, said "Villard begged Halstead to bell the cat and, reluctantly, so the editor said, he had consented." The evidence is overwhelming that Villard's account in his memoirs was duplicitous, aimed more at improving his own image than doing anything to restore Sherman's.

The Ewing-Sherman clan rallied to the general's defense. Philemon Ewing, one of old Tom's boys, demanded that Halstead print a retraction. It appeared on the 13th, stating categorically that the whole story, from beginning to end, was false. But the story by now had taken on a life of its own, and other papers began picking it up.

The *Cincinnati Gazette*'s Whitelaw Reid was in Kentucky when the *Commercial* ran the insanity story. Reid, one of the three or four best reporters in the Civil War, filed a story the next day, and it supported the allegation that Sherman was insane. Reid said:

> The insanity of Brigadier General William T. Sherman, lately commanding in Kentucky, has been a matter of *quasi* secret gossip for some time, but it was the desire to keep it out of the papers. As this desire had failed to be realized, I deemed it proper to telegraph last night that the stories of his having been "stark mad at times, while commanding in Kentucky" were exaggerations. His insanity was not clearly developed until his arrival at Sedalia, but he was all the time

despondent while in Kentucky, was the victim of hallucinations and appears clearly to have been gradually sinking into his present mournful condition.

. . . I had never met General Sherman till some three weeks or a month ago. . . . I was particularly struck by his dreamy, abstracted look and I remarked to a friend that his face and expression might indicate either a self absorbed military enthusiast or a monomaniac.

Ellen smelled a conspiracy to destroy her husband, and wrote Halleck demanding to know who was behind it. "Tell the General I will make a Yankee trade with him," Halleck replied. "I will take all that is said against him if he will take all that is said against me. I am certain to make 50% profit by the exchange."

Ellen wrote Lincoln, too. "As the minister of God to dispense justice to us and as one who has the heart to sympathize as well as the power to act, I beseech you by some mark of confidence to relieve my husband from the suspicions now resting upon him," she said.

When the twenty-day leave was up, Sherman returned to Saint Louis and began training recruits at Benton Barracks. He wrote his brother, John, on January 4, 1862: "I am so sensible now of my disgrace from having exaggerated the force of our enemy in Kentucky that I do think I should have commited suicide were it not for my children. I do not think I can again be entrusted with a command."

Halleck, a shrewd and calculating man, understood that Sherman had friends in high places—two U.S. senators, one his brother, John Sherman, the other his father-in-law, Thomas Ewing, both favored by Lincoln. Halleck knew, too, that both of them wanted Cump back in action. Biographer Lewis concluded, perhaps a little cynically, that Halleck acted entirely out of self-interest in promoting a new fighting career for Sherman.

Whatever his motivation, Halleck did the right thing. He told Sherman to take charge of the District of Cairo, headquartered in Paducah, Kentucky, and begin supplying troops and supplies to Grant, who had just taken Forts Henry and Donelson.

Sherman, finally emerging from his funk, impressed Grant with his zeal and competence. The friendship between these two great generals—one charged with being a drunk, the other thought to be

insane—began then. It was forged a few weeks later at Shiloh, bloody
Shiloh, and it lasted the rest of their lives.

By March, Sherman's rehabilitation had come along so nicely that
he was deemed fit to take command of his own division, the fifth of
six, in Grant's Army of the Tennessee. Grant himself was back at
work after being briefly relieved of his command by Halleck for failing to report regularly on the strength and position of his army. The
suspicion, of course, was that Grant had gone off on a bender. He
hadn't.

Halleck was now the commanding general of all Union armies
west of the Alleghenies. His goal was to concentrate his forces—
Grant's forty-five thousand men and Don Carlos Buell's Army of the
Ohio with thirty thousand more—and then advance together under
Halleck's personal command against the main Confederate base at
Corinth, Mississippi. There, they would defeat the rebels and cut the
Memphis & Charleston Railroad, a vital east-west link in the Con-
federacy. Corinth was held by Albert Sidney Johnston's Army of Mis-
sissippi, its four corps—forty thousand men in all—commanded by
Leonidas Polk, Braxton Bragg, William J. Hardee, and John C. Breck-
inridge.

Lloyd Lewis, in that splendid biography of Sherman, as fresh
today as it was when it was published in 1932, called these two armies
"great mobs of innocents ripe for slaughter . . . two herds of appren-
tice killers, pathetically eager to learn their trade in what Sherman,
then and later, frankly reminded his men was 'horrid war.'"

But how they fought. Shiloh, Bruce Catton wrote, "underlined
one of the basic facts about the war—that it was being fought by men
of enormous innate pugnacity; tenacious men who would quit a fight
once begun only when someone was *beaten*. North and South had not
gone to war in a mere fit of peevish irritability; the men they sent into
their armies had something on their minds and were desperately in
earnest."

It was "the first great modern battle," Shelby Foote said. "It was
Wilson's Creek and Manassas rolled together, quadrupled, and com-
pressed into an area smaller than either. From the inside it resembled
Armageddon."

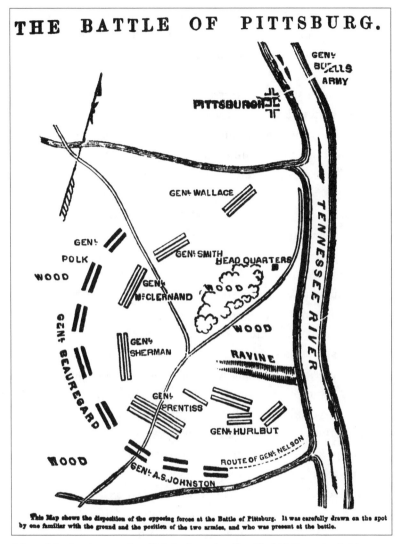

THE BATTLE OF PITTSBURG.

This Map shows the disposition of the opposing forces at the Battle of Pittsburg. It was carefully drawn on the spot by one familiar with the ground and the position of the two armies, and who was present at the battle.

Map of the battleground at Shiloh, from the *New York Tribune*, April 16, 1862. (Clements Library, University of Michigan)

Sherman, on patrol in a navy steamer, was the one who spotted a dilapidated wharf and some old warehouses on the west bank of the north-flowing Tennessee River. The place was called Pittsburg Landing, just twenty miles, overland, from Corinth, and Sherman sent back word that this was the place to concentrate the army. Sherman led his division—mostly raw recruits from Ohio and Illinois—up the bluffs to the heights above the river, where peach trees were just starting to bloom. From his tent, Sherman could see a simple log church, Shiloh Meeting House. He was soon joined by the rest of Grant's army.

To Sherman's left was Benjamin M. Prentiss's division. Beyond Prentiss was Stephen A. Hurlbut. Behind him was John A. McClernand. And down by the landing was W. H. L. Wallace. None of them had dug in; they didn't think they needed to. No one, surely not Grant or Sherman, expected the Confederates would attack.

But that's what Johnston and his deputy, Bull Run Beauregard, decided to do. They would attack Grant at Pittsburg Landing, on those heights hemmed in by the Owl and Lick Creeks, and drive him into the Tennessee River before Buell could come up with his thirty-thousand-man Army of the Ohio. "Tonight," Johnston said the morning of the attack, "we will water our horses in the Tennessee River."

Grant spent most of his time thinking up what he would do to his enemy; he rarely gave much thought to what they might do to him. It was a considerable weakness for a man of such overall genius. Sherman was vulnerable at Shiloh, too, for he couldn't forget what he called his "disgrace" in overestimating the strength of his enemy in Kentucky. He didn't want that to happen again.

The saddest Union figure at Shiloh was Colonel Jesse J. Appler, in command of the Fifty-third Ohio, a part of Sherman's division. Appler kept warning Sherman that rebels were forming in advance of his regiment. He cried wolf so many times that an exasperated Sherman told him to take his damned regiment back to Ohio, for there were no Confederates nearer at hand than Corinth.

Johnston began his attack at dawn on Sunday, April 6, 1862 (and a terrified Colonel Appler fled to the rear, never to be seen in the war again). The battle lasted all day Sunday and most of Monday. It remains to this day the most controversial battle fought during the entire Civil War, and the blame for that is usually placed squarely at the feet of the war correspondents who covered it and wrote it up in their notebooks with their Number 2 Faber pencils.

Grant began his description of the battle that appears in the Shiloh chapter of that classic work, *Battles and Leaders of the Civil War*, with these words: "The battle of Shiloh, or Pittsburg Landing, fought on Sunday and Monday, the 6th and 7th of April, 1862, has been perhaps less understood, or, to state the case more accurately, persistently misunderstood, than any other engagement between National and Confederate troops during the entire rebellion."

The misunderstanding boils down to a single question: Was Grant surprised by the Confederate attack? He and Sherman and the rest of the Union commanders insisted they were not, but sometimes they quibbled. One of them, for a hair-splitting example, said they weren't surprised, but that they were unprepared. Newspaper correspondents, especially Whitelaw Reid, said they were surprised *and* unprepared, and they shouldn't have been.

In terms of controversy, Whitelaw Reid's twelve-thousand-word Shiloh dispatch stands alongside Billy Russell's account of Bull Run.

Reid is an important figure in American journalism, diplomacy, and politics. He became managing editor of Greeley's *New York Tribune* in 1868 and its proprietor after Greeley's death in 1872; his son, Ogden, succeeded him in 1908 and was editor when the *Tribune* merged with its old rival, the *Herald*, to become the *Herald-Tribune* in 1924. In his later years, Whitelaw Reid served as the American ambassador in Paris and London; he ran for vice president on Benjamin Harrison's losing Republican ticket in 1892 (Democrat Grover Cleveland won by 365,000 votes), and he was one of the negotiators of the peace treaty with Spain in 1898. He was a very distinguished American. But for all of this, Americans probably knew him best as the unsuccessful suitor of the beautiful Quaker girl, Anna E. Dickinson, the celebrated girl orator. When Reid met her in Philadelphia in 1863, as she neared the pinnacle of her fame, she was twenty-one, and had, in his lip-smacking words, a "plump, round, supple figure . . . rich mouth, with ripe lips that curve into a score of expressions in an instant."

"White" Reid was born in Cedarville, Ohio, near Xenia and sixty-five miles north of Cincinnati, on October 27, 1837. His parents, Robert Charlton and Marion Ronalds Reid, were prosperous farmers, and their home was large and comfortable and filled with books and musical instruments. They were Presbyterian, Whig to begin with,

Whitelaw Reid of the *Cincinnati Gazette*. (Author's collection)

Republican later, and conservative in personal habits always. Like so many of these Civil War correspondents, Reid attended a small liberal arts college, Miami University (of Ohio), graduating in 1856 with honors in science and the classics. Fresh out of college, he bought the *Xenia News* with borrowed cash and went to work as its publisher, editor, reporter, and typesetter.

He sold the paper in 1860 and took a holiday with an old college classmate exploring the upper reaches of the Mississippi River. He was particularly taken with Agate Bay on Lake Superior; when he returned to newspaper work, he adopted the pseudonym "Agate" for all his serious dispatches.

Ohio's daily newspapers were themselves a battleground during the Civil War. Most of them supported it, but a significant number did not, and the proprietors of those anti-Lincoln journals paid a heavy price. The *Cincinnati Enquirer* and the *Crisis*, in Columbus, led the pack in finding fault with Lincoln and his war aims, but there were lots of others all over the state. The problem, press historian Robert S. Harper pointed out, was that editors of Democratic newspapers "felt that to support the war to restore the Union was to support the Republican Party. In a day when neither party could see an ounce of merit in the other's point of view, this situation was baffling to those out of power at the moment, in this instance the Democrats."

Republicans and prowar Democrats were outraged by these antiwar newspapers. Trouble began the night of August 22, 1861, when an angry mob broke into the offices of the *Stark County Democrat* in Canton and wrecked the place. The same thing happened a month later to the *Bucyrus Forum*. The editor of the *Circleville Watchman*, John W. Kees, was rousted out of his bed and put on a train to the nation's capital, where he was thrown into a cell at the infamous Old Capitol Prison. J. F. Bollmeyer, editor of the *Dayton Empire*, owned by the notorious copperhead congressman, Clement Vallandigham, was shot to death by an angry neighbor. Vallandigham himself was arrested by a Union commander, Major General Ambrose E. Burnside, and turned over to the Confederates.

Reid took a job as war correspondent with the *Cincinnati Gazette*, edited by Richard "Deacon" Smith, in early June of 1861. Smith's newspaper was the bitter rival of Murat Halstead's *Commercial*, but both, like Reid himself, were solidly Republican. Cincinnati was a good place for a journalist to be. Because of its strategic location (and the skills of its newspaper editors), it became the center for reporting the war in the West.

Reid was a very systematic young man and he prepared himself for his new job by reading the standard manuals on war, including one by Old Brains Halleck himself. James G. Smart, the editor of Reid's news dispatches, said "he was familiar, too, with the campaigns of Napoleon and Frederick the Great. His emphasis on geology as a student and his writing of a descriptive log on the trip to [Agate Bay] gave him practice in describing land formations." He had also taught himself to take notes in shorthand.

Reid was something of a perfectionist in his own personal life, and he often expected far too much in the way of perfection from Union generals and Union armies. He was a great reporter, but he was also a bit of a common scold. He complained at great length in one of his earliest dispatches about the uniforms issued to the Ohio troops. "The cloth is made of factory clippings and sweepings and wears out almost as fast as stout wrapping paper would." He couldn't understand why the army didn't get on with it. "The West full of wagons and wagonmakers but the army waiting for wagons. The West full of horses but the army waiting for horses. Cavalry companies clamoring to be accepted months ago but the army waiting for cavalry. Troops everywhere eager for service but the army waiting for reinforcements!"

He saw his first real action with Major General George Brinton McClellan in his brief and successful campaign in July of 1861 against a rebel force commanded by Brigadier General Robert S. Garnett in northwest Virginia. Reid was with the Fourteenth Ohio at the most dramatic moment in the campaign, when Garnett made his last stand with his rear guard at Carrick's Ford on the Cheat River. Reid wrote:

> Just as the Fourteenth came fairly in front of this bluff and before they reached the ford, General Robert Seldon Garnett sprang up on the very brink, waved his hat, and shouted, "Hurrah for Jeff Davis!" The words were scarcely out of his mouth till his whole force, which had been concealed in an ambuscade, poured down a perfect storm of bullets on the Fourteenth, and two of their rifled cannon opened fire.

The Fourteenth was soon reinforced, and the tide of the battle quickly turned.

> General Garnett attempted to rally his men, but they were much too terrified to be stopped in their headlong flight. Just then Major

Gordon with Captain Ferry's company, which led the advance of Dumont's regiment, came to the brink of the river where they could see General Garnett waving to his men to return. In an instant Sergeant Burlingame [one of the rare occasions when a Civil War reporter gave a name to an enlisted man] "drew a bead" on him and fired. He fell instantly, and when Major Gordon reached him but a moment later, his muscles were just giving their last convulsive twitch. The major stooped down by his side, tenderly closed his eyes, bound up his face, and left a guard to protect his body.

Garnett was one of the first general officers to fall in a war that took a very high toll of men with stars on their shoulders—forty-seven for the North, seventy-seven for the South. Carrick's Ford was a Union victory and it made McClellan an instant hero. But four days later Reid was complaining that McClellan hadn't pursued what was left of Garnett's army; he didn't "catch them." The next day, he was grumbling that the defeated Confederates had been equipped with better tents, blankets, and cooking utensils.

Reid was resting in "pleasant quarters" at Crump's Landing, below Pittsburg Landing (remember, the Tennessee flows north), when the guns of Shiloh opened fire. "I was roused by the cry: 'They're fighting above!' Volleys of musketry could sure enough be distinguished, and occasionally the sullen boom of artillery came echoing down the stream." Reid leaped out of bed, rushed down to the landing, and hitchhiked a ride to the battle aboard one of the steamers. Grant, who had been spending his nights in the comfort of Crump's Landing, did much the same thing.

Written by pencil, in notebooks, and after witnessing the bloodiest battle in history (though worse were yet to come), Reid's dispatch was a masterpiece—engaging, carefully organized, filled with penetrating detail. But there was a flaw in it. It's a problem that permeates all of Reid's dispatches. He simply could not resist pointing out—again and again—that his generals were human, and sometimes made mistakes. Grant made mistakes that almost lost the battle the first day; he made up for those mistakes by leading his battered army to victory the second day. But Reid hammered away at the disasters the first day without giving sufficient credit to the turnaround the second.

At the same time, in the aftermath of the battle, Grant and his other generals insisted against all logic that there had been no big mistakes the first day, instead of briefly conceding those mistakes and going on to underline the brilliant success of the second, and deciding, day of the battle.

Reid pulled no punches. In the fourth paragraph of his huge opus, he complained that Grant's army "had lain at Pittsburg Landing, within twenty miles of the rebels that were likely to attack us in superior numbers without throwing up a single breastwork or preparing a single protection for a battery, and with the brigades of one division stretched from extreme right to extreme left of our line, while four other divisions had been crowded in between as they arrived."

In his own defense, Grant said that he had asked his only military engineer to lay out a line for entrenching. But the line he chose, Grant said, "was . . . too far away from the Tennessee, or even from the creeks, to be easily supplied with water. The fact is, I regarded the campaign we were engaged in as an offensive one and had no idea that the enemy would leave strong intrenchments to take the initiative when he knew he would be attacked where he was [in Corinth] if he remained."

Reid was right—Grant should have given some thought to the possibility of an enemy attack and ordered his men to use their spades, but he made too much of it too early in his story.

By the time Reid—and Grant—got to the battlefield, about 8 A.M., a number of Union troops had already skedaddled and were now crouched, terror-stricken, under the bluffs at the landing. Reid wrote that some of these troops were completely taken by surprise by the rebel attack.

> Here began scenes which, let us hope, will have no parallel in our remaining annals of the war. Some, particularly among our officers, were not yet out of bed. Others were dressing, others washing, others cooking, a few eating their breakfasts. Many guns were unloaded, accoutrements lying pell-mell, ammunition was ill-supplied—in short, the camps were virtually surprised—disgracefully, it might be added, unless someone can hereafter give some yet undiscovered reason to the contrary—and were taken at almost every possible [dis]advantage. . . . Into the just-aroused camps thronged the rebel

regiments, firing sharp volleys as they came and springing toward our laggards with bayonets. Some were shot down as they were running, without weapons, hatless, coatless, toward the river. The searching bullets found other poor unfortunates in their tents, and there, all unheeding now, they still slumbered while the unseen foe rushed on.

If the situation at dawn was exactly the way Reid pictured it—remember, he was in bed at Crump's Landing when the attack began—could there be any doubt that the rebels would have swept straight on to the Tennessee and ended the battle right there? It was bad enough, but it wasn't as bad as Reid said it was. Sherman's and Prentiss's regiments bore the brunt of the attack, and they didn't all throw their muskets away and run to the river. Most of them stood their ground and fought tenaciously.

Reid admitted it wasn't entirely disgraceful. "They were raw troops, just from the usual idleness of our 'camps of instruction'; hundreds of them had never heard a gun fired in anger; their officers, for the most part, were equally inexperienced. . . . Certainly it is sad enough, but hardly surprising, that under such circumstances, some should run."

Reid, in fact, saw good things happening on the battlefield. Sherman, he said, "was doing his best to rally his troops. Dashing along the lines, encouraging them everywhere by his presence, and exposing his own life with the same freedom with which he demanded their offer of theirs, he did much to save the division from utter destruction." He was completely in control of himself, not a twitch, not a vacant stare. No crazy man, this. This was a warrior.

And Reid got it exactly right about Prentiss's division, standing firm in a sunken road that history remembers as the "hornet's nest": "The men held their position with an obstinacy that adds new laurels to the character of the American soldiers." Brave Confederates attacked Prentiss time and time again, trying to turn the Union army's left flank and reach the river. A hornet's nest is just what it was, and the stubborn Confederates died by the hundreds trying to take it.

Hurlbut was fighting tenaciously in the middle of the peach orchard. Johnston, seeing that Breckinridge's men were losing heart, took command personally, shouting "I will lead you!" This time, the

Confederates broke through Hurlbut's lines, but Johnston was shot in the right leg, just above the knee, and he was bleeding badly. A surgeon could have applied a tourniquet, but there was no surgeon there. Johnston died about 2:30 P.M. and Beauregard took command of the battle.

Prentiss, isolated now from the rest of the Union army, fought on and on, until he had only two thousand men standing. And then, only then, late in the afternoon, he surrendered. "Sherman and McClernand had saved their divisions by retreating," Shelby Foote wrote, "but Prentiss had saved Grant by standing firm."

Reid reported that

> the rebels occupy the camps of every division save that of W.H.L. Wallace [not to be confused with Lew Wallace, the future best-selling author of *Ben Hur*, who took the wrong road and was late reaching the battlefield]. Our whole army is crowded in the region of Wallace's camps and to a circuit of one half to two thirds of a mile around the Landing. We have been falling back all day. We can do it no more. The next repulse puts us into the river, and there are not transports enough to cross a single division till the enemy would be upon us.

No one who was at Shiloh ever forgot the skulkers huddled under the bluffs. "There are not less than 5,000 of them," Reid said. "Ask them why they don't go to their places in the line. 'Oh, our regiment is all cut to pieces.' 'Why don't you go where it is forming again?' 'I can't find it,' and the hulk looks as if that would be the very last thing he would want to do."

But there, standing with some of his officers, was Grant himself. "The General is confident. 'We can hold them off till tomorrow; then they'll be exhausted, and we'll go after them with fresh troops.'" (In a book he wrote in 1868, Reid said, "I was myself a listener to this conversation, and from it I date, in my own case at least, the beginnings of [my] belief in Grant's greatness.")

It was almost at this precise moment that Reid detected "a rustle" among the skulkers. They had spotted something moving across the river.

It is! It is! You see the gleamings of the gun barrels, you catch amid the leaves and undergrowth down the opposite side of the river glimpses of the steady, swinging tramp of trained soldiers. A DIVISION of Buell's army is here! And the men who have left their regiments on the field send up three cheers for Buell. *They* cheering! May it parch their throats.

First, Buell. And then, an hour after dark, Lew Wallace. The reinforcements streamed in, and now the rebels would never water their horses in the Tennessee.

Reid watched at daybreak on Monday as Buell's men were ferried across the river,

> curious to see how these fine fellows would march out to the field where they knew reverses had crowded so thickly upon us the day before and where many of them must lie down to sleep his last sleep ere the sun, then rising, should sink again. There was little of that vulgar vanity of valor which was so conspicuous in all the movements of our rawer troops eight or nine months ago. There was no noisy and senseless yelling, no shouting of boasts, no calling on onlookers to "show us where the cowardly Secesh is, and we'll clean 'em out double quick." These men understood the work before them; they went to it as brave men should, determinedly, hopefully, calmly.

The *New York Herald*'s Henry Villard was with them. "On landing, we were met by an overwhelming confirmation of our apprehensions," he wrote in his memoirs. "We found ourselves, indeed, amid an immense, panic-stricken, uncontrollable mob. There were between seven and ten thousand men, of all arms and of all ranks, from field officers downward, all apparently entirely bereft of soldierly spirit, with no sense of obedience left, and animated by the sole impulse of personal safety."

Villard said Brigadier General William Nelson was a veritable "Orlando Furioso as he rode up through the packed crowds, waving his hat and shouting, 'Fall in, boys, fall in and follow me. We shall whip them yet.' Finding this did no good, he drew his sword and commenced belaboring the poltroons around him, berating them at the same time with his stentorian voice, in language more forcible than polished."

Nelson took his brigade past the skulkers and up the bluff to the bloody battleground. The rest of Buell's army followed. Now it was Beauregard's turn to be surprised: he had no idea they had arrived.

Reid complained in his dispatch that Grant had no plan of attack on Monday. But he did, and it was simple enough: advance all along the line and recapture the army's original camps. And that's what they did—by noon, they were back in the peach orchard and edging closer to Shiloh Meeting House. The Confederates had no fresh troops to throw into the battle and by now the men who had fought for the better part of two days were exhausted. Beauregard gave the order to begin a withdrawal.

Reid probably saw it happening. He was standing on a hill with troops from W. H. L. Wallace's division when "a rare vision" appeared.

> Away to the front were woods. Through the edge of the timber skirting the fields, the head of a rebel column appeared, marching past in splendid style on the double quick. Banner after banner appeared; the "stars and bars" formed a long line, stretching parallel with Wallace's line of battle. Regiment after regiment followed on, the line lengthened, and doubled and tripled; the head of the column was out of sight, and still they came. Twenty regiments were counted passing through these woods.

Reid thought they were on the move to make a new attack. More likely they were on the move to get into position to make the withdrawal. Either way, it was a sight Reid would never forget. He ended his dispatch with these words: "The camps were regained. The rebels were repulsed. Their attack had failed. We stood where we began. Rebel cavalry were within striking distance. *But we had regained our camps.* And so ended the battle of Pittsburgh Landing."

Villard was roaming the battlefield, too. He described what he saw in his memoirs:

> There was bloody evidence in every direction that the slaughter had been great. Neither the one side nor the other had buried its dead, and there they were, blue and gray, in their starkness, lying here

singly and there literally in rows and heaps. I passed more than a thousand of them. It was morbid, perhaps, on my part, but I lingered to see the effect of sudden violent death on features and limbs. It surprised me that the faces of most of these victims of battle bore a peaceful, contented expression, and that many lay as though they had consciously stretched themselves out to sleep. But there were also many ghastly exceptions, with features repulsively distorted by pain and hatred.

Once the battle was over, the reporters—they were exhausted, too—faced the biggest challenge of all: getting their stories into print, first. Villard ran down to the landing to board the first steamer he could find. He hoped to write his account on his way to Cairo, and mail it at Cairo upon his arrival. Already on board the steamer, a hospital ship, was Reid, whom he had never met. The two reporters—Reid from Grant's army and Villard from Buell's—sat down and exchanged notes.

Villard mailed his story at Cairo. Reid took a train to Cincinnati and delivered his twelve-thousand-word story in person, scoring the greatest scoop of his career. His story was widely reprinted by other newspapers, several of which published special editions.

Villard noted in his memoirs that neither he nor anyone else could write a completely accurate account of a battle on the scale of Shiloh. That, of course, is true. Reid's story is neither complete nor completely accurate, and the fact he complained that Grant was surprised on Sunday morning had reverberations. Grant was criticized for incompetence, for being drunk on the day of the battle. He was a butcher, his critics said. A delegation called on Lincoln and demanded Grant's removal. Lincoln rose from his chair, and said, quietly, "I cannot spare this man—he fights!"

The shock to the public wasn't so much what Reid and the others had reported. It was the slow progress of all those steamships loaded with thousands of wounded soldiers. This, they finally realized, would not be a short and relatively bloodless war.

Franc Wilkie saw Reid in Cairo a day or two after the battle was over and said that Reid's face suggested "an escape from . . . imminent . . . danger, something like fright . . . , as if he had just been witness to some tremendous calamity from which he had narrowly escaped."

But, of course, he had just been witness to what was then the bloodiest battle ever fought on American soil. That, under these terrible conditions, he managed to write twelve thousand coherent words remains a striking achievement.

Sherman was a hero in most of the newspaper accounts, including Reid's, but that did nothing to change his opinion of the press. In a letter written just after Shiloh, he said reporters were "the most contemptible race of men that exist, cowards, cringing, hanging around, gathering their material out of the most polluted sources."

He was still a very angry general.

8

The Court-Martial

So LONG AS Vicksburg was held by the enemy, Grant wrote in his memoirs, "the free navigation of the [Mississippi] river was prevented."

Grant wanted nothing more than to capture the great rebel bastion, standing on a bluff high above the river. And he wanted the job done quickly. "At this stage of the campaign against Vicksburg," he wrote,

> I was very much disturbed by newspaper reports that General [John A.] McClernand was to have a separate and independent command with mine, to operate against Vicksburg by way of the Mississippi River. Two commanders on the same field are always one too many, and in this case I did not think the general selected had either the experience or the qualifications to fit him for so important a position.

McClernand was a former member of Congress from Springfield, Illinois, and a close friend of President Lincoln. To the West Pointers Grant and Sherman he was the apotheosis of a very low form of military life—the political general. Without telling Grant, Lincoln and Secretary of War Stanton had given McClernand permission to raise an army in Illinois, Iowa, and Indiana, assemble it at Memphis, and then head downriver to Vicksburg. Grant fumed that his only role in this enterprise would be to maneuver on land in hopes of pinning down some of the Confederate forces while McClernand sailed down the mighty Mississippi to glory. Grant wired Halleck, the commander in chief, to ask, in a polite way, just what the hell was going on here. Halleck replied that Grant was in charge "and [had] permission to fight the enemy where you please." Grant took that to be an open invitation to start the ball before McClernand could reach the dance floor.

On December 8, Grant ordered Sherman to proceed swiftly to Memphis and sweep up all the troops based there—this was the core of McClernand's army!—"and move them down the river to the vicinity of Vicksburg."

Grant hoped to move on Vicksburg, by land, with his forty thousand troops, while Sherman was steaming downriver with thirty-two thousand men. At the very least, Grant's army would draw the rebel forces under John C. Pemberton, a Yankee from Philadelphia, of all things, away from Vicksburg, making the assault on the fortress by Sherman that much easier. Nathaniel P. Banks, still exhausted, no doubt, from chasing Stonewall Jackson all over the Shenandoah Valley, had recently replaced Ben Butler at New Orleans. Grant hoped Banks would move north from Louisiana and discombobulate the Confederate commanders.

Grant established a large supply depot at Holly Springs, Mississippi, but supplies came to it over two hundred miles of exposed railway line. That was a tempting target for the Civil War's most dangerous cavalry commander, that genius, Nathan Bedford Forrest, the man who had escaped so easily from Fort Donelson. With no more than two thousand men, Forrest began ripping out the rails and capturing, one after another, the Union garrisons up and down the line. He cut the telegraph lines, too, so Grant couldn't tell Sherman how much trouble he was in. Forrest, Sherman once said, was "a devil," and he was certainly proving it in the final days of 1862.

If Forrest wasn't a big enough problem, Earl Van Dorn, the rebel general who had lost at both Pea Ridge, Arkansas, and Corinth, Mississippi, was moving towards Grant's big supply base at Holly Springs. The depot was defended by Colonel R. C. Murphy, and he surrendered all the stores and fifteen hundred men without a fight. Grant said Murphy was either a traitor or a coward. Grant now had no choice but to give the whole business up and fall back into Tennessee, learning, for the first time, just how easily an army could live off the land. The rebels, meanwhile, concentrated their forces at Vicksburg, awaiting Sherman's arrival.

Sherman knew nothing about this, because, thanks to Forrest, the wires were down. It was too late to stop him, and he blundered into a messy defeat that really wasn't his fault.

Sherman issued General Order Number 8 on December 18, stating that "any person whatever, whether in the service of the United States or transports, found making reports for publication which might reach the enemy giving them information and comfort, will be arrested and treated as spies." This time, Sherman swore, he would not be pestered by the "buzzards of the press."

It didn't work. When the expedition—this was, officially, the Right Wing of the Thirteenth Army Corps—set sail on December 22, more than a dozen Bohemians, not one of them sympathetic to the commanding general, were safely tucked aboard one or another of the transports. They included some of the regulars—Knox of the *Herald*, Wilkie of the *Times*, and Browne of the *Tribune*. Knox was aboard the steamer *Continental* with Sherman's Fourth Division under the command of Knox's friend, Brigadier General Frederick Steele.

In his memoirs, Sherman said "the preparations were necessarily hasty in the extreme, but this was the essence of the whole plan, viz., to reach Vicksburg as it were by surprise, while General Grant held in check Pemberton's army about Grenada, leaving me to contend only with the smaller garrison at Vicksburg and its well-known strong batteries and defenses."

In an order dated December 23, Sherman told his four division commanders—Steele, George W. Morgan, A. J. Smith, and M. L. Smith—that he planned to land a brigade at Milliken's Bend, Louisiana, to destroy tracks of the Vicksburg & Shreveport Railroad and then disembark his main body at the mouth of the Yazoo River, on the Mississippi side, and attack Vicksburg, twelve miles away, from the rear by land while David Dixon Porter's gunboats attacked its big gun batteries by water.

Sherman's army reached Milliken's Bend on Christmas Day, and a brigade, following orders to the letter, broke up the rail lines. That same day, Wilkie wrote a story that appeared in the *Times* on January 18.

Milliken's Bend, La., Thursday, Dec. 25, 1862.

A merry Christmas to you all! A queer place this, to wish a merry Christmas from, and not less peculiar are its surroundings. A warm, foggy morning in which overcoats are uncomfortable—miles of steamers extending along the bend of the Mississippi, their long black streamers of smoke scarcely visible against the foggy sky, their flags waving damply in the feeble wind—on one shore a low flat bottom, whose fringes of cotton-wood and cypress are scarcely visible through the heavy fog; on the other a broad, irregular stretch of cotton fields, interspersed with scattered residences of dirty white, among which are the inevitable square-roofed two-story house of the planter, and the unpretending white-washed quarters of the ne- groes: in the background, a notched and scalloped line of trees looking gayly through the mist; in the foreground, scattered groups of blue-coats, and an immense white cotton gin, from whose roof dense volumes of black smoke, with here and there an edging of fleecy white, while occasionally fierce red flames burst out from the centre, as if anxious to assert their supremacy.

That last sentence is more than 150 words long; Civil War corre- spondents were wordy, but no one, surely not their editors, seemed to mind. In fact, if you can hold your breath that long, Wilkie's open- ing paragraph does give a nice picture of Milliken's Bend.

Toward the end of his dispatch, Wilkie took note of General Order No. 8, barring newspaper reporters from accompanying the ex- pedition: " . . . all steamboat captains . . . were strictly enjoined, in case any such person were found along with the flotilla, that he should be turned over to the mates and be required to do duty as a deck hand. 'All newspapermen are spies,' remarked this discriminat- ing chief [Sherman], and hence, they must, along with cotton specu- lators and other rascals, be excluded."

And then Wilkie gave Sherman the needle: "The general's success in reading the characters of correspondents seems to have been greater than his ability to exclude them, as this letter and many more from the same point will prove."

Finally, as if to show his contempt for Sherman and his orders, he described how he and Knox boldly went ashore to look around.

> We walked down to the town, and while passing along a street parallel with the river, noticed several men on horseback, down a lane, some two hundred yards below the town.
>
> "Better not go dar, Masas," said a negro.
>
> "Why so, ivory?"
>
> "Because dem's rebel soldiers," said our intelligent contraband [meaning slave] informant.
>
> We pushed down the lane and saw five horsemen standing by their horses, ready to mount. We hailed them.
>
> "Hullo, rebs!"
>
> "What do you want?"
>
> "Want to talk to you—hold on a minute!"
>
> "Oh, you be d——d! We've seen too many of your Yankee tricks."

The two reporters followed the horsemen on foot until they came to a cornfield, filled with rebel soldiers, in line of battle. "As there were but two of us," said Wilkie, "we 'retired in good order.'"

The main attack began about noon on December 29. This is how Sherman described it in his memoirs:

> A heavy artillery fire opened along our whole line, and was replied to by the rebel batteries, and soon the infantry fire opened heavily, especially on A. J. Smith's front, and in front of General George W. Morgan. One brigade [Colonel John F. De Courcy's] of Morgan's troops crossed the bayou safely, but took to cover behind the bank, and could not be moved forward. Frank Blair's brigade, of Steele's division, in support, also crossed the bayou, passed over the space of level ground to the foot of the hills; but, being unsupported by Morgan, and meeting a very severe cross-fire of artillery, was staggered and gradually fell back, leaving about five hundred men

behind, wounded and prisoners. . . . Part of Thayer's brigade took a wrong direction, and did not cross the bayou at all; nor did General Morgan cross in person. This attack failed, and I have always felt it was due to the failure of General G. W. Morgan to obey his orders. . . . Our loss had been pretty heavy, and we had accomplished nothing, and had inflicted little loss on our enemy.

Sherman ordered another attack, at a different point, beginning at dawn December 31. But the fog rolled in, and then it began raining heavily. "I became convinced the part of wisdom was to withdraw," Sherman concluded.

The army was back at Milliken's Bend on January 3, and on January 4 McClernand showed up to take command. He divided what was now his Army of the Mississippi into two corps, one for Sherman and the other, improbably, for the same General Morgan who had failed to press home the attack at Chickasaw Bayou.

The campaign had been a small disaster—Van Dorn capturing Grant's supply base at Holly Springs, Banks failing to materialize, and Sherman losing seventeen hundred men in a futile attack against Vicksburg.

It was, once again, failure, and the circling buzzards came home to roost. There is no journalistic practice more disreputable than the one called "piling on," in which reporters team up and attack a public figure when he is down. Sherman's reporters piled on, with a vengeance.

Headlined THE VICKSBURGH FAILURE and datelined—wonderful ring to it—"Up the Yazoo," Wilkie struck on January 19 in the *New York Times* with an article complaining that Sherman and his minions had been rifling his mail. Written on January 1, Wilkie aired his grievances right at the top of the story. He said he understood that he was a suspicious character and for that reason had been enclosing his dispatches in innocent-looking envelopes. He said he "put on the proper number of stamps and addressed them to private parties in Cairo, with a request to remail them." He said he supposed that Sherman's officers were "gentlemen" who would never descend "to the small business of robbing mails and opening private letters, but in this my conclusions appear to have been incorrect. All my communications to

Thomas Nast's sketches of the press in the field, from *Harper's Weekly*. (Library of Congress)

newspapers have, whether addressed directly or to private parties in the North, been opened, their contents read and the letters retained." He added:

> It may be remarked here that had the commanding general, W. T. Sherman, and his staff, spent half the time and enterprise in the legitimate operations of their present undertaking, that they have in bullying correspondents, overhauling mail bags and prying into private correspondence, the country would not now have the shame of knowing that we have lately experienced one of the greatest and most disgraceful defeats of the war.
>
> It will, however, scarcely be expected that men whose *forte* lies in sneaking into the private affairs of other parties—in ransacking mail bags, tearing open envelopes and reading private correspondence, are calculated to carry out successfully an operation so gigantic as the reduction of Vicksburgh. The prime mover in the whole affair is a fellow named ——— , a subordinate on Sherman's staff whose aptitude for sneaking, bluster and insult qualifies him

admirably for some business in which crawling under beds, listening at key holes and eavesdropping generally are the main peculiarities.

Wilkie didn't actually identify the "prime mover in the whole affair," but when copies of the *Times* showed up in Sherman's camp everyone knew it was Sherman's chief of staff, Major J. H. Hammond.

Hammond, Wilkie recollected in his memoirs, was so angry he told everyone that "he would shoot me on sight." Wilkie retired from the field himself and took refuge in a steamer, *City of Madison*. Hammond tracked him down "and a murderous look appeared to fill his eyes." But cooler heads intervened, and Hammond departed without firing a shot. Wilkie, observers said, was shaking visibly.

The last half of Wilkie's dispatch that ran in the *Times* on January 19 chronicled the actual battle, and it is a reasonably accurate account of what happened. In it, Wilkie supported Sherman's contention that Morgan's men, and especially Colonel DeCourcy's brigade, had refused to take part in the advance that Sherman thought might have had the best chance of winning the battle.

Because of Sherman's censorship of the mail, news of the defeat didn't reach the public for days. On January 6, for example, the *Chicago Tribune* was speculating that Vicksburg probably had fallen. THE BATTLE YET UNDECIDED, a headline reported on January 8. It wasn't until January 12 that news of a defeat began filtering back. "Sherman's repulse was complete," the *Tribune* said. "All agree that the attack on Vicksburg by Sherman was premature." The unsigned article explained that "General Sherman is charged with having detained the steamers from coming up, in order to conceal his misfortune; to have opened and read letters of correspondents there, and to have suppressed some of them. He also threatened to put correspondents in front and set them carrying powder."

These were perilous times for Union armies. John Pope had been badly beaten in the second battle at Bull Run by Lee and Jackson in August. Ambrose E. Burnside had been beaten even more decisively by Lee and Jackson at Fredericksburg, Virginia, in mid December, a pounding that was still fresh in the minds of newspaper readers. The last thing Union patriots wanted to hear was news that the western armies were being licked, too.

The *Tribune*'s reporter with Sherman, an obscure character named F. C. Foster, wrote his article about Sherman's defeat on December 30. It was finally published on January 15. Here is the way it began:

Battlefield Before Vicksburg
Warren County, Miss. Dec. 30, 1862.

A GRAVE DISASTER

A Fredericksburg in the West! Another national humiliation! More blundering! Immense energy squandered! Heroism thrown away! Defeated, baffled, repulsed, disheartened!

We have made the attack and have failed. Vicksburgh is stronger than we thought, and we are weaker than we supposed. . . .

Foster said Sherman attacked the rebels at the strongest point in their whole line, and did it in such a clumsy way that the enemy commanders knew he was coming in plenty of time to strengthen their position. "Bad generalship and planning and a want of concert would defeat any army in the world," Foster wrote. "The simplest colonel in the army understands that with a line of defense more than twelve miles long, the rebels will have hard work to defend it at all points, and that we have the advantage of menacing at all while seizing any one."

One day, Foster said, a Union general will bag the whole rebel army at Vicksburg—another Fort Donelson. But he doubted it would be Sherman.

To do this, we must have a radical change of commanders. Sherman is most bitterly hated. Any change would be hailed. The reports that he is insane are now believed and sworn to. There is a lack of positive power, that inventive faculty, the adaptability and exhaustive insight of genius in Sherman. Let someone be sent to replace him.

What extraordinary arrogance. Here we have a reporter so obscure his name is attached to no other battle report during the entire war calling for a general's removal. But these were unusual times for reporters in the West. Many of them were involved in buying cotton in the South and selling it in the North, an immensely profitable undertaking. Henri Lovie, the combat artist for *Frank Leslie's Illustrated Newspaper* and one of the original Bohemians, made such a killing that he went home to Cincinnati, bought his parents a farm in their native Germany, and vowed never to see war again.

Wilkie, in his memoirs, told a delightful story about a new Bohemian, DeBenneville Randolph Keim of the *New York Herald*, joining the brigade. A number of the correspondents were sitting around one day, trying to connect a Shakespeare quote to a Shakespeare play.

> "What about it?" Keim was asked.
> "I can't tell you," he replied. "I never read Shakespeare."
> "Never read Shakespeare!" and there was a universal laugh of incredulity. "Never read Shakespeare! Why not?"
> "Because, gentlemen, I am afraid that he would interfere with my style as a writer."

The *Herald*'s Thomas Knox, a big, slow-moving fellow, had once been a schoolteacher, and he tended to lecture people, including generals. He was a little arrogant by nature. His story about the mini disaster at Chickasaw Bayou was written on January 3 and appeared in the *Herald* on January 18.

Like his friend Franc Wilkie, the twenty-eight-year-old Knox began his long dispatch with a complaint about Sherman's staff rifling his mail, and named Major Hammond as the chief villain. "Had they [Sherman and Hammond] acted as earnestly and persistently against the enemy as against the press, there is little doubt that Vicksburg would, ere this, have been in Union hands."

Wilkie and Knox were in collusion. Both men led their stories with the complaints about censorship. Both, in very similar language, said the battle would have been won if Sherman hadn't been so obsessed with the activities of the journalists. Both reporters said Sherman attacked the rebels at their strongest point. Both blamed

Sherman for the expedition's failure, and both suggested, once again, he was insane. Knox put it in these words:

> At noon on Friday the 2d of January, we steamed out of the Yazoo, which we had entered just one week before. In that week we had attacked the enemy in his least vulnerable and best protected point; had fought with him through portions of three days; had once made a valiant and desperate, though badly planned and unsupported assault upon his batteries and rifle pits on a defensible hillside. From this assault we had been repulsed through no fault of the troops making it, but through the sad mismanagement of General Sherman in allowing them to go unaided by all the force at his command. Making a half attempt to execute another plan, that at our first arrival might have succeeded, we finally abandoned the siege of Vicksburg and decided to evacuate both our position on the Yazoo and the river itself. With hearts full of sadness at the failure of our undertaking, we moved down the stream toward the great river of the West. . . . Our failure has dashed the hopes of the nation, and delayed for weeks the progress of our arms. When we again attack the steep bluffs and frowning batteries of Vicksburg we will do so with a better prospect of success.
>
> Insanity and inefficiency have brought their result; let us have them no more. With another brain than that of General Sherman's, we will drop the disappointment of our reverse, and feel certain of victory in the future.

Knox was impertinent, too. Noting that Hammond finally had returned one of his dispatches, he said: "The letter is all right but I fail to find two elaborate maps, drawn with great care. It is possible General Sherman may need them for his instruction. Had he possessed them earlier, it is possible that he would have taken Vicksburg."

It would have required a more philosophical man than William Tecumseh Sherman to ignore this kind of outrageous criticism. Sherman decided he had seen and read enough. He revealed his intentions in a letter to Admiral Porter, dated February 4.

> I am going to have the correspondent of the New York Herald tried by a court martial as a spy, not that I want the fellow shot, but

because I want to establish the principle that such people cannot attend our armies, in violation of orders, publishing their garbled statements and defaming officers who are doing their best. You of the Navy can control all who sail under your flag, whilst we are almost compelled to carry along in our midst a class of men who on Government transports usurp the best state-rooms and accommodations of the boats, pick up the drop conversations of officers, and report their limited and tainted observations as the history of events they never see nor comprehend. This should not be, and must not be. We cannot prosper in military operations if we submit to it, and, as some one must begin the attack, I must assume the ungracious attack.

Sherman at no time seems to have considered the possibility that the army wasn't supposed to court-martial civilian newspapermen. (Osbon the naval specialist, we have seen, was tried illegally, too, before a "military commission.") No one ever raised the question of Knox's First Amendment rights. In fact, Union newspaper editors, including Knox's own at the *Herald*, remained silent throughout what was palpably an illegal proceeding.

Knox recognized he might be in trouble. He wrote a letter to Sherman on February 1 in which he said he didn't know about General Order Number 8, barring correspondents from accompanying the expedition, until the fighting was under way. He said he thought he had written a "correct history of the affair," but admitted he drew his facts from "narrow channels of information." He now realized, he groveled, that he had made any number of errors in his story and was prepared to admit that Sherman's conduct of the battle had been judicious and efficient. "From listening to and examining your plans and orders concerning those operations, I find that nothing could be more full and complete. . . . I am now satisfied that neither to yourself nor any officer of your command can be attributed the failure to accomplish the object of your expedition."

If he had continued to show contrition, Sherman might have relented. But when Knox appeared before the angry general, he was unaccountably cocky. In a letter written in the spring (to Murat Halstead, of all people, the editor whose paper had announced he was insane), Sherman said Knox told him, "Of course, General Sherman,

I had no feeling against you personally, but you are regarded as the enemy of our set, and we must in self-defense write you down." The quotation has a manufactured ring to it, but given the way Knox and Wilkie conspired to write Sherman down, there's no doubt it fairly represented the thinking of Sherman's Bohemian "set."

Knox was arrested, "passed in the care of the provost-marshal," and confined aboard a steamship at Young's Point, Louisiana. He wrote:

A volume of lectures upon temperance and a dozen bottles of Allsop's pale ale were among the most welcome contributions that I received. The ale disappeared before the lectures had been thoroughly digested.

The chambermaid of the steam boat displayed the greatest sympathy in my behalf. She declined to receive payment of a washing-bill, and burst into tears when I assured her the money was of no use to me. Her fears for my welfare were caused by a frightful story that had been told her by a cabin-boy. He maliciously represented that I was to be executed for attempting to purchase cotton from a Rebel quartermaster. The verdant woman believed the story for several days.

The court-martial convened February 5, with a brigadier general, four colonels, and two majors sitting in judgment. They were all Sherman's men. The general was John M. Thayer; the prosecutor (judge advocate) was Captain C. Van Rensselaer; Knox's defense attorney was Lieutenant Colonel W. B. Woods. Sherman himself was in attendance most days. It was serious business, Knox noted, with the members of the court in full uniform, including swords and sashes.

There were three charges placed against Knox:

1. *Giving intelligence to the enemy, directly or indirectly*. In the first specification, Knox was charged with writing an article that included "the names of commanders of corps, divisions, and brigades comprising said army, with the number and description of the regiments . . . thereby indirectly conveying to the enemy an approximate estimate of its strength, in direct violation of the Fifty-seventh Article of War."

In the second specification, Knox was charged with writing an article "purporting to be a history of the operations of the army before

Vicksburg in direct violations of General Orders No. 67, dated . . . August 26, 1861." Number 67 was an obscure War Department order that stated that reporters couldn't write about military movements without the authority and consent of the general in command.

2. *Being a spy.* In the first specification, Knox, "being a citizen and camp follower," was charged with boarding the steamer *Continental* on December 21, "acting as a spy," and remaining on board until January 3, in direct violation of Sherman's own General Order Number 8.

In the second specification, Knox was charged with writing "sundry and various false allegations and accusations against the officers of the Army of the United States, to the great detriment of the interest of the National Government and comfort of our enemies." That was followed by a number of excerpts from Knox's story—entered in the trial as Exhibit B—including his allegations that one general, A. J. Smith, had frittered away his time in erecting a bridge across the bayou, that the medical director (unnamed) hadn't equipped his hospitals adequately, and that Sherman himself had failed to issue proper orders to his divisional and brigade commanders.

3. *Disobedience of orders.* In the first specification, Knox was charged with violating Sherman's General Order Number 8. In the second, he was charged with violating the War Department's General Order Number 67.

Knox's lawyer, Colonel Woods, successfully challenged the second specification of the second charge—the one stating that Knox had written all those false and scurrilous things about Sherman and his officers. Colonel Woods argued that there was no criminal intent in what Knox wrote; he didn't really mean to communicate worthwhile information to the enemy. "The publication of 'false allegations and accusations against the officers of the Army of the United States' does not make a man a spy," Colonel Woods said. "If it did, there is scarcely a newspaper editor or correspondent in the North who is not liable to be capitally punished."

Sherman argued that newspapers routinely were passed back and forth between Union and Confederate lines. He said that he had received Southern newspapers himself—the *Grenada Appeal*, "and very

often the Mobile papers . . . and from them learned that our Northern newspapers were received regularly at Jackson, Holly Springs,
and Senatobia." But, Colonel Woods said, there was no evidence
Knox's story had been picked up by newspapers in the South, even
though "steamers were flying up and down the river in the vain
search for evidence" to make the point. They were looking for a
Southern newspaper—*any* Southern newspaper—containing information about Knox's dispatch. They did come up with a copy of the
Vicksburg Whig, dated January 23, carrying extracts from various Northern newspapers, but not a word from Knox's story in the *Herald*. The
charge was thrown out. Knox pleaded not guilty to everything else.

Colonel Woods pointed out that Knox's dispatch appeared long
after the battle was over "and after the army had moved some 25
miles from the scene of the action." The Confederates had captured
more than five hundred of Sherman's soldiers, and some of them, it
seems safe to say, must have supplied information about the composition of the Union army, including the names of the Yankee commanders.

Sherman really had no case against Knox for giving information to
the enemy and for being a spy. That left disobedience of orders—
violating both Sherman's General Order Number 8 and the War
Department's Order Number 67.

Order Number 8 was a curious document. Paragraph 1 pointed
out that the expedition against Vicksburg was "purely of a military
character" and so "no citizen, male or female, will be allowed to accompany it, unless employed as part of a crew, or as a servant to the
transports." It went on to spell out the role of chambermaids and
nurses. Paragraphs 2, 3, and 4 dealt with buying and dealing in cotton. Paragraph 5 said that violators of the order would be conscripted
into the army and put to work as deckhands. It was only in the final
paragraph, the sixth, that Sherman said, through Major Hammond,
that anyone found "making reports for publication . . . will be arrested
and treated as spies."

In his defense, Knox argued that he had never heard of War
Department Order Number 67 and that, in any event, it had been
superseded by rules laid down by the army's commander in chief

United States
agt
Thomas W. Knox

Exhibit C

HEADQUARTERS RIGHT WING, 13TH ARMY CORPS.
Memphis, Tenn., December 18, 1862.

GENERAL ORDER,
No. 8.

1. The Expedition now fitting out is purely of a military character, and the interests involved are of too important a character to be mixed up with personal and private business. No citizen, male or female, will be allowed to accompany it, unless employed as part of a crew, or as a servant to the transports. Female chambermaids to boats, and nurses to sick, alone, will be allowed, unless the wives of Captains or Pilots, actually belonging to boats. No laundress, officer's or soldier's wives, must pass below Helena.

2. No person whatever, citizen, officer, or sutler, will, on any consideration, buy or deal in cotton, or other produce of the country. Should any cotton be brought on board of a transport, going or returning, the Brigade Quarter Master, of which the boat forms a part, will take possession of it, and invoice it to Capt. A. R. Eddy, Chief Quarter Master, at Memphis.

3. Should any cotton, or other produce, be brought back to Memphis, by any chartered boat, Capt. Eddy, will take possession of the same and sell it for the benefit of the United States. If accompanied by its actual producer, the planter or factor, the Quarter Master will furnish him a receipt for the same, to be settled for, on proof of his loyalty, at the end of the war.

4. Boats ascending the river may take cotton from the shore, for bulk heads, to protect their engines or their crew, but on arrival at Memphis it will be turned over to the Quarter Master, with a statement of the time, place, and name of its owner. The trade in cotton must await a more peaceful state of affairs.

5. Should any citizen accompany the expedition below Helena, in violation of these orders, any Colonel of a Regiment, or Captain of a Battery, will conscript him into the service of the United States for the unexpired term of his command. If he show a refractory spirit, unfitting him for a soldier, the commanding officer present will turn him over to the Captain of the boat, as a deck hand and compel him to work in that capacity, without wages, till the boat returns to Memphis.

6. Any persons whatever, whether in the service of the United States or Transports, found making reports for publication, which might reach the enemy, giving them information, aid and comfort, will be arrested and treated as spies.

By order of Major General SHERMAN.

J. H. HAMMOND,
Maj. and A. A. Gen'l.

Official Copy
JHHammond
Major and A. A. Gen'l.

General William T. Sherman's infamous Order Number 8, from Thomas Knox's court-martial papers. (National Archives)

at the time, General McClellan, "regulating Army correspondence, and directly authorizing such correspondence as should conform to those rules."

But Knox knew he was on shaky ground here. "Here was the rock on which I split," he wrote in his memoirs. "I *had* written a letter respecting military movements . . . 'without the sanction of the general in command.' Correspondents everywhere had done the same thing, and continued to do it until the end of the war. 'Order No. 67' was as obsolete as the Medes and Persians." But it was still on the books, even though it was never enforced against anyone except Thomas Knox.

As for General Order Number 8, Knox had boarded the steamer *Continental* and accompanied Sherman's expedition, in apparent violation of the order. But he figured he had an ace up his sleeve on this one. He had been issued a pass from General Grant's headquarters dated December 16, 1862, and it gave him permission to "go where he pleased within the lines of the 13th Army Corps." Sherman, we have seen, commanded the Thirteenth Army Corps' right wing; Grant commanded the whole corps. "That is the authority of accused for accompanying the expedition," Colonel Woods said, "and it seems to accused that it makes an end to all controversy upon the specification under consideration."

Knox produced several character witnesses, including Brigadier General Frank Blair Jr., brother of Lincoln's postmaster general, the politically powerful Montgomery Blair. He testified that Knox was "a very honorable and respectable gentleman" and that he had never had "the slightest doubt that he was a perfectly loyal man. I have seen him in positions where his loyalty was very thoroughly tested, and I have understood that Mr. Knox's opinions were Radical, although the Herald is a Democratic and conservative journal." Another general, Knox's friend Frederick Steele, said the correspondent was as loyal to the United States as "anyone with the Army. I had never heard his loyalty questioned by anyone."

The trial concluded two weeks after it began. The court found Knox guilty on the first specification of charge one, that he wrote an article in the *Herald* giving the names of the various army commanders, but absolved him of the more serious part of the specification, that he conveyed information to the enemy in violation of the Fifty-seventh Article of War. The court said the facts had been proven in the third charge that he had disobeyed General Order Number 8, "but attach no criminality thereto." He was also found guilty of disobeying the War Department's Order Number 67. He was acquitted on the other charges.

The court sentenced him "to be sent without the lines of the Army and not to return under penalty of imprisonment."

Sherman was displeased by the verdict, even though it was handed down by his own officers. He was especially disturbed by the court's finding that Knox had violated Order Number 8 but that there was no criminality attached to it. In a letter to Colonel John A. Rawlins, Grant's chief of staff, he said:

> The inference is that a commanding officer has no right to prohibit citizens from accompanying a military expedition, or, if he does, such citizens incur no criminality by disregarding such command. . . . If a commanding officer cannot exclude from his camp the very class of men which an enemy would select as spies and informers, and if to prove the conveyance of indirect information to the enemy it be necessary to follow that information from its sources to the very armies arrayed against us, whose country thus far our hundreds of thousands of men have been unable to invade, and yet whose newspapers are made up of extracts from these very Northern papers, then it is fruitless to attempt to conceal from them all the data they could need to make successful resistance to our plans, and to attack our detached parties and lines of communication. To this cause may well be attributed the past reverses to our armies and the failure of almost every plan devised by our generals. I believe this cause has lost us millions of money, thousands of lives, and will continue to defeat us to the end of time, unless some remedy be devised.

Knox's unconstitutional court-martial stands today as the most dramatic attempt ever made by the American military to suppress journalists and the newspapers they represented. In its aftermath, Sherman said he looked for "some remedy to be devised." We know what his remedy would have been—he would have removed correspondents from the battlefield entirely (he did just that in his celebrated March to the Sea). But the United States is a democracy with a written Constitution protecting a free press. The First Amendment protects nasty stories (like the ones Knox and Wilkie wrote) just as it protects simpering ones. On the other hand, generals are properly outraged when they are defamed by journalists and when they see newspapers publishing information useful to the enemy. The American military, 140 years after the Civil War, is still looking for that "remedy" Sherman talked about.

What's puzzling about the Knox trial is the fact that newspapers all over America fell silent. Though the issues were crucial to their well-being, they didn't print a word. It's hard to know exactly why this was so. Perhaps they were intimidated by what was happening at Young's Point. Perhaps they simply failed to appreciate what was at stake. Perhaps they thought it was Knox's mess and it was up to him to find a way out of it. The *Herald*'s silence is even more puzzling. Bennett—not an editor easily intimidated—never offered any support to Knox. There were no telegrams, no letters. The paper might have hired a lawyer for its correspondent and raised the compelling constitutional issues.

It's not that Bennett and his top editors weren't aware of what was happening. An obscure correspondent named Bingham in Memphis wrote a letter dated February 23 to Bennett's managing editor, Fred Hudson, and talked about Knox's predicament. "I fear they have Knox in a bad way at Vicksburg," Bingham said. But he added, gratuitously, his own opinion that Sherman had been "badly treated." Knox, he said, "will come out all right in the end," and perhaps it was that kind of optimism that guided Bennett's thinking in New York.

If the editors weren't intimidated, reporters in the field surely were. Bingham said that both Richard T. Colburn of the *World* and Franc Wilkie of the *Times* skedaddled out of Sherman's reach when they heard Knox had been arrested. "I think they are all worse scared than hurt," Bingham noted.

When word of the verdict reached Washington, a number of reporters, acting individually and led by "Colonel" John W. Forney, absentee owner of the *Philadelphia Press* and secretary of the Senate, signed a memorial to President Lincoln calling on him to set the verdict aside.

Knox's friend, the *New York Tribune*'s Albert Richardson, was working in Washington at the time, and he led a delegation of newspaper reporters and a Colorado congressman that delivered the memorial to the president.

Lincoln told a few stories—in one, he said that if Longfellow's stream was "Minne-haha," a smaller one he and Richardson had seen on a western trip years earlier should be known as the "Minne-boohoo"—they all settled down to talk about Knox. The president said he would set the verdict aside only if Grant agreed.

> We reminded him that this was improbable, as Sherman and Grant were close personal friends. After a few minutes, he replied, with courtesy, but with emphasis:—
>
> "I should be glad to serve you or Mr. Knox, or any other loyal journalist. But, just at present, our generals in the field are more important to the country than any of the rest of us. It is my fixed determination to do nothing whatever which can possibly embarrass any of them. Therefore, I will do cheerfully what I have said, but it is all I can do."

There was so much irresistible good sense in this that it prevented any further discussion. The president took up his pen and wrote, reflecting from time to time, the following:

> Executive Mansion, Washington, March 20, 1863.
>
> Whom it may concern:
>
> Whereas, it appears to my satisfaction that Thomas W. Knox, a correspondent of the New York Herald, has been, by the sentence of a court-martial, excluded from the military department under the command of Major-General Grant, and also that General Thayer . . . and many other respectable persons are of the opinion that Mr. Knox's offense was technical, rather than wilfully wrong, and that the sentence should be revoked; Now, therefore, said sentence is hereby so far revoked as to allow Mr. Knox to return to General Grant's head-quarters, and to remain if General Grant shall give his express assent, and to again leave the department, if General Grant shall refuse such assent.
>
> A. Lincoln

Never let it be forgotten that Abraham Lincoln was a lawyer.

Knox wrote a letter to Sherman on April 6 in which he regretted "the want of harmony between portions of the army and the press" and asked to be reinstated as a western army journalist. He enclosed

Lincoln's statement. Sherman replied the next day in no uncertain language:

> Come with a sword or a musket in your hand, prepared to share with us our fate in sunshine and storm, in prosperity and adversity, in plenty and scarcity, and I will welcome you as a brother and associate; but come as you now do, expecting me to ally the reputation and honor of my country with you, as the representative of the press, which you yourself say makes such a slight a difference between truth and falsehood and my answer is, Never.

There had been a flurry of letters all around in early April. On April 6, Grant had written Knox a letter stoutly defending Sherman and saying he would do nothing for Knox without Sherman's consent. Two days later, Sherman wrote Grant to thank him for refusing to reinstate Knox. Sherman was particularly outraged by Knox's statement that he regretted there was a lack of harmony between "portions of the army and the press." He wrote:

> The insolence of these fellows is insupportable. I know they are encouraged, but I know human nature well enough, and that they will be the first to turn against their patrons. Mr. Lincoln, of course, fears to incur the enmity of the Herald, but he must rule the Herald or the Herald will rule him; he can take his choice. . . . If the press be allowed to run riot, and write up and write down at their pleasure, there is an end to constitutional government in America, and anarchy must result. Even now the real people of our country begin to fear and tremble at it, and look to our armies as the anchor of safety, of order, submission to authority, bound together by a real government, and not by the clamor of a demoralized press and crowd of demagogues.

William Tecumseh Sherman sometimes sounded, terrifyingly, like the man on horseback.

9

Prisoners of War

O N MAY 3, 1863, three well-known war correspondents—Albert D. Richardson and Junius Henri Browne, both of Mr. Greeley's *New York Tribune*, and Richard T. Colburn of the *New York World*—met at Milliken's Bend, twenty-five miles above Vicksburg, to decide their next moves.

"Duty to the paper we represented required that we should join the army [at Grand Gulf, fifty-five miles below Vicksburg] with the least possible delay," Richardson wrote in his memoirs. The question was, how to get there.

> We could go overland, down the Louisiana shore, and, if we safely ran the gauntlet of Rebel guerrillas, reach Grand Gulf in three days. But a little expedition was about to run the Vicksburg batteries. If it survived the fiery ordeal, it would arrive at Grant's headquarters in eight hours. Thus far, three-fourths of the boats attempting to run the batteries had escaped destruction; and, yielding to the seductive doctrine of probabilities we determined to try the short, or water route.

Big mistake.

The three newspapermen were captured, and two of them, the lads from the *Tribune*, languished in seven different rebel prisons before pulling off one of the war's most dramatic escapes. (Colburn, representing the sedate *World*, was released three weeks after his capture.)

In *his* memoirs—both men rushed into print shortly after completing their escape—Browne pointed out that the expedition had the potential for a disaster right from the start. It consisted of a steam tug, the *Sturges*, and two barges loaded with provisions and bales of hay. One steam tug meant a top speed of seven miles an hour; the usual expedition consisted of two steam tugs, increasing the expedition's speed to twelve or thirteen miles an hour.

Some of the hay, Browne and Richardson agreed, was lying loosely about, where any exploding shell might start a fire. If that happened, they had only two buckets to put it out. And, if they were forced to abandon ship, they had only one skiff for the thirty-five men taking part in the expedition. They included the three Bohemians; the tug's captain, a man named Ward, and his crew; Davidson, a surgeon with the Forty-seventh Ohio Infantry; fourteen infantrymen, on hand to repel rebel boarders; and various other officers and citizens.

It was a beautiful moonlit night, in itself a bad sign. "For two or three hours, we glided silently along the glassy waters between banks festooned with heavy, drooping foliage," Richardson recalled. "It was a scene of quiet, surpassing beauty."

"We smoked and laughed and jested and chatted, saying if that was to be our last appearance on any earthly stage, that we would remember it with pleasure when we obtained a new engagement—on some celestial newspaper," Browne wrote.

Captain Ward remembered he had a bottle of Catawba wine in his valise, and he broke it open with his sword. "From a soldier's cup of gutta-percha we drank to the success of the expedition," Richardson remembered.

And then all hell broke loose.

"At one o'clock in the morning," Richardson said,

. . . a rocket shot up and pierced the sky, signaling the Rebels of our approach. Ten minutes later, we saw the flash and heard the boom of their first gun. . . . A shell struck one of our barges, and exploded upon it.

We were soon under a heavy fire. The range of the batteries covered the river for nearly seven miles. The Mississippi here is very crooked, resembling the letter S, and at some points we passed within two hundred yards of ten-inch guns, with point-blank range upon us. As we moved around the bends, the shots came toward us at once from right and left, front and rear.

The Bohemians took refuge behind the hay bales. "Discretion," Richardson said, "was largely the better part of my valor, and I cowered close in our partial shelter." He recalled Bottom's line from Shakespeare's *Midsummer Night's Dream* that "good hay, sweet hay hath no fellow." Two or three times, he stood up to see what was happening. "How the great sheets of flame leaped up and spread out from the mouths of the guns!" he wrote. "How the shells came screaming and shrieking through the air! How they rattled and crashed, penetrating the sides of the barges, or exploding on board in great fountains of fire!"

Skinny little Junius Browne "persisted in standing, all exposed, to watch the coming shots. Once, as a shell exploded near at hand, he fell down among the hay bales. I dared not put forth my hand in the darkness, lest it should rest on his mutilated form. At last he spoke and relieved my anxiety. He had only slipped and fallen."

By now, Browne and Richardson said, the battered expedition was below the town, and in ten minutes more would be safely through. Richardson described what happened next.

A terrific report, like the explosion of some vast magazine, left us breathless, and seemed to shake the earth to its very center. It was accompanied by a shriek which I shall never forget, though it seemed to occupy less than a quarter of the time consumed by one tick of the watch. It was the death-cry wrung from our captain, killed as he stood at the wheel. For his heedlessness in fitting out the expedition, his life was the penalty.

We listened, but the friendly voice from the tug was hushed. We were disabled, and drifting helplessly in front of the enemy's guns.

In his memoirs, Browne reconstructed what would seem to be a somewhat unlikely conversation.

"The play is over," said Richardson. "Hand in your checks, boys," exclaimed Colburn. "A change of base for the Bohemians," remarked the undersigned; and he glanced around and heard the groans and sharp cries of the wounded and the scalded.

We rushed forward and tried to trample out the flames, but they rose behind us like fiery serpents, and paled the full-orbed moon, and lit up the dark waters of the Stygian river far and near. . . . Every one was now bent on saving himself.

Of the thirty-five men aboard the expedition, more than half were killed or badly wounded. The three Bohemians were unscathed; they tossed bales of hay into the water and then jumped in after them, using the bales as rafts. Richardson was paddling along nicely when he saw a rebel shot coming straight at him. "How round, smooth, shining, and black it looked, ricochetting along, plunging into the water, throwing up great jets of spray, bounding like a school boy's ball, and then skimming the river again! It struck about four feet from my hay bale, which was now a few yards from the burning barge."

The Confederates sent out a yawl to pick up the survivors, and they were landed about two miles below the city. "We were all reported lost, we learned afterward," Browne said, "though General Sherman's humorous comment, when apprised that three of the Bohemians had been killed—'That's good! We'll have dispatches now from hell before breakfast'—did not prove a veracious prediction."

One of the survivors whispered to Richardson that it might not be a good idea to tell the rebels that he and Browne were correspondents for Mr. Greeley's *Tribune*. "Tell them you are correspondents of some less obnoxious journal," he advised.

Months earlier, Richardson said, he had asked three Confederate officers—paroled prisoners within the Union lines—what would be the fate of a *Tribune* correspondent were he to be captured by the rebels. "We would hang him upon the nearest sapling," they agreed.

Browne and Richardson realized that they would be the first correspondents representing a radical Republican newspaper to fall into enemy hands. Even so, they decided they had no course but to "stand by our colors and tell the plain truth."

They were marched into Vicksburg—Browne with bloody bare feet—and turned over to the City Guards. "I hope, sir," said Colburn, "that you will give us comfortable quarters." Instead, they were thrown into the city jail, "its foul yard . . . half filled with criminals and convicts, black and white, all dirty and covered with vermin."

In a day or two, the three Bohemians were taken before Major N. G. Watts, the Confederate prisoner-exchange agent; they all signed standard parole papers giving each of them "full leave to return to his country" with the usual stipulations about not taking up arms again.

After three days in Vicksburg, the Bohemians were put aboard a train with forty Union prisoners of war from Ohio and taken to Jackson, Mississippi. There, they were permitted to visit the offices of what had once been the *Memphis Appeal* and was now known as the "moving *Appeal*," perhaps the most admirable newspaper published, North or South, during the Civil War. It kept publishing, every day, for three years while it was on the run from advancing Yankee armies—in Grenada, Mississippi, Jackson, Atlanta, and Montgomery, Alabama. Richardson thought the editors, John R. McClanahan and Benjamin F. Dill, published "the most enterprising and readable newspaper in the South." Maybe that was because the *Appeal* was "noticeably free from vituperation, calling the President 'Mr. Lincoln' instead of the 'Illinois Baboon.' "

The editors gave the three Bohemians clothing and money and agreed to send the news north that they were, in Browne's florid words, "still among the living, instead of waltzing obliviously with the catfish in the turbid eddies at the bottom of the Mississippi." On May 14, the day the Federal forces entered Jackson, the moving *Appeal* crossed the Pearl River in a flatboat with its printing equipment and its mules just minutes ahead of the Yankees, stopped briefly at Meridian, Mississippi, rolling out one edition, and then settled in Atlanta.

Through it all, the moving *Appeal* managed to keep three correspondents in the field. One of them was an Alabamian named John H. Linebaugh, who served with the dyspeptic Braxton Bragg and his Army of Tennessee. Linebaugh's early dispatches were optimistic about Bragg's drive into Kentucky. "But," historian George Sisler wrote, "the steady paean of praise began to fade when Linebaugh filed his account of the bloody battle of Perryville [on October 8, 1862], taking on a critical tone when Bragg, confronted with Federal reinforcements, abandoned his dead and wounded and hastily retired across the Tennessee border."

Linebaugh later reported that "nowhere in our ranks can there be found any degree of confidence in Gen. Bragg." On the eve of the battle of Chickamauga (September 19 and 20, 1863), Linebaugh—whose only son had been killed while serving with Pemberton in Mississippi—was arrested by Confederate army officers and charged with treason. It was Thomas Knox all over again, except in this instance the angry general was a Confederate, Bragg, and not a Yankee, Sherman. Linebaugh's editors (unlike Knox's) immediately hired a lawyer and sought Linebaugh's release on a writ of habeas corpus. The Superior Court judge, O. A. Bull, ruled in Linebaugh's favor, and he was released from prison on October 5. CIVIL LAW VINDICATED, said the *Appeal*'s headline on October 7.

The *Appeal* supported the Confederate cause throughout the war, but not blindly and not intemperately. The editors were often thoughtful and eloquent. A few months before the war ended (when the *Appeal* had moved again, to Montgomery, where the Confederate States of America had been born), Dill wrote that the South's tragedy "has been, that we have been enjoying independence before we had achieved it, and enjoying history before we had made it."

From Jackson, the three Bohemians were put on the cars and taken to Atlanta. They were committed to what Richardson said was "a filthy, vermin-infested military prison." Encouraged by the kindly treatment they had received from the editors of the *Appeal* in Jackson, they sent a card to one of the local Atlanta newspapers asking to purchase whatever out-of-town newspapers they had available. The messenger blundered and dropped their card at what Richardson called the *Confederate* and Browne the *Confederacy*. They were referring to the *Southern Confederacy*, one of the city's eight daily and weekly newspapers.

The next morning, the Bohemians were appalled when they read a copy of the paper, which called them impertinent and impudent for

NEWS FROM THE BATTLE.

Sketch of a correspondent carrying news from the battlefield. (Library of Congress)

asking for the exchange newspapers and went on to argue that what they really deserved was "a rope's end, and will not receive their just deserts till their crimes are punished with death."

The correspondents were not sorry to escape from Atlanta. They were put aboard another train and arrived in Richmond at 5 A.M. on Saturday, May 16. They were taken immediately to Libby Prison.

It was bad enough, Browne said, but "not so bad as I had anticipated. The floor was clean and the walls were whitewashed; but I thought if I were compelled to remain there a month, I should die outright. How little we know of ourselves!"

Lice—"insatiate lice"—were the biggest problem. The prisoners spent hours every day trying to destroy them. "For the first week," said Richardson, "I could not think of them without shuddering and faintness: but in time I learned to make my daily entomological researches with calm complacency."

After a week or so, a Confederate exchange officer received a request from Colburn's editor at the *New York World* for his release. "It proved as efficient as if it had been an order from Jefferson Davis," Richardson said. "After ten days' confinement in Libby, Colburn was sent home by the first truce boat. A thoroughly loyal gentleman, and an unselfish, devoted friend, he was induced to go, only by the assurance that while he could do no good by remaining, he might be of service to us in the North." (Colburn, unable to do much for his captured friends, rejoined Grant and his army and was with them when they captured Vicksburg on July 4, 1863. One of the first Confederates he met inside the fallen city was Major Watts, the prisoner-exchange officer.)

Before he left, Colburn put $50 in U.S. currency in the hands of Captain Thomas P. Turner, commandant of the prison. The money, he said, was for Richardson, so he could buy necessary supplies. "A day or two afterward, Turner handed the sum to me in Confederate rags, dollar for dollar, asserting that this was the identical money he had received. The perpetrator of this petty knavery was educated at West Point, and claimed to be a Virginia gentleman."

Browne and Richardson demanded to know why they weren't being released on parole like their friend, Colburn, and all the other survivors of the Vicksburg expedition. They were told that the parole signed by Major Watts wasn't valid and that they were just the kind of men the South intended to keep. "We knew our case was hopeless," Browne said, "[and] that the Tribune correspondents were in for the War. . . . Never during the war have I known of another instance in which prisoners have been held, as we were, who had been paroled regularly by an accredited agent of exchange at a regular point of exchange." The whole thing, Browne said, was "a farce."

It was too much for Browne. "My system gave way, and ere a week had passed I was prostrate on the floor with a raging fever. Those who felt any interest in me became alarmed, thinking I would die in that wretched place." It went on that way for eight weeks until news leaked into the prison that Vicksburg had fallen. "No cordial of Zanoni's could better have done its therapeutic errand. I rose at once and joined in a tremendous chorus of the 'Star Spangled Banner,' which made the air vibrate. . . . That news, so glorious, proved more potent than any Arabian philter. I had no fever nor any ailment of any kind for many a long month after."

On September 21, the two correspondents were transferred from Libby to another Richmond prison, Castle Thunder, filled mostly with civilians. The commandant there, Captain George W. Alexander, was an extraordinary character—"a regular Bombastes Furioso," Browne said. "Pompous and excessively vain, delighting in gauntlets, top boots, huge revolvers, and a red sash, he was sometimes furiously angry, but, in the main, kind to captives," Richardson added.

Browne and Richardson were joined, briefly, at Castle Thunder by two other Bohemians, Solomon T. Bulkley and S. A. Hendricks, both from Mr. Bennett's *Herald*. Hendricks, Richardson said, was a wag.

> One evening a Virginia ruralist, whose intellect was not of the brightest, was brought in for some violation of Confederate law. After pouring his sorrows into the sympathetic ear of the correspondents, he suddenly asked: "What are you here for?"
>
> "I am the victim," replied Hendricks, "of gross and flagrant injustice. I am the inventor of a new piece of artillery known as the Hendricks gun. Its range far exceeds every other cannon in the world. A week ago I was testing it from the Richmond defenses, where it is mounted. One of the shots accidentally struck and sunk a blockade runner just entering the port of Wilmington. It was not my fault. I did not aim at the steamer. I was just trying the gun for the benefit of the country. But these confounded Richmond authorities insisted upon it that I should pay for the vessel. I told them I would see them ———— first, and they shut me up in Castle Thunder, but I never will pay in the world."
>
> "You are quite right. I would not, if I were you," replied the innocent Virginian. "It is the greatest outrage I ever heard of."

Hendricks and Bulkley were paroled after three months. Browne and Richardson were transferred to yet another prison, the Confederate States Penitentiary at Salisbury, north of Charlotte in western North Carolina. They arrived there on February 3, 1864.

The two Bohemians had been contemplating an escape for months. At Salisbury, they became serious. Salisbury, after ten thousand captured Union infantrymen arrived from Richmond, was hell. "It seems hardly possible to exaggerate the incredible cruelty of the Rebel authorities," Richardson wrote. On November 26, a number of the Union prisoners tried to force their way through the front gate. Sixteen of them were killed and sixty more wounded. Richardson wrote: "After this massacre, cold-blooded murders were very frequent. Any guard, standing upon the fence, at any hour of the day or night, could deliberately raise his musket and shoot into any group of prisoners, black or white, without the slightest rebuke from the authorities. He would not even be taken off his post for it."

Browne said he began thinking of almost nothing else except tunnels. "Tunnels were my thought by day and my dream by night. . . . A Tunnel to me was the greatest work of Man."

"We were constantly trying to escape," Richardson said. "During the last fifteen months of our imprisonment, I think there was no day when we had not some plan which we hoped soon to put into execution."

Browne, Richardson said, was a worrier. He saw the "gloomy side of every picture." Once they escaped, he said, they would be forced to make "this terrible tramp of two hundred miles, by night, in midwinter, over two ranges of mountains, creeping stealthily through the enemy's country, weak, hungry, shelterless!" Quite a lot, in fact, to be gloomy about.

Bushwhackers—armed men operating in a sort of no-man's-land in North Carolina and Tennessee—made it even worse. The rough country between Salisbury and the nearest Union lines was filled with them. They were "vicious, passionate, bloodthirsty," living "in caves, or pits dug in the earth." Their main concern was self-preservation. Browne worried about them.

The Bohemians discovered they had an ally inside the prison—a Confederate officer, Lieutenant John R. Welborn, a member of a mysterious organization called the Sons of America, founded to help Union men seeking to escape to the North. Richardson said the members of the order recognized each other "by the signs, grips, and passwords common to all secret societies."

Browne and Richardson had been joined by a third Bohemian, William E. Davis of the *Cincinnati Gazette*. With Welborn's help, the three journalists were assigned to work in the Union hospital inside the prison, and Davis and Browne managed to secure passes that allowed them to pick up medical supplies from a Confederate hospital located outside the prison lines. Joined by another prisoner, Thomas E. Wolfe, a merchant captain, at half an hour before dark on Sunday, December 18, 1864, they simply walked past the sentries—first Browne, Wolfe, and Davis, and then Richardson—flashing their passes and telling anyone who cared to ask that they were on their way to the Confederate hospital for supplies.

Richardson was the only one to encounter a challenge.

"Have you a pass, sir?" a sentry asked.

"Certainly I have a pass," he replied. "Have you not seen it often enough to know by this time?" Fortunately for Richardson, Browne had found a way to sneak his valid pass back into the prison. Richardson now showed it to the sentry. "Junius H. Browne, Citizen," it said, "has permission to pass the inner gate of the prison, to assist in carrying medicines to the Military Prison Hospital, until further orders." It was signed by Captain J. A. Fuqua, the assistant commandant. "That pass is all right," the sentry said. "I know Captain Fuqua's handwriting."

"At dark," said Richardson, "my three friends joined me. We went through the outer gate, in full view of a sentinel, who supposed we were Rebel surgeons or nurses. And then, on that rainy Sunday night, for the first time in twenty months, we found ourselves walking freely in a public street, without a Rebel bayonet before or behind us."

They made their way to a small plantation, owned by a farmer with Union sympathies. He said he couldn't allow them inside his house because it was full of rebels but he did show them to his barn. Richardson said:

We climbed up the ladder to the hay mow. Davis and Wolfe burrowed down perpendicularly into the fodder, as if sinking an oil well, until they were covered, heads and all. "Junius" and myself, after two hours of perspiring labor, tunneled into a safe position under the eaves, where we lay, stretched at full length, head to head, luxuriating in the fresh air, which came in through the cracks.

Lieutenant Welborn (Brown referred to him simply as "a lieu-tenant of militia") caught up with them the next night, bringing with him another escaped prisoner, Sergeant Charles Thurston of the Sixth New Hampshire Infantry. Richardson said Thurston had "two valu-able possessions—great address, and the uniform of a Confederate private."

Welborn gave what was now a five-man party directions to remote Wilkes County in the Blue Ridge Mountains; he said his family and friends lived there, and they were all loyal to the Union. It was the last the Bohemians saw of the man who had made their escape pos-sible, though they learned afterward that Welborn was forced to run himself three months later. He showed up inside Union lines in Knoxville with thirty Union soldiers he had safely conducted from Salisbury.

They traveled now at night, hiding during the day, cold, shiver-ing, hungry. They were befriended again and again by Negro slaves. In one slave cabin, an old Negro killed two chickens for supper and then, Richardson wrote, stood outside "to watch and warn us of the patrols. . . . It was the first dwelling I had entered for nearly 20 months. It was rude almost to squalor; but it looked more palatial than the most elegant and luxurious saloon. There was a soft bed, with clean, snowy sheets. How I envied those Negroes, and longed to stretch my limbs upon it and sleep for a week!"

"God bless the negroes," Browne said. "During our entire cap-tivity, and after our escape, they were ever our firm, brave, unflinch-ing friends. We never made an appeal to them they did not answer. They never hesitated to do us a service at the risk even of life. . . . They were ignorant, oppressed, enslaved; but they always cherished a simple and beautiful faith in the cause of the Union and its ultimate triumph."

They finally arrived in Wilkes County on Christmas Eve, where they were welcomed by Lieutenant Welborn's mother. Richardson wrote: "We were soon by the great log fire of a house where friends awaited us. Belonging to the secret Union organization, they had re-ceived intelligence that we were on the way. Our feet were blistered and swollen; mine were frostbitten. We removed our clothing, and were soon reposing in soft feather beds."

They were now in the mountain South, poor country without great plantations or very many slaves. Sympathy for the Union was strong, but not overpowering; patrols of the rebel "Home Guards" made their rounds on a fairly regular basis. The escapees were taken to neighboring Yadkin County, and lodged at Lieutenant Welborn's home. When a patrol of Breckinridge's cavalry came thundering up the road, they hid under the beds while Mrs. Welborn "talked to them in a quiet, easy way." As they rode away, Mrs. Welborn called to them, "All is safe, boys."

They were taken back to Wilkes County on Wednesday night, some of them staying with the lieutenant's mother, the rest, including Browne, staying with his sister. Welborn's sister had an adopted daughter, sixteen or seventeen years old. Browne called her "Lucy"— "black-eyed, black-haired, intensely loyal Lucy, who took as much interest in our welfare as if we were lovers and brothers combined."

Browne was having supper with Lucy and her family when they all heard a low whistle, a warning from outside that danger, perhaps a rebel patrol, was approaching. Browne told what happened next:

A minute after I felt some one clinging to my arm, and a voice saying, in a suppressed tone: "Come this way!" I could hardly see the face, it was so dark, but I knew it was . . . Lucy.

"What are you doing here, my dear child?" I enquired whisperingly. "Why don't you . . . let me take care for myself?"

"Oh, I want to stay with you," she answered earnestly. "Do come with me. I will show you where to hide [the loft, possibly, or a connecting shed]. I wouldn't have anything happen to you for the world. I'd rather die than have harm come to you."

Poor girl! Her appeal was resistless. I forgot the danger of the situation in my pity and regard for her. Her voice and manner had touched even my worn-out heart.

The rain was falling in torrents [outside], and the thunder bellowing through the sable vault overhead; but still Lucy clung to my arm. The other, disengaged, I threw about her waist—a taper one, even though she had always lived in North Carolina, and had never worn a corset—and drawing her plump figure close to my bosom, kissed her long and closely—more for gratitude than gallantry, more from a sense of duty than affection; and yet duty just at that moment appeared not disagreeable to discharge.

The sensation was not unpleasant to me.

I do not believe it would have been to any man who had not touched a woman's lips for at least two years.

Browne, always a bit of a rogue, pulled down the veil on what happened next. After he awoke the next morning, he found Lucy "sitting demurely in the chimney corner, preparing our plain breakfast before the fire."

Bidding farewell to the black-eyed Lucy, they set out again on December 28, venturing into a mountainous and lonely countryside fought over by roaming bands of deserters and bushwhackers. They met their first party of bushwhackers Friday night, December 30. Richardson wrote:

These men were walking arsenals. Each had a trusty rifle, one or two navy revolvers, a great bowie knife, haversack, and canteen. Their manners were quiet, their faces honest, and one had a voice of rare sweetness. As he stood tossing his baby in the air, with his little daughter clinging to his shirt, he looked

——— "the mildest-mannered man,
That ever scuttled ship or cut a throat."

He and his neighbors had adopted this mode of life, because [they were] determined not to fight against the old flag. They would not attempt the uncertain journey to our lines, leaving their families in the country of the enemy. Ordinarily very quiet and rational, whenever the war was spoken of, their eyes emitted that peculiar glare which I had observed years before in Kansas, and which seems inseparable from the hunted man.

By January 5, the Bohemians and their party (now numbering almost a dozen) were 135 miles from the Union lines in Tennessee. But they were exhausted, their clothes in tatters. Richardson said Browne was a sight to behold.

Overcoat he had none. Pantaloons had been torn to shreds . . . by the brambles and the thorn-bushes. He had a hat which was not all a hat. It was given to him after he had lost his own in a Rebel barn, by a warm-hearted African . . . who felt with the most touching propriety that it would be a shame for any correspondent of the Tribune to go bareheaded as long as a single negro in America was the owner of a hat! . . .

His boots were a stupendous refutation of the report that leather was scarce among the Rebels. I understood it to be no figure of rhetoric, but the result of actual and exact measurement, which induced him to call them the "Seven-Leaguers." The small portion of his body which was visible between the tops of his boots and the bottom of his hat was robed in an old gray quilt of Secessionist proclivities.

For several days they had been told that if they could only hook up with the legendary Dan Ellis, the famous Union pilot, their trials would be over.

"We *did* find Dan Ellis," Richardson wrote, the night of Sunday, January 8.

Greatly broken down, we reached a point in the road, waited for two hours, when along came Dan Ellis with a party of seventy men—refugees, Rebel deserters, Union soldiers returning from their homes within the enemy's lines, and escaping prisoners. About thirty of them were mounted and twenty armed. Like most men of action, Dan—never without his Henry repeating rifle—was a man of few words. When our story had been told him, he said to his comrades: "Boys, here are some gentlemen who have escaped from Salisbury, and are almost dead from the journey. They are our people. They have suffered in our Cause. They are going to their homes in our lines. Get down off your horses, and help them up."

Down they came, and up we went; and then we pressed along at a terrible pace.

Browne said they traveled twenty-seven miles that miserable night and found "after crossing the Nolechucky that we had lost several of our party, three mules, most of the rations, and I know not what else. The truth was, some of Ellis' men had drank too much brandy, becoming so intoxicated that they parted with their reason, and, when asked, could not tell where any thing was." Among the missing was Richardson; he had trusted his mule and his mule had wandered off in the wrong direction.

"We were unwilling to go on without the Tribune correspondent, so we bivouacked, and sent scouts out to obtain tidings of the missing individuals," Browne wrote. Richardson, after concluding that the mule had led him astray, spent the night curled up against a log. The next morning, a farmer set him off in the right direction, "and in four hours . . . he was in our camp."

"Today," said Dan Ellis on the morning of Monday, January 9, "we must cross the Big Butte of Rich Mountain."

"How far is it?" Richardson asked.

"It is generally called ten miles; but I suspect it is about fifteen, and a rather hard road at that."

Richardson described their journey:

We started at 11 A.M. For three miles we followed a winding creek, the horsemen on a slow trot, crossing the stream a dozen times; the footmen keeping up as best they could, and shivering from their frequent baths in the icy waters.

We turned up the sharp side of a snowy mountain. For hours and hours we toiled along, up one rocky, pine-covered hill, down a little declivity, then up another hill, then down again, but constantly gaining in height. Dan averred he had never crossed the mountain when the travel was so hard; but he pushed on, as if death were behind and heaven before.

Browne was almost ready to give up. He said he had written in his notebook that evening that "I have no more hope now of getting through; yet I will do my utmost, and compel the strong spirit to rule the weak flesh. I will march till I fall fainting on the road from hunger, cold, and exhaustion."

They had just settled down for the night when Dan woke everybody up and said he had just talked to a local Union man, and they were all in deep trouble. "We have walked into a nest of Rebels. Several hundred are within a few miles; eighty are in this immediate vicinity."

Ellis divided the party in half, sending the men on horseback one way, the men on foot the other. "My place," Richardson said, "was near the middle of the cavalcade [on horseback]. . . . We galloped along at Dan's usual pace, with sublime indifference to roads—up and down rocky hills, across streams, through swamps, over fences—everywhere but upon public thoroughfares."

Dawn wasn't far away when the *Cincinnati Gazette*'s Davis fell back from the front of the line to talk to Richardson.

"That young lady rides very well, does she not?" he asked.

"What young lady?"

"The young lady who is piloting us."

Richardson rode forward to have a look for himself.

There she was! I could not scrutinize her face . . . but it was said to be comely. I could see that her form was graceful, and the ease and firmness with which she sat on her horse would have been a lesson for a riding master.

She was a member of the loyal family that Dan had gone [to] for news. The moment she learned his need, she volunteered to pilot him out of that neighborhood, where she was born and bred, and knew every acre. . . . She mounted, came to our camp at midnight, and was now stealthily guiding us—avoiding farm houses where the Rebels were quartered, going around their camps, evading their pickets.

Browne wasn't so exhausted he couldn't ride to the front of the line to observe a pretty young woman. "I confess," he said, "I looked at her with some degree of admiration as she sat there, calm, smiling, comely, with the warm blood of youth flushing in her cheek, under the flood of yellow moonlight that bathed all the landscape in poetic softness and picturesque beauty."

"She led us for seven miles," Richardson reported.

Then, while we remained in the wood, she rode forward over the long bridge which spanned the Nolechucky (now to be crossed a second time), to see if there were any guards upon it; went to the first Union house beyond, to learn whether the roads were picketed; came back, and told us the coast was clear. Then she rode along our line toward her home. Had it been safe to cheer, we should certainly have given three times three for the NAMELESS HEROINE who did us such vital kindness. "Benisons upon her dear head forever."

(In a footnote in his book, Richardson identified the NAMELESS HEROINE as Miss Melvina Stevens.)

At 10 A.M. on Friday, January 13, the ragged little party reached the Union picket line at Strawberry Springs, fifteen miles east of Knoxville. They had traveled 340 miles in twenty-seven days.

"Who comes there?" the sentry called.

"Friends without the counter-sign," one of the Bohemians replied, "escaped prisoners from Salisbury."

"All right, boys, glad to see you."

"I walked within the lines that divided Freedom, Enlightenment, Loyalty, from Slavery, Bigotry, Treachery," Richardson wrote, displaying a certain lack of journalistic objectivity, and "was once more an American citizen, emancipated, regenerated, and disenthralled."

Richardson sent a telegram to his editors in New York.

"Out of the jaws of death," he said, "out of the mouth of hell."

10

Grant Finds a Reporter

SYLVANUS CADWALLADER was already a regular, even though he had been the *Chicago Times'* war correspondent with the western armies for less than nine months when he arrived by steamer at Milliken's Bend in late April 1863. He was greeted at the gangplank by three of his fellow correspondents—Richardson, Browne, and Colburn. They urged him to join them in an expedition they were putting together to run past the Confederate guns at Vicksburg.

"I took an hour to consider the matter and decided to take my chance through the mud," he wrote in his memoirs. "The best I could do was secure a government mule, a thrown-away cavalry saddle and bridle, and one or two extra blankets. Thus mounted I took to the road, over which the army had preceded me."

Cadwallader and his mule made it safely to Grant's headquarters at Grand Gulf, below Vicksburg. As we have seen, Richardson, Browne, and Colburn were captured after the Confederate guns wrecked their little expedition, and Greeley's two *New York Tribune* men, Richardson and Browne, spent twenty months in rebel prisons.

Sylvanus Cadwallader was thirty-six years old when he arrived that day at Milliken's Bend, a mature journalist with a wife and a daughter at home back in Wisconsin. He and Grant became friends, and when Grant needed a friend more than at any other time in his life, Cadwallader was there to help him. It was Sylvanus Cadwallader who rescued U. S. Grant from his biggest drinking binge in the war.

He went on to become the *New York Herald*'s chief correspondent for the Army of the Potomac, organizing the Civil War's most efficient field organization. His role in the Civil War was neglected for years—his memoirs weren't published until 1955—and yet he stands out as one of the war's most important journalists.

The best newspaper in Chicago was Joseph Medill's *Chicago Tribune*, always stalwart in its support of Lincoln and the Republican Party. But right behind it, nipping at its heels, was a little bulldog of a paper, Wilbur F. Storey's *Chicago Times*. Storey (like Cadwallader) grew up in Vermont and worked for a number of newspapers before landing in Chicago in June of 1861. Despite his New England background, Storey sided with the South, intellectually at least, on the question of slavery; he despised the abolitionists. His views struck many as inflammatory and unpatriotic, and for a couple of days in the summer of 1863 an angry Union general, Ambrose Burnside, shut the *Times* down.

Storey—a bear of a man—was threatened so frequently that he kept loaded muskets and hand grenades in the newsroom, according to historian J. Cutler Andrews. An added feature was a hot-water boiler that allowed scalding steam to be pumped into ground-floor rooms that might be occupied by a mob.

But Storey was serious about the news, and he was one of the first editors in the country to recognize the importance of the telegraph in relaying it. Storey is supposed to be the man who told his reporters in a famous line that could apply to any number of cable news shows today, "Telegraph all the news you can get, and when there is no news send rumors."

One of his reporters took that message to heart, perhaps too seriously. His name was Warren P. Isham, and he was married to Storey's sister. By all accounts a first-class writer, Isham telegraphed more rumor than fact to his editors in Chicago, and had been warned about it two or three times by military authorities. "The last offense," Cadwallader said, "was that of sending a 'cock and bull' story about a fleet of rebel iron-clads at Pensacola, which he claimed to have received by 'grape-vine' telegraph through the Southern Confederacy."

On August 8, 1862, an angry Grant instructed Sherman to arrest the offending reporter and pack him off to the penitentiary in Alton, Illinois, "for confinement until the close of the war, unless sooner discharged by competent authority." It's hard to imagine that Sherman could have been given a more delicious assignment. "Your order of arrest of newspaper correspondent is executed," he wrote Grant on August 17, "and he will be sent to Alton by the first opportunity. . . . I regard all these newspaper harpies as spies and think they could be punished as such."

Storey recognized that his brother-in-law had gone too far, and deserved some kind of punishment. But prison for the war's duration struck him as unnecessarily harsh. He wired Cadwallader, then the city editor of the *Milwaukee Daily News,* a journalist with a growing reputation, and asked him if he would take Isham's place with the Army of the Tennessee and do what he could to arrange the poor fellow's release.

"I replied, 'yes,'" Cadwallader wrote in his memoirs.

A second dispatch sent the same day inquired, "When?"

To which Cadwallader answered, "Immediately."

Cadwallader caught up with Grant at Jackson, Tennessee, a few days later. "At that time," he said, "nearly all army correspondents were in bad odor at all army headquarters," and in special bad odor among West Pointers and Regular Army officers. He wrote:

> Candor compels the admission that as a class, the first installment of correspondents sent to the armies deserved no high rank in public or official estimation. Some were so lacking in conventional politeness as to make themselves positively disagreeable. Some unduly magnified their importance as the representatives of leading metropolitan daily newspapers. . . . Others were base enough to make merchandise of personal mentions in their correspondence. Others almost unblushingly took the contract of "writing up" some colonel to a brigadier generalship, for a specified consideration in dollars. And still others were sufficiently ignoble to fasten themselves upon some colonel or brigadier, and pay their bills, whiskey bills and horse hire, by fulsome and undeserved praise of their patrons and protectors in every communication sent back for publication.

There was still another class, more despisable than those already mentioned, who would purloin papers and orders, hang around officers' tents secretly at night hoping to overhear a conversation that could be used by their papers.

The worst of the bunch, Cadwallader concluded, was the *New York Times*' William Swinton, who was caught one night "hiding in the shade of a large stump, playing 'eavesdropper,' and trying to overhear a conversation between Grant and one of his generals." He was dragged from his hiding spot and banished from the army. "He was tall and lanky in build; cold-blooded, conceited, and prejudiced to a surprising extent . . . ," Cadwallader said. "It was matter of small wonder that he was universally hated and despised by all who knew him."

Grant's siege of Vicksburg began on May 19, 1863, three days after he defeated John C. Pemberton at Champion Hill, Mississippi, and forced the Confederate army to fall back into their great bastion city. For reporters and soldiers it was boring work. Franc Wilkie was there again, and so was young DeBenneville Randolph Keim, from Reading, Pennsylvania, the same fellow who said he didn't want to read Shakespeare for fear it would influence his literary style. Keim, Cadwallader said, was "polite, vivacious, and accomplished in manners," but he "was never quite up to Mr. Bennett's estimate of a first-class war correspondent because he could never obtain his own consent to send off a dispatch until he had subjected it to the severest literary and scholarly scrutiny; whereas James Gordon Bennett Senr., exalted late news far above fine writing."

Wilkie, Cadwallader said, was "phlegmatic, cynical, severe in invective, well informed on political economy, and indolent by nature unless stirred into action"—perhaps, as we have seen, by a bottle or two of Catawba wine.

Cadwallader, still reporting for the *Chicago Times* but now also sending private letters to Bennett in New York, was the cleverest of the bunch. He set up camp with Captain E. D. Osband, commanding officer of Company A, Fourth Illinois Cavalry, northeast of the city between positions manned by Sherman and Major General James B. McPherson. Osband's background tells a good deal about the kind of war this was; in peacetime, he had operated a cigar and tobacco stand at the Tremont House Hotel in Chicago. From Osband's camp, Cadwallader could "keep constantly within sight of all Gen. Grant's personal movements; his receipt of news from all parts of the line; and the arrival and departure of couriers and bearers of dispatches."

Cadwallader cut a special deal with Grant's couriers. When a courier "was hurriedly and unexpectedly started with dispatches up the river (or elsewhere), my arrangements were such that when he was mounted and had received his final instructions, he came past my tent and took everything I had in readiness. This enabled me to keep from one to two days ahead of my less fortunate competitors." Cadwallader doesn't say so, but it seems obvious the couriers pocketed some of the *Chicago Times'* expense-account money each time they stopped by the correspondent's tent.

Cadwallader reckoned it was probably during the first week of June—it was June 6, for a fact—that he boarded the steamboat *Diligence*, commanded by Captain Harry McDougall of Louisville, for a foray up the Yazoo River.

"Everything was quiet," he wrote in his memoirs, completed in 1896 when he was seventy years old. The memoirs, edited by Benjamin P. Thomas, were published in 1955, and, with Cadwallader's vivid descriptions of Grant's behavior, have caused something of a stir among Civil War historians ever since. Grant's defenders argue that he wasn't drunk on that boat trip. Sick maybe, possibly suffering a migraine attack, but not drunk. Some even suggest Cadwallader wasn't on Grant's boat.

The *Diligence* was on its way downriver the next day, heading back to Vicksburg, when she encountered another steamboat heading upriver. Grant was aboard with Captain Osband—the cavalry commander from the hotel tobacco shop—and a small cavalry escort. Grant, Cadwallader said, had always liked the *Diligence,* and decided to switch steamboats. Accompanying him was Charles A. Dana, formerly Greeley's man at the *New York Tribune* and now Stanton's assistant secretary of war and chief troubleshooter. The *Diligence* turned around and headed upriver again, towards Satartia.

"I was not long in perceiving that Grant had been drinking heavily and that he was still keeping it up," Caldwallader wrote. "He made several trips to the bar room of the boat in a short time, and became stupid in speech and staggering in gait."

Cadwallader didn't know it, then or later, but Grant's behavior had already caught the eye of his chief of staff and loyal protector, Colonel Rawlins. Grant had begun drinking wine before setting off up the Yazoo. Rawlins had seen the empty bottles. He wrote Grant an emotional letter the night of June 6. "The great solicitude I feel for the safety of this army," he said, "leads me to mention what I had hoped never again to do, the subject of your drinking." He demanded Grant take the pledge, immediately, else he would be forced to resign. But Grant apparently slipped away so early the next morning he never saw Rawlins's extraordinary note.

The chance to write a dramatic firsthand story about Ulysses Grant on a frightening drunken binge might have been irresistible to a fair number of Bohemians. Apparently Cadwallader never gave it a thought. He appealed to the officers aboard the *Diligence*, begging them to close the bar and throw away the bottles Grant had collected in his stateroom. They were too frightened to do it. Cadwallader wrote in his memoirs:

> I then took the General in hand myself, enticed him into his stateroom, locked myself in the room with him (having the key in my pocket), and commenced throwing bottles of whiskey which stood on the table, through the windows, over the guards, into the river. Grant soon ordered me out of the room, but I refused to go. On finding himself locked in he became quite angry and ordered me peremptorily to open the door and get out instantly. This order I firmly, but good-naturedly refused to obey. I said to him that I was the best friend he had in the Army of the Tennessee; that I was doing for him what I hoped some one would do for me, should I ever be in his condition; that he was not capable in this case of judging for himself; and that he must, for the present, act upon my better judgment, and be governed by my advice. As it was a very hot day and the stateroom almost suffocating, I insisted on taking off his coat, vest and boots, and lying down in one of the berths. After much resistance I succeeded, and soon fanned him to sleep.

The *Diligence*'s arrival at Satartia caused a noisy disturbance and awakened Grant, still in something of a drunken stupor. He announced he was getting dressed and was prepared to go ashore, ordering poor Captain Osband to disembark his men and their horses. Satartia, Cadwallader wrote, was "a miserable little hamlet, filled with desperadoes and rebel sympathisers." To go ashore with Osband and his band of cavalrymen struck Cadwallader as suicidal.

Dana was concerned, too. He went to Grant's stateroom and told the general the place was swarming with rebels and suggested it might be a good idea to head back to Vicksburg. Grant, he said, was "too sick to decide." He told Dana, "I will leave it to you."

The *Diligence* began the return trip sometime during the night and tied up at Haynes' Bluff, Mississippi, in the morning. Dana said Grant appeared for breakfast "fresh as a rose, clean shirt and all, quite himself. 'Well, Mr. Dana,' he observed, 'I suppose we are in Satartia now.'" Dana told him they were actually in Haynes' Bluff.

That seemed to be the end of it, but drunks are amazingly devious; somehow Grant procured a few more bottles of whiskey from shore and in an hour he was just as drunk as before. Grant ordered the *Diligence* to get under way and make for the landing at Chickasaw Bayou, which would be swarming with officers and men by the time the steamboat arrived there.

Cadwallader coached Captain McDougall to delay the departure on the excuse the wood for the boilers was green. That worked for about two hours. When the boat did get under way, Cadwallader instructed the captain to run her gently up on a sandbar. That burned up another two hours. By the time the steamboat pulled up alongside a pier at the Chickasaw Bayou landing, it was sundown. But the steamboat occupying the other side of the pier was a headquarters sutler boat, operated by "Wash" Graham, notorious for dispensing free liquor and cigars to Grant's officers.

Cadwallader ran Graham down, and cautioned him not to give Grant any liquor, explaining he'd had more than enough already. Then he hurried back to the *Diligence* and discovered that the commanding general of the Army of the Tennessee had vanished. What he had done, of course, was slip across to the sutler boat. Cadwallader finally found him in a room opening off the ladies' cabin, in front of a table covered with bottles of whiskey and champagne. Graham, the wretch, was pouring.

By now, Cadwallader said, he was "thoroughly indignant." He announced the general's cavalry escort was waiting and it was time he saddled up and returned to his headquarters. Grant, a superb horseman, had borrowed a horse named Kangaroo for the trip, the name deriving from the animal's unfortunate tendency to rear up on its hind feet whenever mounted. Cadwallader continued:

> On this occasion Grant gave him the spur the moment he was in the saddle, and the horse darted away at full speed before anyone was ready to follow. The road was crooked and tortuous, following the firmest ground between sloughs and bayous, and was bridged over these in several places. Each bridge had one or more guards stationed at it, to prevent fast riding or driving over it; but Grant paid no attention to roads or sentries. He went at about full speed through camps and corrals, heading only for the bridges, and literally tore over and through everything in his way. The air was full of dust, ashes, and embers from camp-fires; and shouts and curses from those he rode down in his race. . . .
>
> I took after him as fast as I could go, but my horse was no match for "Kangaroo." By the time the escort was mounted Grant was out of sight in the gloaming. After crossing the last bayou-bridge three-quarters of a mile from the landing, he abandoned his reckless gait, and when I caught up with him was riding in a walk.

Cadwallader seized Grant's bridle rein and told the general he was behaving recklessly. The two men—the reporter and the general—"took refuge in a thicket near the foot of the bluff," and waited for the escort to catch up. Grant was now unsteady and a little sleepy. Cadwallader helped him stretch out, using his saddle for a headrest, under a tree. A trooper finally made an appearance, and Cadwallader sent him off to fetch an "ambulance," a horse-drawn wagon, and a careful driver. But when the wagon arrived, Grant refused to get in it. "We compromised the question by my agreeing to ride in the ambulance also, and having our horses led by the orderly. On the way he confessed that he had been wrong throughout, and told me to consider myself a staff officer, and to give any orders that were necessary in his name."

They reached Grant's headquarters at about midnight, and a furious Colonel Rawlins was waiting for them. Grant bid everyone good night "in a natural tone and manner, and started to his tent as steadily as he ever walked in his life." Cadwallader told Rawlins the whole story, the beginning point of their long friendship. (They roomed together in Washington for a time after the war and Cadwallader named one of his sons Rawlins.)

Grant never discussed the Yazoo drinking incident with Cadwallader, but there is little doubt he never forgot it. "From the date of this Yazoo-Vicksburg adventure until the end of the war," Cadwallader wrote, " . . . my standing with the general and his staff became stronger month by month. I constantly received flattering personal and professional favors and attentions shown to no one else in my position."

Grant's defenders have always insisted he really wasn't an alcoholic. He took up drinking, they said, because he was lonely; he was fine when his wife, Julia, was around. Cadwallader's account, even allowing for a generous interpretation of those events on the Yazoo, lends powerful support to the belief Grant was a binge drinker. Most contemporary historians, including Shelby Foote and Grant's biographer, William S. McFeely, accept that now. Others still disagree.

An analysis of Grant's alcoholism appeared in the *Hayes Historical Journal* in the fall of 1983 and was written by Lyle W. Dorsett. The journal is a publication of the Rutherford B. Hayes Presidential Center in Fremont, Ohio. Hayes, the nineteenth president, served in the Civil War as a brigadier general; he, too, had a drinking problem.

Grant's grandfather, Noah, was an alcoholic, Dorsett noted, and so was his own son, Frederick. Ulysses Grant began drinking when he was just a boy, nipping down to the cellar and imbibing his father's blackberry cordial. He began drinking heavily during the time he served in the Mexican War. By 1851, he was drinking so heavily he joined the Sons of Temperance, a forerunner of Alcoholics Anonymous. Dorsett wrote: "He craved alcohol. Occasionally he succumbed to the temptation. Because his well-meaning but ignorant contemporaries defined his slips and his compulsion to drink as morally reprehensible behavior or a flawed character, the wretched man was laden with guilt. No doubt his soul writhed in the pain of self-doubt and personal inferiority."

Grant, Dorsett said, welcomed his participation in the Civil War as a chance to escape that pain. And because he was an alcoholic, in a strange way he was a better general. "It freed him to challenge fate, damn the consequences, and doggedly pursue Lee's army. After all, in his mind he assumed he had little to lose."

But if Sylvanus Cadwallader hadn't been on that steamboat that night on the Yazoo River, none of it might have happened. Grant was lucky; he found an understanding reporter when he needed one desperately.

11

The Jolly Congress

EVEN TODAY, nearly 140 years later, the "Lost Cause" stirs the passions of millions of Americans. We remember those long gray lines on the march, the wild cavalry raids, the fallen heroes, the stately figure of Robert E. Lee.

There was a romantic quality to the Confederate army that has been matched by no other army in American history. It fought with valor and skill, always (or almost always) against overwhelming odds. It was crushed, finally, by men in Union blue who sometimes didn't even speak English very well.

Nobody loved the Confederate army more, or wrote about it with more passion, than a fascinating group of foreigners who called themselves the "Jolly Congress." Two of them were journalists: Francis Charles Lawley, of the *Times* of London, and Frank Vizetelly, the artist/correspondent for the *Illustrated London News*. The others were soldiers: Heros von Borcke and Justus Scheibert, both Prussians; FitzGerald Ross, an English-born Austrian; and James Arthur Lyon Fremantle, an Englishman.

Lawley and Vizetelly wrote as often as they could, and hoped their dispatches and their drawings would slip through the Union blockade and arrive safely in London. Sometimes they did. The soldiers wrote books—good, descriptive books.

Between them, the members of the Jolly Congress witnessed many of the major battles of the war and knew most of the principal

Confederate commanders. Von Borcke, in fact, became Jeb Stuart's chief of staff and his best friend. The gallant rebel cavalryman died in the Prussian's arms.

Not unlike the Bohemian Brigade itself, these six foreigners spent a great deal of their time together, putting on shows, dancing with all the belles of Richmond society. Several of them watched Gettysburg from the limbs of a tree that shaded General Lee himself. They all anticipated the Confederacy would triumph in the end, and even at the end they refused to admit the possibility of a Union victory. They had all fallen hopelessly in love with the Lost Cause.

Lawley arrived in America in March of 1862, just a few weeks before his colleague, the disillusioned Bull Run Billy Russell, set sail for home. He joined Charles Mackay to form the *Times'* team in America. Mackay rarely ventured out of New York City during the war, griped steadily about Union failures, and never witnessed a battle. He was a complete bust as a war correspondent. Lawley headed south, took up the Southern cause, and spent a great deal of time on battlefields.

Lawley was the fourth (and last) son of Sir Paul Bielby Lawley-Thompson, the first Baron Wenlock, and his wife, Catherine Neville, daughter of Sir Richard Neville, the second Lord Braybrooke. These weren't old titles on either side, but they were titles all the same, making Lawley a minor figure in the British aristocracy.

Lawley attended Rugby, one of the premier boys' schools in England, and was graduated with honors from Balliol College at Oxford University in 1848. He swiftly moved to what seemed to be a fast track, taking a seat in the House of Commons from East Riding, Yorkshire, in 1852. Weeks later, he was named private secretary to the great man himself, the future prime minister, William E. Gladstone.

In July of 1854, Lawley was under consideration for an important overseas post—governor of South Australia. He was rejected after word leaked out that he had developed a passion for gambling on horse races, putting his money on one losing equine cause after another. It was also suggested he had used inside information in a desperate effort to recoup his turf losses on the stock market.

Lawley, disgraced, retired to Yorkshire, and nobody knows what he did with himself the next few years, according to his biographer, Wm. Stanley Hoole.

Why Lawley was plucked out of Yorkshire by editor John Thadeus Delane to be the *Times'* new correspondent in one of the great breaking stories of the day remains a mystery. But plucked he was, and in late September of 1862 he joined forces with the man who would one day be a field marshal and Gilbert and Sullivan's "very model of a modern major general," Colonel Garnet Joseph Wolseley, on leave from his post in Canada. Together they set out to see the rebel South for themselves.

In an article published in *Blackwood's* magazine in January 1863, Wolseley said that because he believed that "little reliance can be placed at any time upon the information published in American newspapers, I was very anxious, if possible, to get to the South, and judge for myself as to the condition of its people, the strength of its government, and the organization of its armies."

They departed Baltimore in a two-horse buggy, rolling along at a snappy pace of thirty miles a day. They rode down the western shore of Chesapeake Bay to Leonard's Town (now Leonardtown), near the mouth of the Potomac River. They had been told to contact a "rude and illiterate" farmer who was making a considerable income on the side by smuggling Southern sympathizers across the river into Virginia. They spent the night in the attic of the farmer's "old tumbledown shed." Wolseley wrote:

> Roused by some noise about midnight, I saw Frank Lawley with the end of a lighted candle in one hand and a stick in the other chasing the rats which swarmed there, and which had been, he said, running over him freely. I laughed and recommended him to take an old campaigner's advice and go to sleep, rats or no rats. . . . This was my travelling companion's debut in campaigning life, and the rats were a little too much for him.

The next day, the farmer/smuggler set sail in a small boat, dodged a number of Federal patrols, and put Lawley and Wolseley ashore in Virginia, five miles from the nearest village. They walked into town, hitched a ride on a horse-drawn cart to Fredericksburg, and boarded a train bound for Richmond with hundreds of wounded rebel soldiers. Wolseley recalled: "The road was extremely rough and jolting, and many in the crowd of wounded men on the train had recently had their legs amputated. That train opened Frank Lawley's eyes to the horrible side of war, made all the more in this instance because no chloroform or medical supplies of any sort were available."

The second English journalist-member of the Jolly Congress was Frank Vizetelly. Though only thirty years old, he was a veteran campaigner. He had covered the war between Austria and Sardinia in 1859 and marched with Giuseppe Garibaldi and his Redshirts in Sicily the following year. The *Illustrated London News* sent him to the United States in the spring of 1861, and he had witnessed—and sketched—a number of important engagements, from first Bull Run to Burnside's expedition to Roanoke Island.

When he began having problems in the summer of 1862 securing credentials to accompany the Union's Army of the Potomac, he decided to switch sides, reaching Richmond just a few weeks ahead of Lawley and Wolseley. Poor Vizetelly was killed in the Sudan while accompanying Colonel William Hicks's ragtag army—sometimes called the worst professional army in history—against the fanatical forces of the Mahdi in 1883, and so he never lived to a comfortable old age and a chance to write his memoirs. But his brother, Henry, another writer—the Vizetellys, Italian in origin, were all writers and artists—filled in for him nicely. Frank Vizetelly, Henry wrote in his own memoirs, started his journey in Baltimore and he made his way to Leonard's Town, too.

> Owing to there being no boats of any kind on the Potomac, he had to embark in a hollow trunk of a tree, usually called a "dug-out," with a buck Negro named Job to paddle him over to the Virginia shore. . . . Under cover of the night Frank V. and Job attempted to cross the river, but the plashing of their paddle was heard by the watch of a Federal patrol steamer, which fired at them, though fortunately without effect. Job was paralysed by fright, and only came round on my brother putting a revolver to his head, when, with his arms flying about like the sails of a windmill, he paddled the dug-out swiftly back to the Maryland shore, among tall rushes, which effectively screened them from observation.

For some hours the patrol steamer's search lights continued playing over the river and its banks, but nothing being discovered, the captain cast anchor, evidently purposing to remain in this part of the river until the little craft [the dug-out] should emerge from its hiding place. For two nights and one tedious day—tortured by mosquitoes during the former and roasted by the burning sun during the latter—they remained crouching in their hollow log among the dank reeds, with the patrol boat close by. All this while, too, they were without a particle of food.

The patrol boat eventually hauled up its anchor and steamed away, and Job and Vizetelly paddled across the river to the Virginia shore. When Lawley and Wolseley arrived in Richmond, Vizetelly was already comfortably ensconced at the Spottswood Hotel.

Wolseley couldn't stay long—he had only a month's leave—and he checked out of the Spottswood a few days later and returned to Canada. The other members of the Jolly Congress were on their way.

Heros von Borcke, an amazing character, came first. Von Borcke was a giant—well over 6 feet tall, weighing 240 pounds. He carried with him, always, "a straight double-edged sword of tremendous size and temper, which I had worn from the commencement of my military career in the Prussian Cuirassiers of the Guards. It was even better known in the Confederate army than myself; and many who were unable to pronounce my foreign name correctly used to speak of me as 'the Prussian with the big sword.'"

In his memoirs, von Borcke said he sailed from Cork aboard a blockade runner called, appropriately, *Hero,* loaded with gunpowder, on April 29, 1862. "With smooth seas and pleasant skies," he wrote, "we made a delightful voyage of twenty days to Nassau." They refueled there and then made their successful dash through the Union blockade.

Next to arrive was thirty-one-year-old Captain Scheibert. He steamed into Charleston aboard a blockade runner on March 15, 1863. He had been sent to the United States on official business, instructed by Prince von Radziwill, chief of the Prussian engineer corps, to observe "the effect of rifled cannon fire on earth, masonry, and iron, and the operation of armor on land and sea."

The thirty-year-old Ross entered the Confederacy by way of what he called the "underground Railway from Yankeeland to Secessia," in May of 1863, following pretty much the same route already taken by Lawley and Vizetelly. He arrived in Richmond on June 18.

Fremantle came to America simply as a twenty-eight-year-old adventurer. There was a war going on, and he wanted to see it. He traveled a roundabout route, landing first in Brownsville, Texas, then moving gradually east, through Texas, Louisiana, Mississippi, and Georgia. He arrived in Richmond on June 17, just twenty-four hours ahead of Ross.

Fremantle came very close to being the perfect caricature of an English gentleman-officer. In the introduction to his memoirs (based largely on his diary), his editor, Walter Lord, wrote:

> He dutifully records all toasts to the Queen. He refuses to go to a party without his evening clothes. He searches in vain for a good old-fashioned cavalry charge with drawn sabers. He's dismayed by the inability of the Confederate infantry to form a hollow square. . . . Yet behind this stiff facade is a man of character. . . . There's no greater proof of his true quality than the warmth and affection he generated wherever he went. He was the pet of everybody, from General Longstreet, to Mr. Sargent, the tough mule driver on the trip across Texas.

Ross's memoirs were published after the fighting had ended. Fremantle's book came out while the fighting was still raging. It made its way from London to the Confederacy, "where its charming spirit and interesting presentment of the situation was greatly welcomed," Constance Cary wrote in her memoirs.

Miss Cary, a member of the Fairfax clan, was an aristocratic young lady from northern Virginia, and a sharp observer in Richmond during the war (she married Burton Harrison, a Skull and Bones man from Yale, after the war ended). She met and danced with almost all the members of the Jolly Congress. Heros von Borcke quite literally swept her off her feet.

> When he first appeared among us in the spring of 1863, he was a giant in stature, blond and virile, with great curling golden

mustaches, and the expression in his wide-open blue eyes of a singularly modest boy. It was said that he rode on the biggest horse and wielded the heaviest sabre in the army. Holding, from the first, high place in the esteem of his fellow-officers and superiors, Von Borcke, whom the troopers styled "Major Bandbox," won brilliant renown in service, and was equally popular in society in Richmond. To dance with him in the swift-circling, never-reversing German fashion was a breathless experience, and his method of avoiding obstacles in the ballroom was simply to lift his partner off her feet, without altering his step, and deposit her in safety farther on.

Miss Cary didn't have much to say about Frank Lawley—he is "cordially remembered," she said—but Vizetelly made a strong impression.

He was a big, florid, red-bearded Bohemian, of a type totally unfamiliar to us Virginians, who could and would do anything to entertain a circle. In our theatricals, tableaux, and charades, he was a treasure-trove. Everything he proposed was according to what they had done in London in the theatrical club of which Charles Dickens was a shining light, and we, of course, bowed before his superior knowledge. He painted our scenery and faces, made wigs and armor, and was a mine of suggestion in stage device. He sang songs, told stories, danced *pas seuls*, and was generally most kind and amusing.

One of the productions was called *Rye,* starring not only Miss Cary and Vizetelly but Generals J. E. B. Stuart and Fitzhugh Lee, the great commander's nephew. In one of the scenes, Miss Cary, playing a "rustic maiden," divided her smiles between Colonel John Saunders, a "humble swain," and Vizetelly, "a plumed cavalier with a purse of gold." She described it in her memoirs:

My scene, charmingly painted [by Vizetelly] as an English thatched cottage wreathed in roses with a glimpse of the Thames in the background, had a garden fence, on the stile of which I was supposed to be perched coquettishly. Just as I had seated myself upon the stile, held up by General Stuart in the rear . . . my perch gave way and

I slid to the ground. In vain General Stuart protested abject penitence for having forgotten for a moment and let go, and promised better behavior. Accused of gross neglect while on duty, he was sentenced to lose his position and sit among the audience for the remainder of the show. General Fitz Lee, virtuously declaring that no young lady could make *him* forget his responsibility as a step-ladder, took and held General Stuart's post.

Poor Stuart, gallant and joyous Stuart! In a few brief months after this brief dalliance with fun in Richmond, he was to ride his last ride, and be shot down by a bullet after the battle of the Yellow Tavern. In all our parties and pleasurings, there seemed to lurk a foreshadowing of tragedy, as in the Greek plays where the gloomy end is never kept in sight.

Ross, the Austrian hussar, said that "there was some outcry, even from the pulpits, against the gaieties that were going on [the poor folks were close to starvation], but General Lee was reported to have said that the young ladies were quite right to afford the officers and soldiers on furlough as much amusement as possible; and balls, tableaux, vivants, and all kinds of social gatherings, were the order of the day."

It *was* romantic in the classic Dawn Patrol, drink-up-because-tomorrow-we-may-die spirit, but with a cast of characters no novel, no movie, could possibly reproduce.

Ross remembered the night von Borcke and several friends, nine of them altogether, "carried us off to the 'Oriental Saloon,' where we had a capital supper, and sat talking till a late hour." Ross included in his memoirs the Oriental's menu and a copy of the bill delivered to their table when the evening ended. The bill of fare included seven soups (terrapin, turtle, mock turtle, and macaroni, among them); four fowls (turkey, goose, duck, chicken); five meats (beef, mutton, lamb, pork, and veal); five steaks; seven fish; four kinds of oysters; six birds (including robin); fifteen vegetables; five wines; five whiskeys; three malt liquors; and various Havana cigars.

The party of nine consumed soup, venison steak, seven birds, various vegetables, and five bottles of Madeira and six bottles of claret. The bill, in Confederate money, came to $631.50.

Stuart was a great favorite among the members of the Jolly Congress. The two journalists—Vizetelly and Lawley—joined the cavalry commander at his tented camp on the grounds of the Bower, Stephen Dandridge's mansion (he was from the same family as Martha Dandridge Custis Washington), near Charles Town in what is now West Virginia on October 16, 1862. Von Borcke had joined Stuart a few weeks earlier and was already an important member of the general's official family.

Stephen Dandridge, von Borcke wrote, was a kindly gentleman with three sons off fighting in the war and a number of very handsome young daughters still at home. "With these amiable people," he said, "I soon contracted a very intimate friendship."

Even before Vizetelly—always the master of ceremonies—arrived, the Bower (surrounded by the military camp) was an extraordinarily joyful place. With Stuart's encouragement, the soldiers formed their own band—Bob Sweeney, "who knew sentimental, bibulous, martial, nautical, comic songs out of number," on banjo; two army couriers, "musicians of inferior talent," on violin; and, best of all, Mulatto Bob, Stuart's servant, "who worked the bones with the most extraordinary and surprising agility." The band played every night at the Dandridge mansion, and "dancing was kept up to a late hour."

Stuart, von Borcke said, "was himself always the gayest and noisiest of the party, ending the evening with a spirited rendition of his favorite song":

If you want to have a good time,
  Join in the cavalry,
  Join in the cavalry.

Just a week before the journalists arrived, von Borcke and his friends staged their greatest theatrical success, a pantomine called *The Pennsylvania Farmer and his Wife*. Stuart's friend, Colonel Bradley T. Johnston, played the farmer; the huge von Borcke, "dressed in an old white ball-dress of Mrs. D's that had been enlarged in every direction, and sweetly ornamented with half-a-bushel of artificial flowers in my hair," played the farmer's wife.

"Our success," Von Borcke said, "greatly outran our expectations. Stuart, exploding with laughter, scrutinised me closely on all sides, scarcely crediting that within that tall bundle of feminine habiliments dwelt the soul of his chief of staff."

Vizetelly and Lawley arrived at Stuart's camp just as Federal troops were making what they would later call a "reconnaissance in force" from their headquarters at Harper's Ferry. Von Borcke was ordered to take a number of couriers and join a small cavalry detachment at Smithfield, about twelve miles from the Bower, "to watch," he wrote, "the enemy's moves on our right." He didn't say so, but it seems probable that Vizetelly and Lawley were with him, at least some of the time. It didn't amount to much, as the Yankees slowly retreated. Von Borcke said he "established my men and myself at the house of an interesting young widow, who, with her sister, enlivened our evening with songs and spirited discourse."

Lawley was obliged to return to Richmond to mail dispatches to London (he usually sent them in the diplomatic pouch of the French consul). Vizetelly—"Major Telly" to many of the rebels—remained at the Bower. Von Borcke wrote:

> Our new guest was an old campaigner, who accommodated himself very readily to the hardships of camp life, and was soon established in his own tent. . . . He was not long in becoming a general favourite at headquarters. Regularly after dinner, our whole family of officers, from the commander down to the youngest lieutenant, used to assemble in his tent, squeezing ourselves into narrow quarters to hear his entertaining narratives, which may possibly have received a little embellishment in the telling, but which embraced a very wide circle of human experience, and had a certain ease and brilliancy beyond most such recitals.
>
> The "ingenuous youth" of our little circle drank in delightedly the intoxications of Mabille and the Chateau des Fleurs, or followed the story-teller with eager interest as he passed from the gardens and boudoirs of Paris to the stirring incidents and picturesque scenery of the Italian campaign, which he had witnessed as a guest of Garibaldi.
>
> V. was greatly pleased with our musical entertainments; and when, after talking for several hours, he had become exhausted,

and, when, from the gathering darkness, we could only distinguish the place where he was reclining by the glow of his pipe, and thus lost all the play of the features in his rehearsal, we proceeded to the great central camp-fire, there to renew the negro dances to the music of the banjo—scenes which Vizetelly's clever pen has placed before the European public in the pages of the Illustrated London News.

Less successful was our friend in his efforts to improve the *cuisine* of our negro camp cook, and we often had the laugh upon him—especially when one day he produced in triumph a roast pig, with the conventional apple in its mouth, which we found to be raw on one side and burned to a cinder on the other . . .

Lieutenant Colonel William W. Blackford, one of Stuart's aides, said Vizetelly

was the most interesting narrator I have ever listened to around a campfire. He had been in all parts of the world, and in several campaigns as a correspondent, and what he did not see and enjoy of social life . . . was not worth seeing. There was not a disreputable . . . place of prominence in the civilized world that he did not know all about, and his accounts of his gallantries were interesting and lively. We had a shrewd suspicion that he drew a great deal from his imagination for his facts, but what difference did it make to us. . . . Mr. Lawley was an exceedingly intelligent . . . Englishman, and in another style we enjoyed his conversation very much, but Vizetelly was entertaining.

These young men—the ones who survived—never forgot those days, and especially those nights, at the Bower.

Vizetelly had seen a great deal of fighting, but nothing prepared him—or anyone else, for that matter—for the slaughter at Fredericksburg on December 13, 1862. He and Lawley had breakfast with General Lee and his staff that morning and then witnessed what Shelby Foote called "the largest—in numbers engaged, if not in bloodshed—as well as the grandest as a spectacle [of] . . . any other conflict of the war . . . it quite fulfilled the volunteers' early-abandoned notion of combat as a picture-book affair."

The slow-moving George B. McClellan was no longer commander of the Army of the Potomac; an impatient Lincoln had fired him on November 7 and replaced him with Ambrose Burnside.

Burnside actually had an interesting idea; instead of trying to slog on down to Richmond the same old way through Manassas, he would take his 120,000-man army to Falmouth, just across the Rappahannock River from Fredericksburg, and push Robert E. Lee and Stonewall Jackson and their 80,000-man army back to Richmond from there. But, because he had to ford so many rivers, he needed pontoons. Ulysses S. Grant was a master in giving explicit, easily understood orders. Burnside was no Grant. His orders for the pontoons were garbled and were more than a week late showing up, giving Lee time to prepare his defenses on the southwestern side of the river, positioning James Longstreet's corps on the left (to the north) and Jackson's corps downriver on the right (to the south). With the pontoons finally in place, Union generals Edwin V. Sumner and Joseph Hooker came across into the the streets of Fredericksburg; William B. Franklin marched across about two miles downriver. Franklin was supposed to roll up Jackson's flank while Sumner and Hooker probed Longstreet's well-defended position on Marye's Heights behind the town.

Franklin actually found a wedge in Jackson's lines, but failed to exploit it, even though Burnside ordered him to keep moving. Fourteen brigades—the men under Sumner and Hooker—tried desperately to reach a stone fence in front of the rebel lines behind the town, and they died there, thousands of them. The attacks were "as courageous and hopeless as anything in the war," acording to James McPherson. The Union lost thirteen thousand men, the Confederates, five thousand.

The battle was just about over when Vizetelly rode into town to watch as hundreds of the Union prisoners were marched to the rear. Von Borcke reported what happened next.

> Having reached the column, he [Vizetelly] had just entered into conversation with a corporal from a South Carolina regiment who commanded the detachment, when the hostile [Union] batteries, mistaking their own men for enemies, opened fire, and one of their very first shells, passing quite close to our friend, tore the head off

the poor fellow with whom he was talking completely off his shoulders, scattering pieces of skull and brain in every direction. Horror stricken at this sad incident, and having no call of duty to remain, the artist at once put spurs into his charger's flanks, and galloped off as fast as the noble steed could take him. But the hostile gunners seemed to take particular pleasure in aiming at the flying horseman, and even closer and closer flew the unpleasant missiles about his ears, while we who from Lee's Hill were spectators of the unenviable position in which our guest was placed, were for some time seriously alarmed that we would never again hear his merry laugh and joyous songs; but at last he reached us in safety, though much exhausted, and was received with loud cheering in our midst.

Lawley was appalled by the bloodshed.

A ride along the whole length of the lines told . . . a sad tale of slaughter . . . Not for 50 years to come will that scene ever fade from the memory of those who saw it. There, in every attitude of death, lying so close to each other that you might step from body to body, lay acres of the Federal dead. . . . In one small garden, not more than a half acre in size, there were counted 151 corpses. I doubt whether in any battle in modern history the dead have ever lain so thick and close. By universal consent of those who have seen all the great battles, nothing like it has been seen before. . . . So tremendous was the [Confederate] fire, chiefly emanating from Cobb's brigade, posted in the lane at the foot of Marye's Heights, that even chickens in the gardens in front fell pierced by it. It was remarked by a Confederate general immediately acquainted with the Federal general Sumner, who commanded the Federal right, "Was there ever any other general but Sumner who would have got his men into a place in which not even chickens could live?"

The town itself was in ruins, filled with the dead and the dying. Lawley continued:

Death, nothing but death everywhere; great masses of bodies tossed out of the churches as the sufferers expired; layers of corpses stretched in the balconies of houses as though taking a *siesta*. In one yard a surgeon's block for operating was still standing, and, more ap-

THE SCENE OF SATURDAY'S ACTION.

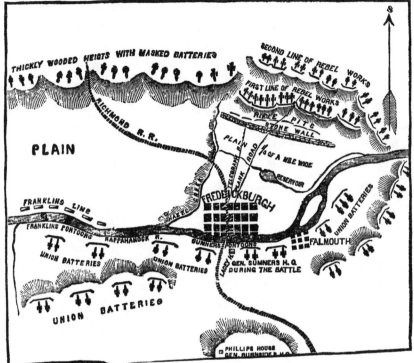

From the *New York Times*, December 17, 1862, a map of the battlefield at Fredericksburg. (Clements Library, University of Michigan)

palling to look at than even the bodies of the dead, piles of arms and legs, amputated as soon as their owners had been carried off the field, were heaped in a corner. There were said to be houses literally crammed with the dead; but into them, horrified and aghast at what I saw, I could not look . . .

Reporters, then and now, usually do their best work when they restrict their observations to events they have actually witnessed. Lawley was so captivated by the Confederate cause that he was utterly worthless as an analyst, but in reporting what he had seen—at Fredericksburg and elsewhere—he was outstanding.

Where, here at Fredericksburg and other battles, were reporters for Southern newspapers? Lawley and Vizetelly and the soldier members of the Jolly Brigade rarely took note of their existence. Part of the reason is that many of them appeared on battlefields sporadically. Perhaps another reason involves caste; the Europeans enjoyed the company of aristocratic Confederate officers, the men Vizetelly called "these Saxons of the South." They may not have found the Southern reporters quite so congenial.

Only three Southern reporters managed to get to the Fredericksburg battlefield, and they were all from Richmond papers. The sad part of it is, we don't even know their names. The only Southern reporters we know very much about were Peter Wellington Alexander, who wrote most of the time for the *Savannah Republican,* but also contributed to the *Mobile Daily Advertiser and Register* and the *Richmond Daily Dispatch,* and Felix Gregory de Fontaine of the *Charleston Daily Courier,* who contributed to two Richmond papers (the *Daily Enquirer* and the *Whig*) and the *Savannah Republican.*

As Southern cities fell to Union armies, newspapers closed down or moved (as did Memphis' proud "moving *Appeal"*). The result is that copies of many daily issues of Southern newspapers have simply disappeared. And, when the war was almost over, only one of the Southern reporters, de Fontaine, sat down to write his memoirs. But his book, called *Marginalia, or Gleanings from an Army Notebook,* is little more than a collection of short items that appeared in various Southern papers.

The forty-three daily newspapers in the South relied more heavily than their counterparts in the North on the official reports filed by their own generals—Lee's reports, especially, were outstanding. They relied even more heavily on their own wire service, the Confederate Press Association, founded in February 1863; it supplied most of the battlefield reporting for the rest of the war. The member newspapers received their telegraph news over the wires of the South-Western Telegraph Company and the army's own Military Telegraph Lines, according to historian Quintus C. Wilson. Each newspaper paid $12 a week for a news report not to exceed thirty-five hundred words. That, of course, was hardly more than a day's work for the likes of Billy Russell or Whitelaw Reid.

(Newspapers in the North relied less heavily on their own wire service, the New York Associated Press. It was used largely for bulletin material and short articles summing up events of the day. Its reporters were called "agents" and they weren't very good. The North's major newspapers preferred to use their own people.)

Southern papers were constantly faced with shortages in paper (in one or two instances, they used rolls of wallpaper) and ink. They also had trouble finding help—typesetters, especially. They had to keep most of their stories short.

The result was that Southern reporters didn't get many chances to write the kind of long, discursive stories that appeared with some frequency in journals in the North. Peter Alexander probably was the best of all the Southern reporters. "The Prince of Correspondents," the *Charleston Courier* called him. A graduate of the University of Georgia, he studied law and opened his own practice before the war in Thomaston, Georgia. He wrote for a number of newspapers under a confusing blur of bylines, including "A" and "P.W.A." and "Sallust."

Alexander arrived on the Fredericksburg battlefield the day after the battle and put together a creditable reconstruction. Here's the way he described the Union army's bloody charges against the rebels behind the stone wall:

> As the fog rolled away and the sun came out, the enemy were seen advancing from the town in great force. Coble's and Kershaw's brigades, posted at the base of the hill about a fourth of a mile from the edge of the town, were the first to receive the shock. Their position was behind a stone fence, while the heights in the rear were occupied by . . . artillery. These batteries poured a devouring fire into the ranks of the multitudinous foe as they advanced across the open plain between the town and our front line. The enemy made a desperate attempt to gain these heights. Assault after assault was made, each time with fresh columns and increased numbers. They never succeeded, however, in getting nearer than seventy or eighty yards to the stone wall, from which the brave Georgians and Carolinians saluted them with a fire that no mere human force could face and live.

[We] repulsed the foe with a slaughter that is without a parallel in this war. I went over the ground this morning, and the remaining dead, after two-thirds of them had been removed, lay twice as thick as upon any other battlefield I have ever seen.

Just in front of our line is a thin plank fence, behind which the enemy took shelter as they advanced to the attack. Some of the planks in his fence were literally shot away from the posts to which they were nailed, and one could hardly place his hand upon any part of them without covering a dozen bullet holes. Just at the foot of the stone wall behind which our men were posted, thousands of flattened musket balls may be picked up, whilst the hills behind it have been converted into a lead mine.

Alexander made some mistakes in his story. Coble is almost certainly Thomas R. R. Cobb, mortally wounded in the action by a Union sniper. Joseph Kershaw's South Carolinians came forward during the action to reinforce Cobb's Georgians. Even so, it is a fair description of what took place in front of that now-famous, still-standing stone wall.

Covering the battle for the North were a number of familiar figures—the ubiquitous Charles Carleton Coffin for the *Boston Journal,* William Swinton of the *New York Times,* and Henry Villard, once Mr. Bennett's top reporter but, since November, working for Mr. Greeley's *Tribune* as chief correspondent with the Army of the Potomac. (Villard replaced George W. Smalley, a Yale man who rowed stroke for his boat in the first Yale-Harvard race. His enduring contribution to Civil War journalism was a single story—his epic description of Antietam in September of 1862.)

By late 1862, many of these Northern correspondents were captains of journalistic teams. At Fredericksburg, Villard was captain of a four-man team, but none of his three reporters came up with anything useful, and one of them simply disappeared. Villard was forced to do what he had been doing all along—collect the information himself. Villard was a Union patriot and he quickly concluded that Burnside had blundered badly, putting the entire army in "grave peril."

Deeply distressed by what he had seen, he set off for Washington on horseback at 3 A.M. on Sunday, and wrote later: "Never before or since have I had such a terrible ride. It was pitch dark. . . . There was no distinct road, but the army trains, in trying to avoid mud and move on solid ground, had made tracks of a seemingly infinite width, but all reduced to a miry state. Hence I traveled most of the way through a sea of mire from one to two feet deep."

It was 9 A.M. by the time he reached the boat-landing area at Aquia Creek. The quartermaster in charge told him that Burnside had given strict orders that no one—and certainly no newspaperman—would be allowed to board a steamboat for the trip to Washington. To Villard's further "disgust," Coffin, "whom I knew as one of the most intelligent, energetic, and indefatigable reporters in the field," turned up at the quartermaster's tent just as he was finishing his breakfast.

But if the steamboats wouldn't come to him, Villard saw a way for him to go to the steamboats. Two Negroes were fishing nearby; he hired them to row him out into the middle of the channel where he waved down a passing steamer. Coffin missed the whole thing; he had dropped into a cot and was fast asleep.

Villard was in the *Tribune*'s office on Fourteenth Street by 8 P.M., only to be told that all the telegraph lines had been shut down to newspaper dispatches. He put a messenger with his long report—in which he said the Union army had suffered another terrible, blundering defeat—on the night train to New York and repaired to Willard's Hotel for a late supper. Prowling the hotel's corridors was Senator Henry Wilson of Massachusetts, "the most persistent news-hunter in Washington." Villard told him that he should go to the White House and tell the president to order Burnside to begin a withdrawal as soon as possible.

Villard had no sooner returned to the *Tribune* offices when Wilson reappeared. The president, he said, wanted to see him "at once." Villard described the interview.

> We found Mr. Lincoln in the old reception room on the second floor, opposite the landing. He greeted me with a hearty handshake, saying, "I am much obliged to you coming for I am very anxious and have heard very little." He then asked me to give him, as far as my personal knowledge permitted, a general outline of what had happened, which I did as fully as I could in a few minutes. He

followed up my account with one question after another for over half an hour.

At the end of the interview, Villard said he "made bold" to tell the president "that success is impossible, and that the worst disaster yet suffered by our forces will befall the Army of the Potomac if the attack is renewed, and unless the army is withdrawn at once to the north side."

The president replied, with a melancholy smile, "I hope it is not so bad as all that."

But it was as bad as all that, a terrible, humiliating defeat, "for which," Villard said, "Ambrose E. Burnside will, to the end of time, stand charged with the responsibility."

Villard had filed a long dispatch pinpointing the dimensions of the disaster at first Bull Run, only to have his weak-kneed editors at the *Herald* gut it for fear of offending some of the New York regiments that had failed to cover themselves in glory. The same thing happened to his Fredericksburg dispatch. "The editor [presumably Mr. Greeley himself] was afraid to let the Tribune solely assume the whole responsibility for what would no doubt prove a great shock to the public, lest I might be mistaken in my opinion, and, accordingly, the report was very much modified, but was printed as an extra issue the next morning."

Lawley returned to Richmond after the bloody battle, and tried to come to grips with what he had seen. He was in despair, for there was nothing jolly about this war any more. In a story dated March 17, he urged the great European powers to intervene.

> Will not England and France rush in to bring an end to this slaughter? It may be that the civilized Powers of Europe see no hope of moral interference. But if they could only witness the misery which is, from every acre of this once favoured continent, crying aloud to Heaven, it could scarcely be that they would risk some chance of failure rather than permit humanity to be outraged by a continuance of such excess of anguish as had visited no nation since the sword first leaped from its scabbard, and the human heart was first sown with the bitter seed of vindicativeness and hate.

With defeats and stalemates piling up, one upon another, the Union now faced its bitter winter of discontent. "With a management worse than has disgraced any modern war we have wrested from a desperate enemy *one-third* of his territory and one-half of his valuable strategic points of resistance," Whitelaw Reid wrote from Washington in early February. "We are weary and exhausted—so are they; we are disgusted with the result of our prodigious efforts—so are they. . . . Now let us hold out, as we can far better do, than can our antagonists, and we shall win the rest."

Burnside was finished; the new man was Joe Hooker. He would lose in another great battle, Chancellorsville (but the South would lose Jackson, mortally wounded by his own men). No one was going to intervene. The fighting between two exhausted armies would go on, and on.

12

Gettysburg

"IF LEE ADVANCES with nearly all his force into Pennsylvania, there must be a collision of the two armies not many miles west of Gettysburg . . . ," Charles Carleton Coffin predicted in the *Boston Morning Journal* on June 26, 1863.

Smack on target. And Coffin was there, albeit a day late, when the most celebrated of all Civil War battles began on July 1. No one knows exactly how many reporters covered the battle, but a good bet is that it was close to fifty—forty or more from the North, the usual corporal's guard from the South. A sickly Francis Lawley was there, too, for the *Times* of London, along with a number of members of the old Jolly Congress.

By July 1, 1863, the war-reporting business had come a long way from those heady days late in 1861 when almost all of the western reporters shared Room 45 at the Saint Charles Hotel in Cairo, Illinois. Historian J. Cutler Andrews, the man who has done the most to keep track of Civil War correspondents, estimated Bennett's New York *Herald* had ten reporters at Gettysburg, closely trailed by Greeley's *Tribune*, with nine. The *New York Times* had three.

But more was not always better. The three major New York dailies put so many men in the field, with instructions to send short dispatches by telegraph, that they lost focus. Most of the time it was bits and pieces, written in breathless prose and far too much of it wildly inaccurate. In their battle to be first, they failed to give their readers a comprehensive account of what was really happening.

Henry Villard, a very fine war correspondent himself, didn't think much of the new gang. "Corrupt, and following their new occupation only from necessity and with mercenary intentions," he wrote in 1865, "they were not long in becoming the servile tools of scheming officers. . . . Others had good intentions, but no capacities. Men turned up in the army as correspondents more fit to drive cattle than to write for newspapers." Maybe even worse, many of them "added to these defects a lowness of habits and vulgarity of manners that rendered them unfit for association with the higher ranks of the army."

Villard never thought seriously of making a career in journalism. Deep down, he was an aspiring capitalist, and he would go on to become a very wealthy railroad tycoon. As a reporter, he did sometimes seem to side with management. If he had been a general, he once said, he would have been the first to impose strict censorship on the press. No Bohemian, Henry Villard.

But he was right—too many reporters were corrupt and incompetent and too many editors encouraged sloppy and inaccurate work. "Our civil war has produced no model army reporter," Villard complained, but that's a little harsh. With the possible exception of Billy Russell in the Crimea, it's difficult to come up with a model army reporter for any war.

Gettysburg was a difficult battle to write about because the town was fairly remote from railroad depots and telegraph offices. But, for all of Villard's grumbling, some of the reporting was distinguished. "White" Reid and Charles Carleton Coffin, the two veterans, wrote the best accounts. It is no accident that both of them worked for smaller, more patient newspapers that couldn't afford to send whole squads of reporters into the field. Reid and Coffin were professionals, the Civil War's foremost battlefield correspondents.

Reid was attending a copperhead political meeting in Ohio when he first heard news that "Lee's whole army [was] moving through Chambersburg in three grand columns of attack!" His editors in

Cincinnati told him to forget Clement L. Vallandigham and make tracks for the front.

He arrived in Washington on June 24 and reported that the capital had "become the most *blasé* of cities. She has been 'in danger' so long that to be out of danger would give her an unnatural, not to say unpleasant shock." He set off for the front a day or two later, in the company of Sam Wilkeson, of the *Times* (the same fellow who crossed up Sherman at the Galt House in Louisville and who would write the Civil War's most poignant story when the battle was over), Uriah H. Painter of the *Philadelphia Inquirer*, and Coffin. They arrived in Frederick, Maryland, to witness a New England regiment, bands playing, flags and guidons flying, "marching—home!" They were a nine months' regiment, and their time was up. "Would that Stuart could capture a train that bears them!" Reid had lost none of his capacity for moral outrage.

"Frederick is Pandemonium," he wrote. "Somebody has blundered frightfully; the town is full of stragglers, and the liquor-shops are in full blast. Just under my window scores of drunken soldiers are making night hideous. . . . The worst elements of a great army are here in their worst condition; its cowards, its thieves, its sneaks, its bullying vagabonds, all inflamed with whiskey, and drunk as well with their freedom from accustomed restraint."

Coffin, a deeply religious man who didn't drink, smoke, or swear, was outraged, too. "It is time there was a reform in the police of the army," he reported from Frederick on the twenty-ninth. "Yesterday was Sunday, and the liquor shops were not open, but today the streets emit terribly of whiskey. . . . There are thousands of men who have bottles of whiskey. There are hundreds lying about the streets, on door steps, under fences. . . . It is a shame, a disgrace. Today I saw a sergeant of artillery, his face all aflame, strike a private with his sword, three heavy blows over his head."

The enterprising Reid headed for the battlefield on horseback, while his three companions returned to Baltimore, hoping to hitch a ride on a train. Reid caught up with the Army of the Potomac headquarters, near Taneytown, Maryland, on July 1, just as the great three-day battle was beginning.

Reid hadn't thought much of Lincoln's removal of Joe Hooker as the army's commanding general. But he was fully prepared to give the new man, George Gordon Meade, a chance:

In a plain little wall tent, just like the rest, pen in hand, seated on a camp-stool and bending over a map, is the new "General Commanding" for the Army of the Potomac. Tall, slender, not ungainly, but certainly not handsome or graceful, thin-faced, with grizzled beard and moustache, a broad and high but retreating forehead, from each corner of which the slightly-curling hair recedes, as if giving premonition of baldness—apparently between forty-five and fifty years of age [forty-seven, in fact]—altogether a man who impresses you as a thoughtful student than a dashing soldier—so General Meade looks in his tent.

"I tell you, I think a good deal of that fine fellow Meade," I chanced to hear the President say a few days after Chancellorsville. Here was the result of that good opinion. There is every reason to hope that the events of the next few days will justify it.

Reid had barely arrived outside Meade's tent when a horseman galloped up and hastily dismounted. He wrote:

It is a familiar face—Lorenzo L. Crounse, the well-known chief correspondent of the New York Times with the Army of the Potomac. As we exchange hurried salutations, he tells us that he has just returned from a little post village in Southern Pennsylvania, ten or fifteen miles away; that a fight, of what magnitude he cannot say, is now going on near Gettysburg between the First Corps and some unknown force of the enemy; that Major General John F. Reynolds is already killed, and that there are rumors of more bad news.

Mount and spur for Gettysburg is, of course, the word, with Crounse as guide.

It is hard work, forcing our way among the moving masses of infantry . . . and we make but slow progress. Crounse seems to know every body in the army, and from every one he demands the news from the front. "Everything splendid; have driven them five or six miles from Gettysburg." "Badly cut up, sir, and falling back." "Men rushed in like tigers and swept everything before them." (Rushing in like tigers is a stock performance, and appears much oftener in the newspapers than on the field.) "Gettysburg burnt down by the rebels. . . ." "D——d Dutchmen of the Eleventh Corps broke and ran like sheep, just as they did at Chancellorsville. . . ."

This, Reid wrote, "is the substance of the information we gain by diligent questioning of scores," and it is, of course, almost entirely wrong. And then Reid made this revealing observation: "It is of such stuff that the 'news direct from the battlefield,' made up by itinerant liars and 'reporters' at points twenty or thirty miles distance, and telegraphed thence throughout the country, is manufactured. So long as the public, in its hot haste, insists on devouring the news before it is born, so long must it expect such confusion and absurdity."

It was a little unfair to blame the worst sins of the press on the public. Even so, simply substitute today's gossipy and irresponsible web sites on the Internet for the Civil War telegraph and it becomes shockingly clear how little reporting the news has changed in 140 years.

A short-handed Jolly Congress was approaching the battlefield, too, with Lee's Army of Northern Virginia. Missing from it were the gallant Prussian, Heros Von Borcke—he had been badly wounded at the cavalry engagement at Brandy Station on June 6—and the artist, Frank Vizetelly—he was out west, watching Grant's efforts to capture Vicksburg. Traveling together were Lawley of the *Times*, Justus Scheibert, the Prussian; FitzGerald Ross, the English-born Austrian hussar; and James Arthur Lyon Fremantle of the Coldstream Guards.

Lawley, Fremantle reported, was so ill on Saturday, June 27, that he couldn't get out of bed. Fremantle borrowed his horse and set out "in search of the generals." He was with Lafayette McLaws's division when it crossed into Pennsylvania.

I entered Chambersburg at 6 P.M. This is a town of some size and importance. All its houses were shut up; but the natives were in the streets, or at the upper windows, looking in a scowling and bewildered manner at the Confederate troops, who were marching gaily past to the tune of "Dixie's Land. . . ." One female had seen fit to adorn her ample bosom with a huge Yankee flag, and she stood at the door of her house, her countenance expressing the greatest contempt for the barefoot Rebs; several companies passed her without taking notice; but at length a Texan gravely remarked, "Take care, madam, for Hood's boys are great at storming breastworks when the Yankee colors is on them." After this speech the Yankee lady beat a precipitate retreat.

By noon Sunday, Lawley, feeling a little better, was ensconced in the Franklin Hotel. With him was Captain Ross, dressed in the glorious uniform of his elite regiment. Fremantle warned him of "the invariable custom of the Confederate soldiers of never allowing the smallest peculiarity of dress or appearance to pass without a torrent of jokes, which, however good-humored, ended in becoming rather monotonous." But Ross was adamant; he wore his uniform until it finally fell apart.

On Tuesday, June 30, Lieutenant General James Longstreet introduced Fremantle to General Lee, "almost, without exception, the handsomest man of his age I ever saw. He is fifty-six years old, tall, broad-shouldered, very well made, well set up—a thorough soldier in appearance; and his manners are most courteous and full of dignity. He is a perfect gentleman in every respect."

Later in the day they set out for Gettysburg, Fremantle riding Lawley's horse, Lawley and Ross bumping along in an army ambulance. They met Longstreet again toward evening, and he told them he had heard that Meade had replaced Hooker. "Of course he knew both of them in the old army, and he says that Meade is an honorable and respectable man, though not, perhaps, as bold as Hooker."

Fremantle—he was a lieutenant colonel but had yet to see action—lectured Longstreet on the proper use of cavalry. They should be used more in the European model, he said, pursuing broken infantry formations. But Stuart's cavalry,

> though excellent at making raids, capturing wagons and stores, and cutting off communications, seems to have no idea of charging infantry under any circumstances. Unlike the cavalry with Bragg's army, they wear swords, but seem to have little idea of using them—they hanker after their carbines and revolvers. They constantly ride

with their swords between their left leg and the saddle, which has a very funny appearance; but their horses are good, and they ride well. The infantry and artillery of this army don't seem to respect the cavalry very much, and often jeer at them.

We don't know what Longstreet thought of Fremantle's foolish monologue—swords against artillery and the new repeating rifles!—but we do know he had a point about Stuart and those cavalry raids; he was off on one of them again, depriving Lee of a scouting force he desperately needed.

Neither side actually planned to fight a decisive battle at Gettysburg; it simply happened, as so many things do during warfare. The battle began on Wednesday, July 1, a mile or two west of Gettysburg, just as Coffin had predicted. Two Confederate brigades, part of Henry Heth's division, had set off for Gettysburg to pick up a large supply of shoes. They found, instead, John Buford's two Union cavalry brigades, equipped with the new seven-shot Spencer repeating carbines. And not far behind him was John Reynolds and the Union army's entire First Corps. Buford held his ground until Reynolds's men began arriving to back him up. Heth sent two brigades, James Archer's from the west and Joseph Davis's from the north, against the Union lines. Archer immediately came under heavy fire from infantrymen wearing distinctive black hats—the Iron Brigade, tough westerners, the best fighting outfit in Meade's army. The Confederates skedaddled, and in their hasty retreat Archer was captured. But before they left one of them, a sharpshooter, killed Reynolds with a single shot behind the ear. Davis, the nephew of the Confederate president, fared no better in his attack from the north. He and his men bumbled their way into a cut for a railroad that hadn't yet been built—and were trapped. Davis managed to escape, but more than half of his men were either killed or captured. The morning's action belonged to the Union.

The afternoon belonged to the rebels. Lawley and his companions didn't arrive on the battlefield until 4:30 P.M.; they joined Lee and Hill "on the top of one of the ridges which form the peculiar feature of the country around Gettysburg. We could see the enemy re-

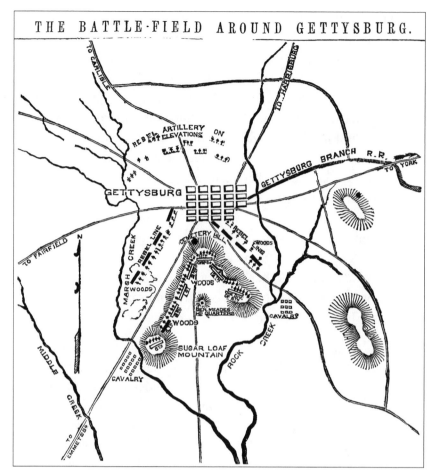

THE BATTLE-FIELD AROUND GETTYSBURG.

The battlefield at Gettysburg, from the *New York Tribune*, July 7, 1863. (Clements Library, University of Michigan)

treating up one of the opposite ridges, pursued by the Confederates with loud yells." General Hill said the enemy had fought (earlier in the day) with unusual determination and had made a "good stand" at a railway cutting.

In his first dispatch, Lawley said that Lieutenant General Richard S. Ewell's men, north of the city, routed whole regiments of German-American troops—the "flying Dutchmen" from Chancellorsville—while Heth ran into a "fiercer conflict."

What really happened was that Ewell launched an attack from the north, soon to be joined by Jubal Early, and drove the outnumbered Union forces back through the town itself. Heth pulled himself together and began a new attack from the west. At about 4 P.M., Major General Oliver O. Howard, commander of the Union Eleventh Corps (the one that included the "flying Dutchmen"), ordered both his corps and the First Corps to fall back to a defensive position on Cemetery Hill, south of the town. It was a retreat, and the Dutchmen really didn't fly the way they had at Chancellorsville.

At the end of the day, Lawley said, "hope reigned triumphant in every Confederate breast . . . A cry for immediate battle louder and more peremptory than ever ascended from the Highlanders of Claverhouse or Montrose swelled the gale."

Like almost all the other reporters, White Reid missed the fighting on the first day. He was riding to the front early the next day—Thursday, July 2—when he heard someone

> calling my name from a little frame dwelling, crowded with wounded soldiers. It proved to be Colonel Luthur S. Stephenson, the Librarian of Congress. He had run away from his duties in the capital, and all day yesterday, through a fight that we now know to have been one of the hottest in the war, had been serving most gallantly as aide on General Solomon Meredith's staff. [Meredith commanded the Iron Brigade.] Congress should make an example of its runaway official!

Reid arrived on Cemetery Hill by mid-morning and began interviewing officers who had taken part in the previous day's fighting. Reid was always careful to say what he had seen himself and what he had reconstructed from talks with others. "I have now conversed with four of the most prominent generals employed in that action and with any numbers of subordinate," he wrote on July 2. "I am a poor hand to describe battles I do not see, but in this case I must endeavor to weave their statements into a connected narrative." And weave it he did, with great skill.

Coffin arrived on the battlefield about 8 A.M. on July 2. From the cemetery gate, he could see almost the entire battlefield. In one of several books he wrote about his war experiences, he said:

To understand a battle, the movements of the opposing forces, and what they attempt to accomplish, it is necessary first to comprehend the ground, its features, the hills, hollows, woods, ravines, ledges, roads—how they are related. A rocky hill is frequently a fortress of itself. Rail fences and stone walls are of value, and a ravine may be equivalent to ten thousand men.

Tying my horse and ascending the stairs to the top of the gateway building, I could look directly down upon the town. The houses were not forty yards distant. Northeast, three-fourths of a mile, was Culp's Hill.

On the northern side of the Baltimore pike were newly mown fields, the grass springing fresh and green since the mower had swept over it. In those fields were batteries thrown up by Howard on Wednesday night. . . . Howard's lines of infantry were behind stone walls. The cannoneers were lying beside their pieces,—sleeping perhaps, but at any rate keeping close, for, occasionally, a bullet came singing past them. Looking north over the fields, a mile or two, we saw a beautiful farming country,—fields of ripened grain,—russet mingled with the green in the landscape.

Coffin got back on his horse and toured the Union lines, making careful notes all the while. Franc Wilkie, remember, made fun of an innocent Coffin touring and sniffing the battlefield at Fort Donelson. But this was a mature Coffin, and he probably knew as much about making war as most of the generals on July 2, 1863.

Having surveyed the field, he joined General Howard in the cemetery, where he had spread his maps and plans on the ground.

"We are just taking a lunch," the general said, "and there is room for one more." Then removing his hat, he asked God to bless the repast. The bullets were occasionally singing over us. Soldiers were taking up the headstones and removing the monuments from their pedestals. "I want to preserve them; besides, if a shot should strike a stone, the pieces of marble would be likely to do injury," said the general.

Lawley and what was left of the Jolly Congress were taking up a position to observe the fighting that morning on the Confederate side of the battlefield. "We all got up at 3:30 A.M., and breakfasted a little

Sketch of Charles Carleton Coffin of the *Boston Morning Journal* interviewing a Union officer. (Author's collection)

before daylight," Fremantle wrote in his diary. "Lawley insisted on riding, notwithstanding his illness." Ross, the hussar, "had shaved his cheeks and *ciréd* his mustaches as beautifully as if he was on parade at Vienna."

They determined the best spot to observe the fighting was atop Seminary Ridge, next to a large oak tree. Scheibert and Fremantle climbed into the tree to get an even better prospect. "From here," Scheibert said, "the battlefield lay before us like a panorama." The observation post was so perfect, he added, that he didn't move from the tree for two days. His white horse, he said, grazed peacefully "in the grass below."

They were not alone. Seated at the foot of the oak tree were Generals Lee, A. P. Hill, Longstreet, and John B. Hood, in consultation. Longstreet and Hood, Fremantle said, were "assisting their deliberations by the truly American custom of *whittling* sticks."

At about 7 A.M., Fremantle joined Longstreet "and saw him disposing of M'Laws division for today's fight. The enemy occupied a series of high ridges, the tops of which were covered with trees, but the intervening valleys between their ridges and ours were mostly open, and partly under cultivation. The cemetery was on their right, and their left appeared to rest upon a rocky hill."

Close to 2 P.M., Longstreet told Fremantle he had better get back into the tree with Scheibert because the attack was about to begin. Lawley, feeling stronger all the time, managed to climb up into the tree as well.

The firing didn't really begin until about 4:45 P.M., when Longstreet's and Ewell's guns opened on the enemy lines. Fremantle watched in amazement as Lee calmly observed what was happening through his field glasses, occasionally saying something to Hill or to Colonel A. L. Long of his staff. "What I remarked especially was, that during the whole time the firing continued, he only sent one message, and only received one report. It is evidently his system to arrange the plan with the three corps commanders, and then leave to them the duty of modifying and carrying it out to the best of their abilities."

Lawley sensed that one man, James Longstreet, was unhappy. He "shook his head gravely over the advantages conferred by the Union position," Lawley wrote, and urged Lee to throw the Confederate army around the Union left, so it would be between Gettysburg and the nation's capital. That would force the Union troops to attack well-prepared Confederate lines, and they would be beaten. "No," Lee said, "the enemy is there and I am going to attack him there."

Lawley was convinced that Lee's great mistake was attacking prematurely on July 2. Part of the problem, he said, wisely, was that the memories of all their earlier victories "combined to inspire the leading Confederate generals with undue contempt for their enemy, although he was fighting on his own soil, with his back to the wall, and in a position which for strength and eligibility for defence had not been surpassed during 27 months of warfare." Lawley thought Lee should have made his grand assault on the third, after Pickett had arrived.

"General Lee," he said, "struck me as more anxious and ruffled as I had ever seen him before, though it required close observation to detect it."

Lee was a brilliant general, especially when he was on the defensive. But he was not himself at Gettysburg. Lawley understood that.

The second day at Gettysburg, Bruce Catton wrote, "was made up of many separate fights, each one a moment or an hour of concentrated fury, with a blinding, choking fog of blue powder smoke over the hillsides and the rocky woods, hammered down by unending deafening noise, sparkling and glowing evilly with constant spurts of fire."

Confederate élan was matched by stubborn Union bravery—the Iron Brigade again, Joshua Chamberlain's Twentieth Maine, George Greene's upstate New Yorkers, William Colvill's First Minnesota Volunteers—swirling around places familiar now to millions of us: the Devil's Den, Big Round Top and Little Round Top, the Wheatfield, the Peach Orchard, Culp's Hill.

The three New York dailies struggled to keep up with the fighting hour by hour, using the telegraph lines without budgetary concerns. This was an entirely different way of reporting the news than that favored by Lawley, Coffin, and Reid. Some of the reports, especially those by the *New York Times*' Lorenzo Crounse, were sensible and mostly accurate. Others were wildly off the mark. "Longstreet was mortally wounded and captured," the *Tribune* reported on Monday, July 6, well after the battle was over. (Crounse had already reported in the *Times* on Saturday, July 4, that there was no reliable information suggesting the general had been killed.) The *Herald*, the worst offender of all, even invented a battle a few days after the fighting at Gettysburg ended. The *Tribune*'s A. Homer Byington wrote his managing editor, Sydney Howard Gay, to complain that the *Herald* had "at least a half-dozen men . . . picking up everything & telegraphing *ad-libitum*. They are the most *drunken*, irresponsible crew that ever squandered a newspaper's money—and they use it without sense and reason."

Thursday's fighting had been confusing. Friday's fighting was so straightforward—Pickett's famous charge—that almost all the reporters understood it.

Lee had hoped to open Friday's fighting at dawn with a coordinated attack by Ewell on the north against Culp's Hill and Longstreet in the center against Cemetery Ridge. But Major General George E. Pickett and his fresh troops—the men selected to lead the charge against Cemetery Ridge—were still three miles away. Lee decided he would postpone the attack until at least 10 A.M., but by the time his messenger reached Early the battle around Culp's Hill was already blazing. It would go on for five more hours.

Lee caught up with Longstreet—"Old Peter"—about dawn, west of the Round Tops, to talk about the day's plans. Longstreet still wanted to take his corps on a flanking movement that would invite an attack from Meade. Lee was even more adamant. No, he said, the attack would be made by Longstreet's whole corps, led by Pickett's three brigades (the fourth in reserve) and Heth's division, now commanded by James Pettigrew, plus two brigades from William Dorsey Pender's division, commanded by Isaac Trimble—15,000 men in all. "It is my opinion," Old Peter complained, "that no 15,000 men ever arrayed for battle can take that position."

Fremantle and Ross couldn't make up their minds where they should post themselves to watch the attack. They rode into Gettysburg itself early in the morning, only to be exposed to heavy Union artillery fire. "We then returned to the hill I was on yesterday," Fremantle said, where Lawley and Scheibert were still camped under the old oak tree. Later in the day Fremantle set off to find Longstreet, passing a large column of wounded Confederates, "as great as the crowd on Oxford street in the middle of the day." He continued:

> When I got close up to General Longstreet, I saw one of his regiments advancing through the woods in good order; so, thinking I was just in time to see the attack begin, I remarked to the general

New York Herald field headquarters. (Library of Congress)

that "I wouldn't have missed this for anything." Longstreet was seated at the top of a snake fence at the edge of the wood, and looked perfectly calm and imperturbed. He replied, laughing, "The devil you wouldn't! I would like to have missed it very much; we've attacked and been repulsed. Look there!"

For the first time I then had a view of the open space between the two positions, and saw it covered with Confederates slowly and sulkily returning towards us in small broken parties, under a heavy fire of artillery.

Fremantle had missed the single most dramatic moment in the Civil War.

Lawley, on the other hand, from his post near the oak tree, saw it all. The more desperate the action, the more inscrutable Lawley's prose. The Confederate artillery created such a racket, he said, that it must be left to the reader's imagination "to conczive [sic] the diapason of 400 guns." He added:

The thundering roar of all the accumulated battles ever fought upon earth rolled into one volume could hardly have rent the skies with fiercer or more unearthly resonance and din. . . . Vast cumuli of cloud, such as would have shrouded 10,000 Homeric goddesses, had they cared in these days of villainous saltpetre to mingle in the *melee*, floated over the strife; horses, the suffering and tormented ministers of man's fury and wrath, lay thickly dead or horribly mutilated upon the ground; constantly from out of the white pall of vapour issued wounded and mangled men . . .

It was, in fact, Shelby Foote wrote, "the greatest concentration of artillery ever assembled for a single purpose on the continent, and Lee appeared to have no doubt that it would pave the way for the infantry by pulverizing or driving off the batteries posted in support of the Union center."

Lawley was impressed with Pickett as he prepared to attack.

Nobly did he spring to head of his undaunted men, and marshal them to the attack. With long floating locks, with a seeming recklessness, which is, perhaps, partly assumed, but which stamps him of the Murat type, General Pickett, of more demonstrative courage than other generals, but not less unflinching than his own sword, seemed as he advanced to lead his men into the very jaws of death.

Over on the Union side, Reid watched the attack from a mile away, atop Culp's Hill, scene of the day's opening round. His description—let's give it in detail, for it is the great moment of the war—was almost as florid as Lawley's.

Around our center and left, the rebel line must have been from four to five miles long [about a mile, according to most historians], and over that whole length there rolled up the smoke from their two hundred and fifty guns [about 170, actually]. The roar, the bursting bombs, the impression of magnificent power, "all the glory visible, all the horror of the fearful field concealed," a nation's existence trembling as the clangor of those iron monsters swayed the balance—it was a sensation for a century! . . .

The great, desperate charge came at four [closer, in fact, to three]. The rebels seemed to have gathered up all their strength and desperation for one fierce, convulsive effort, that should sweep over and wash out our obstinate resistance. They swept up as before [on Thursday], the flower of their army to the front, victory staked upon the issue. In some places they literally lifted up and pushed back our lines, but, that terrible position of ours!—wherever they entered it, enfilading fires from half a score of crests swept away their columns like merest chaff. Broken and hurled back, they easily fell into our hands, and on the center and the left the last half-hour brought more prisoners than all the rest.

So it was along the whole line; but it was on the Second Corps that the flower of the rebel army was concentrated; it was there that the heaviest shock beat upon and shook and even sometimes crumbled our line.

We had some shallow rifle pits, with barricades of rails from the fences. The rebel line, stretching away miles to the left, in magnificent array, but strongest here—Pickett's splendid division of Longstreet's corps in front, the best of A. P. Hill's veterans in support—came steadily and as it seemed relentlessly sweeping up. . . . The rebels reserved their fire till they reached [the] Emmetsburg road, then opened with a terrific crash. . . . The rebels—three lines deep—came steadily up. They were in point blank range.

At last the order came! From thrice six thousand guns there came a sheet of smoky flame, a crash, a rush of leaden death. The line literally melted away. . . . Up to the rifle pits, across them, over the barricades—the momentum of their charge, the mere machine strength of their combined operation swept them on. . . . But they had penetrated to the fatal point. A storm of grape and canister tore its way from man to man and marked its track with corpses straight down their line! They had exposed themselves to the enfilading fire of the guns on the western slope of Cemetery Hill; that exposure sealed their fate.

The line reeled back—disjointed already—in an instant in fragments. . . .

It was fruitless sacrifice. They gathered up their broken fragments, formed their lines, and slowly marched away. It was not a rout, it *was* a bitter crushing defeat. For once the Army of the Potomac had won a clean, honest, acknowledged victory.

Coffin was in the cemetery, in better position to watch Pickett's charge than Reid. "Boom! Boom!" he began his account of Friday's fighting. The two guns, fired at 3 P.M., signaled the beginning of the charge. It had been preceded, Coffin said, by a tremoundous carronade, noisier than Antietam or Fredericksburg. "Never have I heard such a roar of field artillery."

After an initial burst of gunfire, the Union batteries fell silent. Reid was too far away to understand that it was a brilliant ruse, orchestrated by Henry Hunt, the Union artillery commander, to convince the Confederate gunners they had silenced his guns. Coffin gave the credit to Howard, but no matter; he called to the attention of his readers one of the most significant details of the battle.

Coffin couldn't restrain himself in summing up the battle, either (in words that sometimes have an eerie echo of Lincoln's famous address).

> The invasion of the north was over, the power of the Southern Confederacy broken. There at that sunset hour I could discern the future—no longer an overcast sky, but clear, unclouded starlight—a country redeemed, saved, baptized, consecrated anew to the coming ages.
>
> All honor to the heroic living, all glory to the gallant dead. They have not fought in vain; they have not died for naught. No man liveth to himself alone. Not for themselves, but for their children, for those who may never have heard of them in their nameless graves, have they yielded life—for the future—for all that is good, holy, true—for humanity, righteousness, peace—for paradise on earth—for Christ and for God—they have given themselves a willing sacrifice. Blessed be their memory forever.

He signed the dispatch, which filled four-and-a-half columns in his Boston paper on Monday, simply, as always, CARLETON.

Lawley and Fremantle were standing next to General Lee when one of his officers, Cadmus Wilcox, rode up with tears in his eyes and exclaimed, "General, I have tried to rally my men, but as yet they will not stand." Lee replied, "Never mind, general, the fault is all mine. All that you have to do is to remedy it so far as you can."

It was impossible to look at Lee, Fremantle wrote, "without feeling the strongest admiration, and I never saw any man fail him except the [dead] man in the ditch."

Late the next day, July 4, Independence Day, the day the Confederates' mighty bastion at Vicksburg fell, the *Times*' Sam Wilkeson began writing his account of the day's events at Gettysburg. It was the most poignant story written during the Civil War.

> Headquarters, Army of Potomac.
> Saturday night, July 4.

> Who can write the history of a battle whose eyes are immovably fastened upon a central figure of transcendingly absorbing interest—the dead body of an oldest born, crushed by a shell in a position where a battery should never have been sent, in a building where surgeons dared not to stay?

With extraordinary fortitude—kneeling beside the freshly dug grave of his own son, an artillery officer—he then wrote his article for the *Times*. He concluded his story with these agonizing words:

> My pen is heavy. Oh, you dead, who at Gettysburgh have baptized with your blood the second birth of freedom in America, how you are to be envied! I rise from a grave whose wet clay I have passionately kissed, and I look up and see Christ spanning this battlefield with his feet and reaching fraternal and lovingly to heaven. His right hand opens the gate of Paradise—with his left hand he beckons to these mutilated, bloody, swollen forms to ascend.

13

The Reporter Who Was Kissed by Lincoln

WITH MEADE'S DEFEAT of Lee at Gettysburg and Pemberton's surrender of Vicksburg and its thirty-thousand-man garrison to Grant, Lincoln believed "one more push" might topple the Confederacy (and guarantee his own reelection in 1864). But Meade had the old Army of the Potomac willies—fear of pressing the enemy too hard. He let Lee slip away. In the West, Major General William Rosecrans was now in command of the Army of the Cumberland, facing Braxton Bragg, the most inept commander in the whole Confederate army (he had already been defeated at Perryville, Kentucky, and had fumbled the chance for a big victory at Stones River, Tennessee). But Rosecrans botched the battle at Chickamauga (saved only by Major General George H. Thomas's rocklike defense), and fell back on Chattanooga.

A disgusted Lincoln fired Rosecrans and gave Grant the command. Grant, a general who didn't know the meaning of the willies, routed Bragg in a stunning victory at Missionary Ridge, above Chattanooga, on November 25, 1863. Four months later, he was called to Washington, promoted to lieutenant general, and put in charge of the whole shooting match. Wasting no time, he gave Sherman the western command and brought Phil Sheridan east to take charge of the cavalry.

"Lee was the last of the great old-fashioned generals, Grant the first of the great moderns," historian T. Harry Williams wrote, memorably. Lee understood battles, Grant understood war. He and Sherman would now begin a total war campaign in which he would seek to destroy Lee's army while Sherman, in his March to the Sea, would seek to destroy the Confederate economy.

Neither felt any urgent need to take reporters along.

Early in March of 1864, Secretary of War Stanton issued an order stating that no civilians other than those already attached to the Army of the Potomac would be allowed to join it. That spelled big trouble for the *New York Tribune,* because all of its correspondents with credentials to accompany the army happened to be in the paper's Washington offices the day the order was issued.

The new bureau chief was Sam Wilkeson, still grieving for his son; he had moved from the *New York Times* to the *Tribune* after Gettysburg. He was furious, and demanded that his four accredited correspondents saddle up and join the army, posthaste, orders from Stanton notwithstanding. At first they all demurred. Too dangerous, they said; they would be arrested as spies and thrown into that odious Old Capitol Prison.

The youngest member of the bureau, nineteen-year-old Henry E. Wing, then spoke up and said he was willing to try even though he had no credentials. He challenged the accredited reporters to join him. One of them, T. C. Grey, accepted, and within forty-eight hours they were inside the Union lines, some sixty miles south of Washington. (Two others caught up later, bringing the *Tribune*'s strength in the field to four.)

Henry Wing may be the only truly endearing reporter to cover the war for either side. He was a gentle, innocent (though persistent) young man, serving after the war as a Methodist preacher in Iowa and Connecticut. And surely he was the only reporter who was ever kissed by Abraham Lincoln.

Wing was reared in Litchfield, Connecticut, the son of a fire-breathing, abolitionist preacher, Ebenezer Wing. He and his father didn't get along very well, so when the chance came young Henry slipped away and joined the army. He was posted to the color guard of the Twenty-seventh Connecticut Regiment.

In the final months of his long life, he told his story to an unlikely biographer—Ida Minerva Tarbell, the tough, turn-of-the-century muckraker. Her best-known work was a two-volume history of the Standard Oil Company, but she had also written a biography of Pres-

HENRY E. WING
War Correspondent

Henry Wing of the *New York Tribune*. (Author's collection)

ident Lincoln. It was during the time she was researching the Lincoln
book that she tumbled onto Henry Wing's dramatic wartime career.

Wing's regiment saw action for the first time on December 13,
1862, taking part with Winfield Scott Hancock's division in that
deadly assault up Marye's Heights at Fredericksburg. Wing was
quoted in Ida Tarbell's book.

> It was early in the morning when we went in. We were mighty
> proud of ourselves for a minute. The Confederates let us come on
> until we got to the very heights, and when we started up they

opened on us and we went down like wheat does under a scythe, hardly a head standing. I was hit pretty quick in the leg, and I guess I didn't know much for a time. When I came to I raised up and looked for the flag. I could see it going down—coming up—going down—coming up . . .

[Then] I could not see the flag any more and I began to worry about it. I just had to be sure that our boys still had it, and I started to crawl where I thought it might be, and then I got hit in the hand. After a little I crawled on again, and then I found the flag. And I found some more of our boys dead; there were ten killed there.

I don't know much what happened after I found the flag. The next thing I knew I was lying on top of a piano. There were doctors beside me, and they had made a mark around my leg and another around my arm; and when I saw they meant to cut off my leg and my arm it made me mad, and I began to curse them. They just took me off the piano and threw me out on the grass.

A young Catholic nun, Sister Mary, saved Wing's life. "Sister Mary," he told Ida Tarbell,

was young and pretty. She cut off those two fingers with a pair of scissors and picked all the proud flesh out of my wounds. Day and night for a week she sat there, flushing them with tepid water and Castile soap. . . . I began to get well right away. She was the first girl I ever wanted to marry . . . (but) it could not be, . . . Sister Mary was a bride of Christ. . . . They dismissed me in March—on crutches. And, of course, that was the last of me as a soldier.

Wing returned to Connecticut and began writing occasional pieces for local newspapers. Someone at the *Tribune* spotted his work and Horace Greeley offered him a job in New York. No, Wing said, he would rather be in Washington, nearer the army. He arrived in the capital late in 1863, fully recovered from his wounds except for two missing fingers and a permanent limp.

Grant took command of all the Union armies, as general in chief, on March 9, 1864. He commanded two big armies—his own, officially still under Meade's direct command, and Sherman's army in the West. But he also had to deal with three smaller armies—Benjamin Butler's Army of the James, Franz Sigel's scattered regiments in West

Virginia and the Shenandoah Valley, and Nathaniel Banks's Army of the Gulf in Louisiana. Grant didn't have much confidence in any of those three generals, but he hoped they could at least hold a leg while he did the skinning. They turned out to be virtually useless.

He faced two major Confederate armies—Lee's Army of Northern Virginia, below the Rapidan River, protecting Richmond, and Joseph E. Johnston's Army of Tennessee, in northern Georgia, covering Atlanta. His strategy was pretty basic—he and Meade would pursue Lee day after day until his army was defeated. Sherman would move against Johnston's army, defeat it, and then march to the sea, raising all the hell he could along the way. The biggest problem was holding the armies together. Most Union soldiers—the best of them, at least—had enlisted in regiments to serve in the army for three years. Those enlistments were now running out. "Of 956 volunteer infantry regiments," Bruce Catton wrote, " . . . 455 were about to go out of existence because their time would very soon be up." More than half the artillery batteries were in the same situation. To make up for the departures, the government in Washington offered big bonuses to sign up. Thousands of men took the money, deserted, turned up somewhere else, and took the money again. The draft was a disaster, too. Anyone getting his draft notice could simply pay $300 to be excused until his number came up a second time. Or, better yet, he could pay a substitute to go to war for him and never worry about being pestered again. The Union armies were saved because more than half of the volunteers reenlisted, but the regiments were never quite the same.

Confederate veterans had no such options. They had signed up for the duration, and many of them would fight to the bitter end. Lee's strategy was simply to hold on, inflicting such heavy casualties that a weary Northern electorate would swing to the Peace Democrats in November. That, Lee hoped, would lead to a negotiated settlement of the war favorable to the Confederacy.

Grant and his army crossed the Rapidan on May 4, 1864—the preservation of the Union literally in their hands—and *disappeared*. For the next three days, no one in the North knew what had happened to them.

Henry Wing knew, for he was there, widely respected by soldiers and officers because he had been a soldier himself, walking with a limp (and two missing fingers) to prove it. One of four *Tribune* correspondents in the field, he had witnessed the first day's terrible fighting in the Wilderness, a huge tract of second-growth timber with nothing more than paths leading through it. Grant had hoped to take his army through the woods and engage Lee in clear country on the other side. Lee would have none of that; he attacked Grant on the morning of May 5, in woods so dense that artillery was useless. The Wilderness campaign was fought with rifles, against an enemy no one could really see. It was so fierce the woods caught fire.

Wing published his own book in 1913, fourteen years before Ida Tarbell published hers. At the close of the first day's fighting, he wrote,

> we [the four *Tribune* correspondents] came together at army head-quarters to compare notes and to lay plans for the future. The battle was to be renewed the next morning. . . . It was quickly decided that one of us should start for the North with the several reports of the stirring events of the last few days. As I was the youngest, I knew the task naturally belonged to me, and my offer to undertake it was instantly accepted by the others.

Before saddling up for the seventy-mile ride to Washington, he strolled over to Grant's tent, hoping for a last word from the generalissimo.

"Well, yes," Grant said, "you may tell the people that things are going swimmingly down here." Wing wasn't fooled. He continued:

> The remark was so evasive, or purposely misleading, at the close of a battle in which every one of his plans had evidently gone wrong that I smiled as I entered the exact words in my notebook, thanked him, and turned away. I had only taken a step or two when he got up and joined me. When we had walked out of the hearing of his companions he laid his hand upon my shoulder and, quietly facing me, inquired, "You expect to get through to Washington?"

I replied that was my purpose, and that I should start at day-break.

Then, in a low tone, he said, "Well, if you see the President, tell him from me that, whatever happens, there will be no turning back." He silently gave me his hand in farewell greeting, and we parted.

Wing's favorite horse was a Kentucky-bred racing horse, called Jesse, that he had borrowed from a member of Meade's staff. He set off at 4 A.M. on May 6, after three hours' sleep and a light breakfast, general reports of the march and the first day's fighting in his sad-dlebags, bags of oats strapped behind "for my trusty comrade."

His first stop was at the home of a well-known Union sympa-thizer, Mr. Wyckoff, near Culpeper, Virginia. "My scheme now was, to get Mr. Wyckoff to go along with me, at least across the country to the Rappahannock River, guiding me by by-roads and cattle-trails with which he must be familiar through that portion of my route, in the immediate rear of our army, and most likely to be overrun by bands of guerrillas and scouting parties of the enemy's cavalry."

It was "a splendid plan—for getting captured."

Wyckoff said he was so well-known as a Union supporter that "no course could be devised that would more surely defeat my purpose than to be found in his company." But when Wyckoff became con-vinced that Wing was dead set on getting to Washington he came up with a plan of his own. So, he said, this would be Wing's story: "There had been a great battle, in which the Yankee army had been badly defeated, and I was hurrying the good news to our friends in Washington. To fortify me in the prosecution of this adventure Mr. Wyckoff made me familiar with the names of a half dozen prominent Southern sympathizers in the capital city."

But Wing's clothing was all wrong. "The Tribune took pride in having its representatives well equipped," he wrote, "and my outfit included pantaloons of the most costly Irish corduroy, a fine 'buck-skin' jacket, a dark, soft felt hat, calf-skin boots, and Alexandra kid gloves. These I exchanged for a regular 'butternut' suit, with coarse, broad 'brogans,' and a disreputable hat of quilted cotton."

While he was changing clothes, Wing spotted a troop of gray cavalry passing up the river on the opposite bank,

> and it became nearly certain that I was to fall in with many such parties. No loyal man would take through our lines, where there was possibility of capture, a scrap of paper that would convey information to the enemy; so I destroyed my precious budget of correspondence and all notes and memoranda that could possibly disclose information of value. And, for my own safety, I divested myself of all private papers, by which I could be identified. Then, bidding farewell to the loyal man whose wise counsel I undoubtedly owe my life, I set out on my long and hazardous journey.

He hadn't gone eight miles when he bumped into a troop of John Mosby's legendary rangers.

> They were lying about in a dooryard, with their horses feeding outside the fence. As I was riding leisurely by they naturally hailed me, and, gathering about, received my good tidings of Lee's victory with great rejoicing. But, as to my going on alone!—the woods were full of skulking "nigger" soldiers, stragglers from Ferraro's division of colored troops, and the life of a good rebel, like me, would not be worth "a chaw-er-terbacker." The sequel was that they furnished me an escort of two men to protect me on the way.

Wing had supposed they were leading him to Field's Ford, where he and Jesse could splash their way across the Rappahannock River. Instead, they led him to Kelly's Ford. The terrible-tempered Mr. Kelly himself, a one-armed secessionist, watched as they approached. Kelly had "entertained" Wing a few days earlier. "He would almost surely recognize me in even this disguise unless I could slip by unobserved. So I dismissed my companions with many thanks."

But Kelly was already suspicious; he walked over and tried to grab Jesse's bridle.

> As he did so I touched Jesse with the spur and he sprang forward and rushed for the river. In answer to Mr. Kelly's shouts, my erstwhile comrades, joined by two other mounted men, came dashing

after me. In my confusion we missed the ford, but Jesse swam boldly through the deep waters to the upper shore. As we scrambled up the deep bank a volley of scattering shots spattered about us.

They were no match for Jesse. Wing and his Kentucky-bred speedster easily escaped. "I was now in excellent spirits," he said. But instead of taking the main road to Warrenton Junction, he took a left on a forest path

and in ten minutes burst into a clearing at Rappahannock Station, on the Orange and Alexandria Railroad. The place was teeming with Confederate patrols. While my story was finally accepted by everyone I met, my progress was constantly interrupted, and somewhere behind me were my comrades of the morning, gathering recruits as they came and bent on my capture.

Just then my apparently ever-present good fortune again came to my aid. A clump of trees with thick underbrush a few yards from the road offered "shelter for man and beast." Watching an opportunity, when no one was in sight, I led Jesse into this safe retreat. Slipping off saddle and bridle and hiding them away, I tied my good friend by a long rein to an overhanging branch, poured the oats upon the ground, and bade him a really "affectionate farewell."

Before I crept out of my hiding place a dozen men, led by my quondam friends, came galloping by. They were evidently in quest of a good-looking youngster, in a butternut suit, riding a handsome chestnut Kentucky thoroughbred.

Wing said he "crawled over to the railroad and started on my long tramp up the track for our lines about Washington." He was stopped by a Union picket who

proved to be a private of one of our Irish regiments (I think the Sixty-ninth New York). They had been here all winter, I believe, as guard of the bridge across Cedar Creek. . . . I got a good dinner here and lots of good cheer. As there were several parties in sight, and I was to resume the role of Southern sympathizer, I arranged with these people to fire a volley toward me as I "escaped" across the bridge.

His luck ran out at Manassas Junction. He stumbled into "a regularly organized Confederate cavalry camp," recently abandoned by Union troops. "I got caught at last," he said. But not for very long.

> At last dusk came on and then I did a very ungentlemanly thing. . . . I crawled out between the guards and broke away up the track for the Bull Run river, six miles distant. Reaching there, as I came across a trestle, a Union picket took me in and sent me to the post headquarters at Union Mills, near-by. . . . And here, at last, safe within my own lines, my story of adventures might end; except that here, at last also, difficulties less exciting but, if possible, much more annoying, were awaiting me.

The nearest public telegraph station was in Alexandria, twenty miles away. To get there, Wing needed a horse, and no one would give him one or sell him one, even for $500, cash. There was, however, an army telegraph at Union Mills, and Wing figured maybe he could send a message over it to his old friend, Charles A. Dana, once the *Tribune*'s managing editor and now Stanton's assistant secretary of war. Permission was given and the short message was sent to Dana in Washington: I AM JUST IN FROM THE FRONT. LEFT GRANT AT FOUR O'CLOCK THIS MORNING. The response was immediate, and it came from Stanton, not Dana: "Where did you leave General Grant?"

This was a shocker to Wing, for he hadn't figured that no one in Washington knew where Grant was. Wing concluded he was dealing from a pretty good hand. "If Mr. Stanton would let me send one hundred words over the government line [to the *Tribune*], I would tell him all that I knew."

Stanton would have no part of it. He wired the post commander and ordered him to arrest Wing as a spy. Wing was disgusted. He had news, he said, "that the whole country was lying awake for, [and it] was tied up here with a strip of dirty red tape. And the young man who to get it here had been shot at, and chased, and captured; who had masqueraded as a loathsome 'copperhead,' and who had even seriously contemplated committing a felony, was to be locked up in a moldy, rat-infested guard house!"

Then something occurred, Wing said, "that I cannot explain." It wasn't all that mysterious: Lincoln himself had got wind of Wing's predicament, and he sent off a telegram of his own. As the message was being ticked off on the tape, Wing guessed it was for him. "What is it?" he asked. "Mr. Lincoln wants to know if you will tell him where Grant is," the post commander said. Wing wrote: "I repeated my offer—to communicate whatever information I had, for the use of the wire to transmit one hundred words. He accepted my terms without hesitation, only suggesting that my statement to my paper be so full as to disclose to the public the general situation."

The story, without a byline of any kind, led the *Tribune* on Saturday, May 7. The lead sentence said the Union army had crossed the Rapidan on Wednesday and Wing didn't get around to noting that "a severe action" took place on Thursday until the sixth paragraph. But it didn't make any difference. The country now knew that Grant and his army were at a place called the Wilderness and that a battle with Lee's whole army was under way.

Ida Tarbell was a tough reporter, but Henry Wing's adventures simply turned her to jelly. She described the situation at the White House:

> Back in Washington the revived President received [Wing's] message at his desk, and he read between the lines the truth: here was a spirited young correspondent, who, caring for his trust, resented the arbitrary decision of his great Secretary of War. He read it as if it were all written there before him. His eyes twinkled, his lips parted into something like a smile—"Wasn't that like Stanton?" and "Wasn't it like a boy?"

Let Henry Wing tell what happened next.

> A locomotive was sent down for me, and about two o'clock in the morning I reached the White House, where the President had gathered his official family to meet me. As I stepped into the room where they were seated my glance caught a quick gleam of surprise and apprehension in Mr. Lincoln's eyes, and I was awakened to a sense of my disreputable appearance. My hair was disheveled, my

shabby old coat was dusty and wrinkled, my pantaloons, much too long, were folded back at the bottom and gathered about my ankles with pieces of cotton twine, and my coarse clothes were coated three or four layers thick with "sacred soil."

I had met, perhaps, every one of this company at public functions or in private interviews, but not one of them recognized me in this garb. As my glance swept around the group it rested on the genial countenance of a particular friend, Mr. Welles, of Hartford, Connecticut, the Honorable Secretary of the Navy. As I advanced and accosted him he recognized me by my voice. He then presented me, with much embarrassing formality, to the others.

A half hour or more was spent in description of the movements of the troops, and in explanation, from a large map on the wall, of the situation at the time when I left. Then, as the company was dispersing, I turned to Mr. Lincoln and said, "Mr. President, I have a personal word for you."

The others withdrew and he closed the door and advanced toward me. As he stood there I realized as never before how tall he was. I looked up into his impressive face, ready to deliver Grant's message. He took a short, quick step toward me, and, stooping to bring his eyes level with mine, whispered in tones of intense, impatient interest, "What is it?"

I was so moved that I could hardly stammer: "General Grant told me to tell you, from him, that whatever happens, there is to be no turning back."

The vision that opened through those wonderful eyes from a great soul glowing with a newly kindled hope is the likeness of Mr. Lincoln that I still hold in my memory. And the hope was never to be extinguished. Others had "turned back." Every other one had. But there had come an end of that fatal folly.

Mr. Lincoln put his great, strong arms about me and, carried away in the exuberance of his gladness, imprinted a kiss upon my forehead.

We sat down again; and then I disclosed to him, as I could not do except in the light of that pledge of the great commander, all the disheartening details of that dreadful day in the wilderness. But I could assure him that the Army of the Potomac, in all its history, was never in such hopeful spirit as when they discovered, at the close of a day of disappointment, that they were not to "turn back."

After a few hours' sleep in his room at the National Hotel, then a bath and clean clothes, Wing reported for duty at the *Tribune*'s crowded office on Fourteenth Street. Sam Wilkeson was standing on a desk shouting that the news was a fraud, and that Wing was still with the army. Wing pushed his way through the crowd. "Here I am, Mr. Wilkeson!"

Ida Tarbell, in describing the scene, was almost more excited than Henry Wing or Sam Wilkeson.

> Such a shout as went up! They caught him in their arms and passed him over their heads to the table beside his chief; and there, with many interruptions, he told them the truth: he had left Grant's army at four o'clock on Friday morning; it had fought all day Thursday; Lee still held his position; when he left, Grant was to attack again in the morning; he had been all day getting out; when he reached Union Mills and asked for Mr. Dana and that a message be sent to the Tribune, Stanton had refused him the lines and ordered him to be shot as a spy.
>
> Such a groan as went up. And how had he escaped?
>
> "The President found it out and sent a train for me," he said proudly.
>
> There were cheers and cheers. Sam Wilkeson patted him on the back, overwhelmed with pride that one of his staff had . . . achieved the biggest scoop in the whole history of the war.

Wing reported back to the White House for another talk with the president late Saturday afternoon. Sam Wilkeson exercised his rights as a bureau chief and went along. According to Ida Tarbell, the conversation went something like this:

> "I see you've cleaned up, Henry," said Mr. Lincoln. "What are you going to do now?" And very promptly Henry replied, "I am going after Jess."
>
> "Jess?" said the President. "Who is Jess?"
>
> "My horse. I left him tied in the thicket down near Warrenton. The Confederates were too thick for me to get through with him any farther, and I promised him to go back. I never break a promise to a horse, Mr. President."

"You had to leave him?" said the President. "You better tell me about it, Henry."

When he had finished telling the story, the president said, "Well, I think we owe you something. I will have to help you with that."

And so he did. The next morning, Henry set out from Alexandria aboard a special train—a locomotive, a boxcar, and a few soldiers as escorts. They stopped near the woods where Wing had tied up Jesse (the horse's real name). Ida Tarbell was still in rollicking form:

> His anxiety was almost unbearable as he crawled out from the underbrush to the spot where he calculated he had left Jess, and raised his eyes to look.
>
> There the horse stood—head stretched out, eyes alert, ears forward, legs far apart, not a muscle moving, not a sound—the very picture of intentness. And when he saw Henry it was as if he would spring to meet him, for with one snap of his white teeth he bit almost entirely through the leather strap which held him. . . . With tears streaming down his cheeks, the youth threw his arms around Jess's neck, while Jess nuzzled his neck, whinnying softly his delight.

Ida Tarbell took liberties in telling Henry Wing's story. But, basically, it's all true. And there's no doubt that when Henry and Jesse arrived back in Washington, some of his colleagues—Whitelaw Reid and Uriah Painter among them—took up a collection and bought the horse for the Civil War's most endearing correspondent.

14

"There Is to Be No Turning Back"

In NOVEMBER OF 1863, Grant's favorite reporter, Sylvanus Cadwallader, was out West, writing for both the *Chicago Times* and the *New York Herald*. He watched as Joe Hooker's eastern soldiers took Lookout Mountain, south of Chattanooga, on November 24. The next day, standing on Orchard Knob, he had a clear view of one of the most spectacular sights of the whole war—"Pap" Thomas's westerners from the Army of the Cumberland, twenty thousand of them, attacking Bragg's supposedly impregnable position on Missionary Ridge.

Cadwallader described his good fortune this way:

> No battle ever fought on this continent afforded such opportunity. The day and the ground conspired to give an unbroken view of the whole field, and probably no great battle ever fought on the American continent equaled it in this regard. With bands playing, flags flying, soldiers cheering and yelling, our men three lines deep in perfect alignment, poured out through the young cottonwood timber, swept the rebel skirmishers out of the underbrush into the open cotton field, and pursued them on the run under a severe musketry fire to the first line of rifle pits.

Grant had expected to win the battle with Sherman's four divisions advancing against the rebel positions from the left and Hooker's three divisions coming down from Lookout Mountain on the right, but they were stalled. And here was Thomas and his four Cumberland divisions rolling them back in the center. Thomas's old veterans,

Cadwallader wrote, had learned a thing or two. "They were not much given to waiting for orders from officers who knew but little, if any, more than themselves. In their own language, 'When they saw a good thing, they knew it, and took it.'"

Historians say Grant was upset as he watched Thomas's men charge up the hill. They were supposed to make a feint, not a real attack. What was happening was not a part of Grant's plan. Cadwallader saw it somewhat differently:

> The propriety of commanding a halt from headquarters was seriously discussed for a few minutes. But Grant could not find it in his heart to dampen the enthusiasm of his men, and said, "Let us wait a few minutes and see what the boys will do. They are not so badly scattered as they seem to be. We see much more bare ground between them on the hillside than we would if they were on a level with us. We shall soon see. The boys feel pretty good. Let them alone awhile."

Cadwallader was so excited that he and one of Grant's engineers, Lieutenant Colonel James H. Wilson, mounted the breastworks on Orchard Knob and remained there until the victory was won. "We were stormed at, scolded, threatened, and repeatedly ordered down; but the fascination of the great battle wholly overcame all prudential considerations. My own experience and observation is probably that of most men similarly situated. Personal danger was forgotten till the excitement was over."

For the Cumberlands it became a race to see which unit would scale the heights first. "Looking down from the crest," Bruce Catton wrote,

> the Confederates kept on firing, but the foreknowledge of defeat was beginning to grip them. . . . No one could determine afterward what unit or what men won the race; and the business was argued at soldiers' reunions for half a century. Apparently the crest was reached at half a dozen places simultaneously, and when it was reached, Bragg's line—the center of his whole army, the hard core of his entire defensive position—suddenly and inexplicably went to pieces. By ones and twos and then by companies and battalions,

gray-clad soldiers who had proved their valor in a great many desperate fights turned and took to their heels.

It was a soldiers' victory for the Union army—a *western* soldiers' victory won by the Cumberlands.

When the battle ended, Cadwallader saddled up and rode for Stevenson, Alabama, the nearest railway station, sixty-five miles away. He arrived at the station just as a train was pulling out. "One of Gen. Grant's couriers returning from Nashville saw me dashing up on horseback, and came elbowing through the crowd to where I was. To him I entrusted my gallant little mare, with orders in Gen. Grant's name to remain in Stevenson until he could ship her by car to Nashville."

Cadwallader's train was delayed until a wreck could be cleared from the tracks and then his own train broke down in sight of Nashville, "and I had to walk three or four miles to the city." By then, he had written an account of the dramatic Union victory; he sent it to both his newspapers by telegraph. His work done—he figured he had scored a scoop—he repaired to Donneganna's restaurant for his first real meal in several days. He had just left the restaurant and was on his way to the Saint Cloud Hotel for a good night's sleep "when I saw Mr. W. F. G. Shanks, correspondent-in-chief of the New York Herald in the Department of the Cumberland, coming up the street on a half-run, and nearly breathless."

William Shanks, it turned out, had arrived in Nashville in his own locomotive after paying the engineer $100 in greenbacks to make the trip. But the whole brilliant achievement was at risk because "a dirty, greasy civilian" had swung aboard the locomotive just as it and its tender were pulling out. Shanks was outraged when he discovered this freeloader was a man named Woodward, a correspondent from the *Cincinnati Times*. Cadwallader wrote: "I was called into play at once to intercept and delay Woodward, while Shanks hastened to get his budget of telegraphic correspondence approved and deposited in the telegraph office. I took him into the restaurant and ordered an elaborate supper for two, composed of such dishes as would consume the most time in preparation."

By the time Woodward got to the telegraph office it was closed for the night. He said that was all right, he would get up at daybreak and file his story when the telegraph office opened for the day. He left an early wake-up call at the front desk, and went to bed. The mischievous Shanks ambled up to the clerk and slipped him $5 to erase Woodward's name from the wake-up list. "Woodward's failure to transmit his accounts cost him his place," Cadwallader said, "and my success led to many subsequent promotions in the New York Herald service."

Cadwallader went home to Milwaukee to see his family and to get some much-needed rest. He severed his relationship with the *Chicago Times* and then began to wonder if he would ever cover another battle. A month later, though, he heard from Fred Hudson, the *Herald*'s managing editor, urging him to report to New York as soon as possible.

> I arrived in New York at 12:20 p.m., April 27th 1864. In the afternoon I had my first visit with Mr. Hudson. He said, smilingly, that . . . I could never sit quietly at home till the war was ended. . . . He at length flatly admitted that the Herald needed my services [at Grant's Army of the Potomac] headquarters—that he had sent two or three capable and discreet correspondents there, but none of them had been able to gain any recognition deserving mention.

The *Herald,* in fact, was in serious trouble. The paper needed a correspondent who would be recognized and trusted by Grant and his associates, and it didn't have one. Shanks recommended Cadwallader as the man for the job. Hudson agreed. Smart decision.

The *Herald*'s chief correspondent with the Army of the Potomac was the same Frank Chapman who had ducked down into the *Louisville*'s engine room as the Confederate shot and shell began flying at Ford Donelson. When Cadwallader arrived in Washington to take up his new duties, he found Chapman at his desk instead of at the front. That posed a problem, for Stanton's order forbidding civilian passage between Washington and the army was still in place. But Cadwallader had connections in high places, and he had no trouble getting a pass signed by Grant. He joined the army on May 2, with a horse he had purchased for $250 in gold, "a good army saddle, pouches, horse equipments," and blankets.

He watched the fighting unfold the first day at the Wilderness. Late in the day he was given permission by one of Grant's aides to talk to Confederate prisoners. He wrote:

> Gen. [Marsena] Patrick was Provost Marshal General of the Army of the Potomac. He was then (and so remained till the day of his death), in my opinion, the finest existing fossil of the Cenozoic age. From his position on an eminence near at hand, he discovered me among the prisoners, and sent one of his staff to put me under arrest. As I neared the august presence of the old martinet, he was pompously strutting back and forth for a few yards, looking as black as a thunder cloud.

Cadwallader gave Patrick his pass and the credentials signed by General Grant; Patrick simply put them in his pocket and told a file of soldiers to march the enraged correspondent off to the "bull pen." At this critical juncture, one of Grant's aides, Colonel W. L. Duff, rode up and demanded to know what was going on. "Release this man instantly, and return his papers," he told a red-faced Patrick.

From that moment on Patrick was Cadwallader's implacable enemy. "He and his subordinates were systematic in subjecting me to annoyances. My horses were thereafter only safe from wrongful seizure when inside the line of Gen. Grant's stable guard. My correspondents and messengers were often hindered and dismounted—sometimes stopped at the gang-planks of steamboats, and kept there til the boat departed."

That night, Cadwallader tried to get some sleep next to the smoldering fire in front of Grant's tent. For the first time in the war, he wrote, he began to have doubts about the commanding general. Briefly, though, only briefly.

> I happened to look obliquely to the right, and there sat Gen. Grant in an army chair on the other side of the slowly dying embers. His hat was drawn down over his face, the high collar of an old blue army overcoat turned up above his ears, one leg crossed over the other knee, eyes on the ashes in front, causing me to think him half

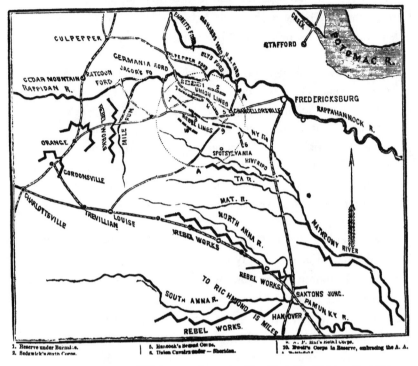

SCENE OF THE RECENT AND COMING BATTLES.

Typographical Map showing the Scene of the Great Battles of Thursday and Friday, with the Rebel Defenses on the Route to Richmond.

A map of the battle of the Wilderness, from the *New York World*, May 10, 1864. (Clements Library, University of Michigan)

asleep. My gloomy thoughts of but a few minutes were instantly chased away by my study of the figure before me. His nervous dangling of one leg over the other showed me he was not asleep. His whole attitude showed him to be in a brown study.

In a short time, however, he straightened up in his chair and finding that I was not asleep, commenced a pleasant conversation upon indifferent subjects. . . . I then remarked that if we were to get any sleep that night, it was time we were in our tents. . . . He smilingly assented, spoke of the sharp work Gen. Lee had been giving us a couple of days, and entered his tent. It was the grandest mental sunburst of my life. I had suddenly emerged from the slough of despond, to the solid bedrock of unwavering faith.

Cadwallader's "mental sunburst" might have been dimmed a little by the arrival the next day of the egregious Frank Chapman, crestfallen at being caught absent from his post for so long and now complaining he wasn't feeling very well. Chapman "besought" Cadwallader to assume leadership of the *Herald*'s ragtag collection of reporters and messengers with Grant's army.

Cadwallader, taking charge, asked for volunteers to carry the *Herald*'s dispatches to the capital through a no-man's-land behind Union lines infested by Confederate cavalry and bushwhackers. When no one raised a hand, Cadwallader said he would take the news reports to Washington himself.

With two cavalry pouches filled with dispatches and "with the most complete list of casualties I ever obtained," Cadwallader set out for Washington at 3 P.M. on Saturday, May 7. He was joined unexpectedly by two reporters, J. C. Fitzpatrick, the *Herald*'s man with Burnside's corps, and the *Philadelphia Inquirer*'s Edward Crapsey.

They were approaching the Rappahannock River at nightfall

> when five mounted men plunged into the road from the thicket that skirted it, in our front and rear, and the click of revolvers were at our ear in an instant. "Surrender." "Give up your arms." "Speak and you die," in suppressed excited tone of voice, were the persuasive words that greeted us. . . . A dozen strong arms seemed to have seized us. We were jerked violently from our horses, dragged into a thicket at the roadside, thrown sprawling on the ground, and found the cold steel of revolver barrels jammed against our heads.

The reporters' captors were nervous troopers from the Ninth Virginia Cavalry, and they were convinced from the start that the smartly dressed Cadwallader was an important Union officer, probably a colonel. After persistent questioning, they concluded he probably was a general. The troopers reckoned Crapsey and Fitzpatrick were too shabbily dressed to be officers of any rank.

Cadwallader wrote:

> We expected to be hurried past the left flank of the Union army that night—perhaps taken to Fredericksburg. But neither was done,

and I have never been able to account for the slow, undecided, dila-
tory march of that night. We went through dark forests, across deep
ravines, by deserted farms, through family door-yards, by blind
paths, often with no path at all, till the roar of falling water proclaimed the presence of some mill dam on the Rappahannock. . . .
We forded the Rappahannock at an obscure place well known to
these partisans, far from house and road.

They put up for the night at a small farmhouse. In the morning, the rebel captain announced he was going to turn them over to
General Fitzhugh Lee in Fredericksburg. "Libby Prison with all its
recounted and unrecounted horrors seemed gaping to receive us,"
Cadwallader said.

On the way to Fredericksburg Sunday morning, they stumbled
into a lively skirmish between Union and Confederate infantrymen.
In the confusion, Cadwallader slipped a rebel sergeant a roll of green-
backs. He looked the other way as the three reporters made their
escape. They spent Sunday night in the woods, got up early, and
reached the mouth of Aquia Creek, emptying into the Potomac River,
about 9 A.M. Monday.

Cadwallader wrote:

> We correspondents all fell to work and by noon had a raft or a float
> barely capable of bearing up three persons. My recollection is that
> the Potomac is nearly five miles wide between the mouth of Acquia
> Creek and Point Tobacco, on the Maryland shore; but we pushed
> and paddled into the sluggish current of the river, hoping to get
> across before dark.

They were picked up by a government transport, *Rebecca Barton*,
at about 2 P.M. and delivered to the Seventh Street wharf in Washington late that afternoon, May 9. Up until that time, Cadwallader
said, "the Herald had not received a line from any of its many special
correspondents. All other papers, however, were in the same predicament." Cadwallader was wrong about that. As we have already seen,
young Henry Wing scooped everyone with his front-page story in the
New York Tribune on May 7. But Cadwallader, at least, was runner-up,

and he had news to report about the second day's action in the Wilderness.

Cadwallader took a carriage to Willard's Hotel, ordered a long bath, sent for new clothing and underclothing, and then held what he called a levee with hundreds of people desperate for information about Grant's army. He went from the hotel to the *Herald*'s office on Fourteenth Street and began writing his account, all from memory, for the written dispatches were still somewhere back in the woods with those fellows from the Ninth Virginia Cavalry. He sent page after page to the telegraph office before fatigue—and half a bottle of whiskey—caught up to him. He was roused out of bed early the next morning and put on the first train to New York. There, in a room at the Astor House, he began writing some more.

When he was finished, Fred Hudson, the managing editor, told him he had done good work and ordered him to go to bed until he was recovered from his ordeal. "Great hearted, chivalrous, magnanimous Fred Hudson!" Cadwallader wrote. "I cannot write of him . . . with dry eyes. He was to Mr. James Gordon Bennett what Rawlins was to Grant, which exhausts human praise."

William Shanks, the *Herald*'s chief western correspondent—the reporter who hired his own locomotive to file his Chattanooga dispatch in Nashville—wrote an article in *Harper*'s magazine shortly after the war ended in which he nicely captured Mr. Bennett's expectations in hiring battlefield correspondents. The *Herald*, Shanks said,

> maintained a corps of sixty-three of the most enterprising, though by no means the most learned, correspondents. But a fair knowledge of English; a clear head, not a concise style; and common sense, not a collegiate education, were the qualifications demanded in a Herald war correspondent. Not elegance of description, though it was not objected to, was urged on the correspondent; but he was carefully impressed with the idea that to be "ahead" of his rivals was to be successful. The correspondents were told, in a printed circular issued by the editor of the Herald, that there was no particular merit in being "up" with his rivals; dismissal was to be expected if he fell behind them; but advancement in position and salary would follow if he came in "ahead."

Cadwallader was just the sort of fellow to command this kind of reporting corps.

Bennett and the editors at the *Herald* wouldn't have thought much of the *New York Tribune*'s Charles A. Page, another reporter with Grant's army. He was not a great battlefield reporter, and he was rarely "ahead" of his competitors. But he was the closest thing the Civil War produced to Ernie Pyle, the GIs' friend in World War II. More than anyone else, Page found time to celebrate the daily life of soldiers and armies.

He was a farm boy from Illinois and attended little Cornell College in Mount Vernon, Iowa. Following his graduation, he edited the local newspaper, the *Mount Vernon News*, and played an enthusiastic role in local Republican politics. As a reward for his loyal party service, he was given a Washington job as a clerk at the Treasury Department. When the war began, he negotiated an unusual deal with Mr. Greeley's newspaper and his supervisors at the Treasury Department: if his desk was clear, he could take the field as a war correspondent.

He took the field in May of 1864 and saw much of the bloody action at the Wilderness, Spotsylvania, and Cold Harbor. Because of the new journalism created by the telegraph, most of his stories were written in bits and pieces. But they contain some wonderful stuff.

"I have never seen the army move with more exact order, with a less number of stragglers, and with so little apparent fatigue to the men," he wrote in a story datelined 8 A.M., Thursday, May 5.

> All had a full ration of sleep last night—which is a better augury of victory than a re-inforcement of thousands. The roads are in excellent condition, the weather delightful, and so warm that whole divisions abandoned their overcoats and blankets on the march. At one point I noticed some hundreds of overcoats had been thrown into a stream to improve the crossing. Overcoats and blankets are decidedly better for the purpose than rails.

In a story written at 2 P.M. the same day, Page paid tribute to the first soldier killed in "this (God willing) last grand campaign on the war"—Charles Wilson of Franklin, Massachusetts, a private in

Company I, Eighteenth Massachusetts, Colonel Joseph Hayes commanding.

He wrote a third story at 9 P.M. The fighting by then was fierce. "The work," he said,

> was at close range. No room in that jungle for manoeuvering; no possibility of a bayonet charge; no help from artillery; no help from cavalry; nothing but close, square, severe, face-to-face volleys of fatal musketry. The wounded stream out, and fresh troops pour in. Stretchers pass out with ghastly burdens, and go back reeking with blood for more. Word is brought that the ammunition is failing [running low]. Sixty rounds fired in one steady, stand-up fight, and that fight not fought out. Boxes of cartridges are placed on the returning stretchers, and the struggle shall not cease for want of ball and powder.

In a story written at 5 P.M. on Saturday, May 7, the twenty-six-year-old Page chronicled this moving vignette:

> Far down the plank road where Hancock fought, beyond the thickest Rebel dead, lay a boy severely wounded, perhaps not less a soldier that he was but a boy. He had fallen the day before when we were farthest advanced, and he was alone with the dead when I rode up. The poor fellow was crawling about gathering violets. Faint with loss of blood, unable to stand, he could not resist the tempting flowers, and had already made a beautiful bouquet. Having caused a stretcher to be sent for, I saw him taken up tenderly and borne away, wearing a brave, sweet, touching smile.

Page could also be amusing. Here's part of a dispatch he wrote on May 31:

> A Sixth Corps staff officer dismounted near me a moment ago. I inquired where he had been riding. He informed me that he had been sent out on a general "scyugle," that he had "scyugled" along the front, where the Johnnies "scyugled" a bullet through his clothes; that, on his return he "scyugled" an ice house; that he should "scyugle" his servant—who, by the way, had just "scyugled" three fat chickens—for a supply of ice; that after he had "scyugled"

his dinner he proposed to "scyugle" a nap, and closed by asking how I "scyugled."

Page said he had no idea where the word came from, but the soldiers in the Army of the Potomac knew what it meant. The soldiers knew, too, all about Grant's grand flanking strategy. Page wrote:

> The rank and file have a pretty good appreciation of the strategy of the campaign. They understand that it has been a series of splendid flank movements, and "flanking" has become the current joke with which to account for everything from a night march to the capture of a sheep or a pig. A poor fellow, terribly wounded, yesterday, said he saw a shell coming, "but hadn't time to flank it." And he enjoyed the joke with a smile and a chuckle, when his quick eye had sought and found appreciation among the bystanders. The shell had "flanked" him, by taking off an arm.

No one ever described the trials of a Civil War correspondent better than Page, "sick with fatigue," did in a discursive dispatch composed in a hospital bed on June 25. The "beautiful weather" Page wrote about in May had now become uncomfortably hot.

> It is hot. It is hotter than yesterday. Yesterday was hotter than the day before. The day before hotter than its immediate predecessor, and *it* than *its*, and so on indeterminately. Purgatory is at least a week back, and hell itself not far behind. How hot it is now, no thermometer of words will begin to indicate. The boy who extended the definition of the adjective from hot to hottest, then began again with Hottentot and ended with Hottentotest, made a creditable effort but failed. . . . It is hot.
>
> This indescribable hotness is part of the misery of correspondents. Dust is a part of the misery of correspondents.
>
> A Scene: Three "specials" of metropolitan journals, smoking meerschaums, and conning letters yet to be. Mail arrives with New York papers. Each reads one of his own letters.
>
> Herald special swears oaths both loud and deep. "They have rewritten my dispatch!" Times special finds something he spoke of as "impudent" pronounced "important." Tribune special is amused.

Had said certain troops are "handled skillfully;" he is made to say they "were traveled skillfully. . . ."

Verily, reading their own letters is a part of the misery of correspondents.

Mr. [Henry] Winser of the Times had his horse shot under him at Cold Harbor. Mr. [Finley] Anderson of the Herald was hit in the arm at Wilderness. Richardson and Browne of the Tribune have been sixteen months in rebel prisons. . . .

Constant danger, without the soldiers' glory, is a part of the misery of correspondents.

You broil; you pant; you thirst; your temples throb with thrills of mighty pain; you are threatened with *coup de soleil;* you wish yourself anywhere—anywhere out of such torment.

Pooh, man! You forget that you are a "special," and that therefore not supposed to be the subject to the laws which govern other mortals. You are a Salamander. You are Briareus. You are Argus. You are Hercules. . . . Be jolly. Ride your ten, fifteen hours; your twenty, thirty, forty, fifty miles. Fatigue is your normal condition. Sleeplessness, too. "Tired nature" is yours; the "sweet restorer" somebody else's. "Balmy sleep" is for babies. You are a "special," I tell you.

Incessant riding in the sun is part of the misery of correspondents.

Composition is pleasant, sometimes. I don't mean the mighty joy of creation of the great author, but the simple pleasure of ordinary mortals writing ordinary things. . . .

It is far into the night when you begin. You rode all day and a part of this night, and have only now had your ablution and supper. You begin—"squat like a toad" before a camp fire; a stumpy lead pencil, and smoke in your eyes, dingy paper, and ashes puffed in your face; no part of you that has not its own special pain and torment. Your brain is in a state of "confusion worse confounded." Your eyes will shut, your pencil will drop from your nerveless fingers, but I say unto you, Write! . . . Force yourself to the rack, tug away, bear on hard, and when you are done, do not read it over, or you will throw it into the fire. Now arrange with the guard to have yourself awakened at daybreak, an hour or two hence, and then lie down, wondering who wouldn't be a "special."

You will inevitably write things that will offend somebody. Somebody will say harsh things of you, and perhaps seek you out to destroy you. Never mind. Such is a part of the misery of correspondents.

Was your horse stolen last night? Are your saddle-bags and all that they contain missing this morning? No matter. It is a thing of course. It is a part of the misery of correspondents.

You are a "special," and who wouldn't be?

There is news at the front, for I hear great guns, but I am too sick to ride till the sun is lower down the sky. Now, "sweet restorer," now is your time!

Battles such as Fredericksburg and Gettysburg and Chattanooga were easier to write about because the correspondents could see the action. But Grant's battles in May and early June of 1864 were fought in dense woods that blurred the action. Cold Harbor, one of the deadliest of all Civil War battles, was decided on June 3. The reporters had trouble pulling it all together into a coherent whole. Page, for example, failed to grasp the horror of Grant's uncoordinated attack on Lee's well-defended position. In not much more than eight minutes, Grant lost several thousand men. It was bad generalship, Grant's worst performance in the war. Lee, almost always brilliant in defensive warfare, lost fifteen hundred men. It was one of his finest hours.

On June 7, four days after Cold Harbor, the *Philadelphia Inquirer*'s Edward Crapsey rejoined the army following a short respite back home in Pennsylvania. Minutes after arriving in camp, he was arrested by the terrible-tempered General Meade.

His crime had been a story that was published in the *Inquirer* on May 27 in which he tried to explain the relationship between Grant and Philadelphia's favorite son, Meade. Grant, Crapsey wrote,

> plans and exercises a supervisory control over the army, but to Meade belongs everything of detail. He is entitled to great credit for the magnificent movements of the army. . . . In battle he puts troops in action and controls their movements; in a word, he commands the army. General Grant is here only because he deems the present campaign the vital one of the war, and wishes to decide on the spot all questions that would be referred to him as General-in-chief.

So far, so good. But then Crapsey wrote:

History will record, but newspapers cannot, that on one eventful
night during the present campaign Grant's presence saved the army,
and the nation too; not that General Meade was on the point of
committing a blunder unwittingly, but his devotion to his country
made him loath to risk her last great army on what he deemed a
chance. Grant assumed the responsibility, and we are still on to
Richmond.

Meade figured Crapsey, this "damned correspondent," was ac-
cusing him of timidity in the face of the enemy, something that had
been suggested about his behavior in failing to follow up his victory
at Gettysburg. Meade was enraged, and no Civil War general, not
even Sherman, could work himself into a more towering rage than
George Gordon Meade. He called Crapsey on the carpet and demanded to know where he had picked up such scurrilous information.
It was "the talk of the camp," an intimidated Crapsey replied. No,
said Meade, bellowing in anger, it was a wicked lie.

Meade turned Crapsey over to Cadwallader's nemesis, Provost
Marshal General Patrick, and told him to see that the correspondent
was promptly expelled from the army. Patrick, Cadwallader wrote,
"added every insult and indignity" he could devise. "Crapsey was
mounted and tied on the sorriest looking mule to be found, with his
face to the mule's tail; when preceded by a drum corps beating the
'Rogue's March,' he was literally paraded for hours through the ranks
of the army." Cadwallader failed to note that a sign reading "Libeler
of the Press" had been hung on Crapsey's back.

That night, seated around a camp fire after supper, Cadwallader
and members of Grant's staff discussed Crapsey's punishment. Cadwallader said Meade would live to regret what he had done. "Meade
had abused his military power, to wreak his personal vengeance on an
obscure friendless civilian, and that it was likely the general would
get the worst of it in the end."

Cadwallader observed that Grant's staff divided almost evenly—
the West Pointers in favor of the punishment as delivered, the volunteers leaning to the opinion that it had been excessive.

It didn't take Whitelaw Reid long to work himself into a lather of
moral outrage as soon as he heard the news. In a letter to his paper,

the *Cincinnati Gazette,* he said Meade had abused his power by seizing a gentleman "as well born, as respectably connected, as well educated as himself, to placard an infamous slander on his back, to humiliate him by the coarsest & most unfeeling exposure through the lines of the army, & to endeavor to disgrace him in his profession & before the country by using the influence of his office to publish in the wildest manner the punishment he had inflicted!"

Reid said Meade might well be a brave man in battle, "but he is as leprous with moral cowardice as the brute that kicks a helpless cripple on the street, or beats his wife at home. He does not care to grapple with newspapers that (in the kindest & most delicate manner) hint the truth about him."

He went on to declare that Crapsey's analysis was right on target—it *was* widely known within the army that Meade would have retreated back across the Rapidan following the battle at the Wilderness if Grant hadn't intervened.

Reid's editors decided they wouldn't print his outburst.

"The consequences of Meade's act extended farther than he expected," Cadwallader wrote.

> Every newspaper correspondent in the Army of the Potomac, and in Washington City, had first an implied, and afterward an expressed understanding, to ignore General Meade in every possible way and manner. The publishers shared their feelings to a certain extent, and it was soon noticed that General Meade's name never appeared in any army correspondence if it could be omitted. If he issued an official or general order of such prominence as to require publication, it would be printed without signature, prefaced with the remark, "The following order has just been issued, etc." From that time till the next spring, General Meade was quite as much unknown, by any correspondence from the army, as any dead hero of antiquity.

Following bloody Cold Harbor, the two armies dug in, exhausted. Grant saw no future in that, so he took his army and quietly slipped away in a brilliant move that briefly surprised Lee himself. Grant traveled southeast, across the James River, and arrived June 15 on the outskirts of Petersburg, a key link in Lee's line of defense. The city was wide open, but apprehensive Union commanders lost their chance to seize it. Lee rushed in reinforcements, and a stalemate began all over again.

One of the regiments in the Union army's Ninth Corps was the Forty-eighth Pennsylvania from Schuylkill County in hard-coal country in the eastern part of the state. Most of the soldiers in the Forty-eighth were miners; they proposed digging a tunnel under the Confederate lines and blowing a hole with blasting powder big enough to let half the army through. The miners did their job; it was a grand tunnel and the explosion on July 30 was powerful enough to open a crater in the middle of the rebel lines 150 feet wide. Unfortunately, though, Ambrose Burnside was still on active service and in command of the Ninth Corps. He ordered four divisions—one of them composed of black men—to take part in the breakthrough.

Burnside directed the attack from a post far to the rear, and fell once again into a funk that prevented him from giving timely and sensible orders. "The opportunity was completely lost," Shelby Foote wrote. "The mine itself could not have worked better, but the arrangements for exploiting it could not have worked worse." The Union soldiers found themselves milling around in the crater, a perfect blue bull's-eye for Confederate gunners. It was at this point that Burnside committed his black troops, and they were cut to pieces, too. So, instead of taking advantage of the greatest opportunity the Army of the Potomac had ever been offered, Grant lost four thousand men in one of the war's greatest fiascoes.

The *Tribune*'s Sam Wilkeson (Henry Wing's boss) witnessed the action at the crater and was appalled by newspaper reports that tried to give it a positive glow. "Glorious news from Petersburg?" he asked in a dispatch August 6.

Why, O swindled people! the ink that made the lie that gave the false information in New York its last sensation was not yet spread on the types, while every drummer boy and mule driver in the Army of the Potomac knew that a crowning disaster and a crowning disgrace had happened. . . . I tell no secret when I say that Grant wrapped himself in silence on Monday, and that his heart was gnawed by disgust and rage.

The ubiquitous Charles Carleton Coffin was there, too. This time, he took the field with an assistant—his young nephew, Edmund Carleton, using the future surgeon as a messenger most of the time. Coffin worried constantly that harm might come to the young man. He was late returning to camp one night, and when he finally showed up, Coffin breathed a sigh of relief. "You're a brick, Ed," he said.

More than most, Coffin understood just how terrible the fighting had been, so terrible that it was causing serious political problems at home. With the presidential election only weeks away, anti-Lincoln newspapers were seizing on the butcher bill as a reason to vote for the Democratic candidate, General McClellan, and bring the war to a negotiated conclusion.

Lincoln needed good news, and he got it, without a lot of time to spare. Old Davy Farragut damned the torpedoes (mines, in fact) and took Mobile Bay on August 5. A few weeks later, on September 1, William T. Sherman licked John Bell Hood and marched into Atlanta.

The most controversial reporter with Grant's army was the *New York Times*' William Swinton. A fair-to-middling battlefield correspondent when he wanted to be, he was that rare creature—a reporter despised by both the army and his colleagues.

He had earlier been caught eavesdropping on General Grant and banished from the army. But now he was back, under the protective wing of a visiting VIP, Congressman Elihu Washburne, from Galena, Illinois, Grant's hometown. Swinton said he wasn't a war correspondent any more. He had graduated from that, he told his colleagues, and he was now "a literary gentleman of leisure," compiling information for a history of the war.

Swinton, Cadwallader said,

> was an Englishman by birth and education, with many of the vices and few of the virtues of his countrymen. He was tall and lanky in build; cold-blooded, conceited, and prejudiced to a surprising extent. He had such inordinate and national self-esteem, as to think it pitiable ignorance in any one to deny English superiority in all

things. When added to this it was found, that so far as he had sympathy for any person, or any cause, he was heartily in sympathy with the Southern Confederacy; and that the thick-skinned imperviousness to argument, ridicule or reason, so often found in his class, was colossal—monumental—it was a matter of small wonder that he was hated and despised by all who knew him.

A young Union officer, Captain Edward P. "Ned" Brownson, youngest son of the philosopher Orestes A. Brownson, saw a good deal of Swinton during the war. He talked about the correspondent in unpublished letters to his sister, Sarah Brownson. Captain Brownson didn't think much of Swinton, either.

"Swinton is eating dinner with the rest [of us]," he wrote on January 18, 1863. "I do not like Swinton's [most recent] letter much. Newspaper correspondents are an abomination."

"Swinton is a bother," he wrote four days later. "If I were Cmdr. In Chief, I would have him beyond the lines in a minute."

Brownson was badly wounded at the Wilderness early in May, but returned to the army as a staff officer with General Hancock late the next month, his left arm useless and carried in a sling. In a letter to his sister on July 1, 1864, he reported with a good deal of pleasure that Hancock had seen enough of Swinton's work. Brownson wrote: "Gen. Hancock has forbidden any of his staff to give any official information, or information on official subjects, to Mr. Swinton, because said Swinton has lied rather too much about this [Second] Corps' conduct. . . . And he has told me to write him to that effect, which I do not altogether unwillingly."

Brownson was wounded again on August 25. He died—just twenty years old—a few days later.

Soon after Petersburg, Cadwallader officially took charge of the *Herald*'s team with Grant's army. He did it in grand style. Mr. Bennett, he said, had impressed upon him

the importance of running an independent mess of my own, and entertaining liberally, as advertisement for the *Herald*. I therefore kept "open house." My dinners equalled those of Gen. Grant, and were free from restraints which often attended his. We could discuss men and measures as we pleased, whilst such conversations would have been indecorous in the general's presence. My preparations consisted in procuring ample supplies of eatables and potables; a professional cook; a tent for his kitchen; one large hospital tent for a reception room, and another opening out of it for a dining room; an old plantation house servant to always be in attendance on any one who called; and white jackets and aprons for him, for Cook George, and for Albert my hostler. . . .

My ambulance [carriage] would convey a party wherever it wished to go, if that mode of conveyance was preferred. I kept four saddle horses and equipments; and could mount two or three friends for a day at any time. Cigars of excellent quality, stood open and free to all guests, or callers. In those times of deprivations, Herald headquarters soon became well known and famous.

George, the professional cook hired away from Willard's Hotel in Washington, must have been a paragon. One night, Cadwallader said, he served potatoes, tomatoes, and onions, canned fruits of many kinds, excellent fresh white bread, standard imported sauces and pickles, good fresh butter, a large, genuine full cream cheese, bologna sausage, canned corn beef, oysters and lobsters, fruit pudding, "and pies far surpassing any 'your mother' ever made."

Cadwallader had almost everything he wanted—except free passage for the *Herald*'s dispatches to headquarters in New York. Secretary Stanton was the problem; he wouldn't let the *Herald* use the mail or the telegraph to file the dispatches. Cadwallader went to Washington to see Stanton personally, but he couldn't get past the waiting room.

So Cadwallader set up his own delivery system. He hired several "intelligent men, familiar with army life," to carry the dispatches from the field to Baltimore, where they were picked up by other messengers and taken to New York. That way, Cadwallader said, "all correspondence could be delivered at the Herald office . . . by my own messengers, free from military censorship by mail or telegraph, and appear in the same issue of the *Herald* as if telegraphed from Washington."

Cadwallader was now in such a charitable mood that he began to have second thoughts about the blackout of General Meade's name in the *Herald* and the rest of the Northern press. Meade, slowly but surely, began reappearing in the *Herald*. Meade noticed the change and wrote Cadwallader a nice note saying he appreciated it.

Grant never wavered in his support for Cadwallader, and the Cadwallader papers at the Library of Congress are filled with examples of the commanding general's generosity. Grant, for example, issued a pass for Cadwallader to bring his wife to camp; he issued another to allow a large shipment of cheese to be delivered to the *Herald* headquarters. On September 24, Grant wrote the kind of letter to Cadwallader that removed any doubt of the special relationship that existed between the two men. "For the years past," Grant wrote,

I have seen more of you personally probably than of all the other correspondents put together. I have read your accounts of operations in the field. . . . It affords me pleasure to bear testimony that in all your correspondence you have, as much if not more often than any other in the profession, stuck to the legitimate duties assigned to you, i.e., reported facts without giving political bearing. You have avoided building up one general or brigade or larger command at the expense of another. Had your course been pursued by all of the profession from the start much of the mortification felt by many would have been arrested and all would have been received as friends and not, as often happens, as something to be dreaded and avoided.

Five days before Grant wrote his letter, the provost marshal's office in Milwaukee wrote a less welcome letter to Cadwallader. "Sir," the letter stated, "you are hereby notified that you were on the 19th day of September, 1864, legally drafted in the service of the United States for a period of one year. You will . . . report the third day of October."

The next day, Cadwallader's wife, the former Mary Paul, telegraphed the *Herald* in New York. PLEASE WRITE TO MR. CADWALLADER THAT HE IS DRAFTED, Mrs. Cadwallader said. A family friend, George

Sylvanus Cadwallader's notice of exemption from the draft. (Library of Congress)

Western Union telegram to Sylvanus Cadwallader notifying him that his friends had bought someone to take his place. (Library of Congress)

Paul, probably related to Mrs. Cadwallader, was enlisted to find someone to take Cadwallader's place. "Am doing everything possible," Paul wired Cadwallader on September 30. "Hope to succeed tomorrow." And then, on October 1, Paul sent this Western Union telegram to Cadwallader: ALL RIGHT HAVE SECURED NIGGER FOR SEVEN HUNDRED (700) DOLS. DEPOSIT BALANCE AS BEFORE.

Cadwallader's papers contain the official "certificate of exemption on account of having furnished a substitute." In it, Cadwallader is described as being thirty-eight years old, five feet six-and-a-half inches tall, with a dark complexion, brown eyes, and brown hair.

The black man who took $700 to serve in Cadwallader's place for one year was identified simply as "George Washington 3rd (col'd)."

15

The Fall of Richmond

LINCOLN WAS REELECTED PRESIDENT on November 8, 1864. Sherman entered Savannah on December 21. On January 23, 1865, the steamship *Greyhound*, a captured Confederate blockade runner, steamed out of Boston harbor with $15,000 worth of food and provisions for the needy citizens of Savannah tucked in her hold. Leading the relief expedition was the *Boston Morning Journal*'s own Charles Carleton Coffin.

Newspapermen have often been a little uncomfortable in the company of churchgoing folks with deeply held religious faith. Coffin's colleagues were a little uncomfortable with him; he was, after all, a man who didn't drink or smoke or swear. But Coffin was the real thing—a decent, honest, hardworking, compassionate Christian. It was God's will, he said, to help the starving people in Savannah. He wrote in a dispatch:

A store at the corner of Bay and Barnard streets was taken for a depot, the city canvassed, and a registry made of all who came for food. I passed a morning among the people who came for food. . . . There was a motley crowd. Hundreds of both sexes, all ages, sizes, complexions, and costumes; gray-haired old men of Anglo-Saxon blood, with bags, bottles, and baskets; colored patriarchs, who had been in bondage many years, suddenly made freemen; well-dressed women wearing crape for their husbands and sons who had fallen while fighting against the old flag, stood waiting patiently their turn to enter the building, where through the open doors they could see barrels of flour, pork, beans, and piles of bacon, hogsheads of sugar, molasses, and vinegar.

After seeing the supplies were being properly distributed, Coffin prepared to go back to work as a war correspondent. He thought at first he might join Sherman (though other reporters were finding that was a daunting challenge). Or perhaps he should return north and follow Grant as the generalissimo made plans for his final campaign. Instead, Coffin decided to go to Charleston, where the war had begun, a city under blockade for almost two years and now, cut off from supplies by land, ready to surrender. "He longed to see the old flag wave once more over Sumter," his worshipful biographer, William Elliott Griffis, wrote. "So, bidding farewell to Sherman's army, he took the steamer *Fulton* at Port Royal, which was to stop on her way to New York at the blockading fleet off Charleston."

Coffin's timing was always impeccable. This time, it was almost miraculous. He entered Charleston harbor at 2 P.M. on February 18, 1865, just in time to see the Union flag being hoisted over what was left of Fort Sumter. His dispatch to the *Boston Morning Journal* began with these words:

The old flag waves over Sumter . . .
   I can see its crimson stripes and fadeless stars in the warm sunlight of this glorious day.
   Thanks be to God who giveth us the victory.

The other correspondents handed over their dispatches to the purser of the dispatch steamer *Arago* and told him to deliver them to the proper newspaper authorities when the steamer reached New York. Coffin, a trusting sort of fellow, put his dispatches in the hands of one of the passengers aboard the steamer who struck him as reliable and gave him careful instructions. "When your steamer comes close to the wharf in New York," he said, "it will very probably touch and then rebound before she is fast to her moorings. Do you stand ready on the gunwale, and when the sides of the vessel first touch the dock, do not wait for the rebound; but jump ashore, and run as for your life to the telegraph office, send the telegram, and then drop this letter [a longer version of the story] in the post office."

When the steamer docked in New York, Coffin's judgment was confirmed; his passenger was the first on shore, minutes ahead of everyone else. He arrived at the telegraph office about 8 A.M., and, after initial resistance by the telegraph operators (they worried the dramatic news might be inaccurate and affect the price of gold), sent Coffin's story. The purser, meanwhile, held on to the other dispatches until his own duties had been attended to. Coffin's story, published as an extra, caused a sensation.

Coffin stayed in Charleston only a few days. One evening, while he and several companions were eating dinner at the Mills House, they heard what he described as "the sound of drums and a chorus of voices." They went outside to see where the music was coming from. "Looking down the broad avenue," he recalled later,

> we saw a column of troops advancing with steady step and even ranks. It was nearly sunset and their bayonets were gleaming in the level rays. It was General [Robert] Potter's brigade, led by the 55th Massachusetts—a regiment recruited from the ranks of slavery. Sharp and shrill the noises of the fife, stirring the drum-beat, deep and resonant the thousand voices singing their most thrilling war song—
>
> *"John Brown's body lies a mouldering in the grave."*

Coffin hastened north, joining the Army of the Potomac "in season to be an observer of Grant's last campaign."

THROUGHOUT THE WAR there was a huge demand in the North for Southern newspapers (and, of course, an equal demand in the South for Northern newspapers). The *Herald*'s Cadwallader, a thoroughly well-organized chief correspondent, decided he would establish a formal arrangement in which papers from the North and the South could be easily exchanged on a daily basis. "To this end," he wrote, "I conferred with Gen. Godfrey Weitzel, commanding the Eighteenth Corps, on [Ben] Butler's front, to make some permanent arrangement for passing through the lines daily, and exchanging files of New York City papers for those from Richmond and other southern cities."

With Weitzel's approval, he assigned one of his assistants, John Brady, to make the exchange with Confederate representatives. It worked perfectly, "and the Herald was filled with southern editorials, showing the animus of the writers and the state of southern opinion in the Confederacy."

The problem was that Cadwallader's operation was so efficient it dried up every other avenue for making newspaper exchanges, even General Butler's. The general, always an unpleasant man, was incensed and ordered Cadwallader's arrest. Cadwallader decided to settle the matter by making a personal visit to Butler's headquarters.

"You have reported under arrest, I suppose?" Butler asked, when Cadwallader entered his tent. Not at all, Cadwallader replied. "Consider yourself under arrest, sir, from this instant," Butler said.

Cadwallader tried to explain the situation, but Butler wouldn't listen for a minute. He

> burst out in great rage at what he considered the severity of my offense and asked if I realized that he could have me shot by drumhead court-martial in about fifteen minutes? Without waiting for my reply, he went on, swaggering and towering in speech and behavior; said affairs had come to a pretty pass when a civilian could assume to pass through the lines of the enemy in broad daylight, and hold communications with the enemy, and he intended to make short shrift of all such work.

Cadwallader played his trump card—an order from General Grant himself, instructing "all guards and all picket guards, in all the armies of the United States, to pass me by day or night, with horses or vehicles." Arrest me, Cadwallader challenged Butler, and allow General Grant "to vindicate his own authority." Butler, sly old politician that he was, folded his hand, and Cadwallader made his way back to Grant's headquarters at City Point, Virginia. "No one stopped me," he said.

Cadwallader was on safe ground. Grant didn't trust Butler, either, and his bungled attempt in late December to capture Fort Fisher at the mouth of the Cape Fear, protecting Wilmington, North Carolina, the Confederates' only working seaport, was the last straw. Cadwallader's friend, John Rawlins, Grant's chief of staff, tipped him off that something was in the works. After supper, Cadwallader wrote, Grant came into Rawlins's tent and told Cadwallader that one of his friends "had come to grief." Which one? Cadwallader asked. "General Butler," the commander in chief replied.

That, of course, was a huge story. The cockeyed Butler was a leading Democratic politician, and the most hated Union general in the South (dating from his occupation of New Orleans; he and his troops stole so much silver that folks in the South's largest and most cosmopolitan city nicknamed him "Spoons").

Lincoln issued 1865's General Order Number 1 on January 7, relieving Butler from command of the Department of Virginia and North Carolina and its Army of the James and putting an able officer, Edward O. C. Ord, in his place.

Cadwallader filed a very brief story, saying simply that Lincoln had issued General Order Number 1 relieving Butler of his command and that it "is causing much comment, but as far as I can learn little or no animadversion." The story was one of the great scoops of the war.

Butler stormed off to Washington and sought to defend his reputation in testimony before the Joint Congressional Committee on the Conduct of the War. In the midst of his passionate testimony, word reached the hearing room that Fort Fisher had fallen. "Impossible," Butler said. But it was true enough. On January 15, after a tremendous naval barrage, the fort surrendered to Admiral David Dixon Porter's warships and an assaulting force of soldiers and sailors under General Alfred Terry that included two brigades of black troops.

Butler muttered that Grant and Cadwallader had conspired to bring about his fall. He charged that at Grant's request he had appointed Cadwallader a second lieutenant of the Second U.S. Volunteers, so the correspondent wouldn't be drafted into the army. Cadwallader admitted there was a "small element" of truth in the allegation. Butler had made the appointment, but Cadwallader argued neither he nor Grant knew anything about it. Perhaps, Cadwallader speculated, Butler made the appointment "to at least partly silence my dreaded strictures" in the *Herald* about him.

In any event, the appointment was never taken up, and Cadwallader, as we have seen, *was* drafted.

GEORGE ALFRED TOWNSEND was the only war correspondent who seemed to understand that there was money to be made on the lecture circuit (a source of an astonishing amount of cash for a number of modern-day celebrity journalists).

Townsend was born in Georgetown, Delaware, the son of an itinerant Methodist preacher who traveled up and down Maryland's eastern shore and the Delaware peninsula. He covered a number of battles for the *New York Herald* in the early part of the war—he was with McClellan through the Seven Days in June and July of 1862—and then decided to sail to England and cash in on his experiences by undertaking a lecture tour through the provinces. It was a surprising success; hundreds of Englishmen turned out to listen to the twenty-one-year-old American talk about the nation's "sanguinary battlefields."

He came home late in 1864 and took the field as a correspondent for the *New York World.* He was with the army in Virginia when it repulsed Lee's last offensive movement at Fort Stedman the night of March 24–25. He interviewed Phil Sheridan hours after the little cavalryman turned Lee's flank at Five Forks, on Saturday, April 1, 1865. "I am sitting by Sheridan's camp fire," Townsend wrote in the *World,*

> on the spot he has just signalized by the most individual and complete victory of the war. All his veterans are around him, stooping by knots over the bright fagots, to talk together, or stretched upon the leaves of the forest, asleep, with the stains of powder yet upon their faces. . . . A cowed and shivering silence has succeeded the late burst of drums, trumpets, and cannon; the dead are at rest; the captives are quiet; the good cause has won again.

Townsend was impressed with Sheridan's performance. "In this last chapter," he wrote, "Sheridan must take rank as one of the finest military men of our century." Well, it had been a great victory, a *personal* victory, for without Sheridan madly dashing up and down the battlefield on his great black horse, Rienzi, it might never have been won so decisively. "Sheridan himself was there," Townsend said, "short and broad and active, waving his hat, giving orders, seldom out of fire, but never stationary, and close by fell the long yellow locks of [George Armstrong] Custer, sabre extended, fighting like a Viking."

The Confederate defenders were led by the unfortunate George Pickett. He lost all but two thousand of his men, a disaster rivaling the famous charge at Gettysburg. Townsend, with Sheridan's help—he even drew a map for the correspondent—wrote the most complete account of Five Forks, and his story was widely read. But events were moving very rapidly now. After defeating Pickett and capturing Five Forks, Sheridan closed off the last railway tracks into Petersburg. Sensing the end was finally at hand, Grant ordered the entire Army of the Potomac to "attack vigorously all along the line."

Jefferson Davis was worshiping in Saint Paul's Church Sunday morning, April 2, when a messenger slipped down the aisle and handed him a telegram from Lee. All preparations must be made to abandon Richmond tonight, it said. Lee and his staff figured their only chance of survival was to make their way to Danville, Virginia, and join Joe Johnston's army ("Old Joe" was in command of the Army of Tennessee again).

The Confederate army began its withdrawal about an hour after sunset, and the whole army was on its way to Amelia Court House, forty miles away, by midnight. Davis and members of his cabinet boarded a train, and pulled out of the capital, too. They hoped to reconstitute the Confederate government in Danville.

The retreating rebels set fire to the tobacco warehouses and strong winds spread the flames to other buildings, including the national arsenal packed with munitions. It blew up with a huge roar about 2 p.m. The flames consumed every newspaper plant in the city except the one occupied by the *Richmond Whig*. The editor put out an edition blasting Jeff Davis and his government for the "ruthless, useless, wanton" way they handed their "fair city" over to the flames.

Coffin entered the burning capital soon after sunrise on Monday. Troops were "pouring in from all quarters, cheering, swinging their caps, helping themselves to tobacco, rushing upon the double-quick, eager to overtake Lee." It was mid-afternoon when he checked in at the Spottswood Hotel.

"Can you accommodate me with a room?" he asked.

"I reckon we can, sir," the clerk replied, "but like enough you will be burnt out before morning. You can have any room you choose. Nobody here."

Coffin continued:

I registered my name on a page which bore the names of a score of Rebel officers who had left in the morning, and took a room on the first floor, from which I could easily spring to the ground in case the hotel should be again endangered by the fire.

Throwing up the sash I looked out upon the scene. There were swaying chimneys, tottering walls, streets impassable from piles of bricks, stones, and rubbish. Capital Square was filled with furniture, beds, clothing, crockery, chairs, tables, looking-glasses. Women were weeping, children crying. Men stood speechless, haggard, woebegone, gazing at the desolation. . . .

The colored soldiers in Capital Square were dividing their rations with the houseless women and children, giving them hot coffee, sweetened with sugar,—such as they had not tasted for many months.

Coffin had led his story about the surrender of Charleston by noting the old flag was flying over Fort Sumter. His first story from Richmond, dated April 8, began much the same way. "The stars and stripes wave over Petersburg and Richmond tonight," he said. "There is no longer a Confederacy, and the rebel army is broken and demoralized. The whole rebellion tonight has disappeared."

Charles Page was at his desk at the Treasury Department in Washington on Monday morning, April 3, 1865, as the great concluding events of the war began to unfold. Earlier in the war, he wrote, he had "climbed tall trees to see the glinting spires of Richmond,— always careful to keep the body of the tree between my own body and those spires, the former being better calculated to stop bullets."

It was no time to be a Treasury clerk, he concluded. "And so, all-athrob with the thought of seeing Richmond, I set about the requisite preparations, in quite as much haste to get there as was Davis himself to get away from there."

But, here at this moment of dizzying triumph, Stanton's War Department refused to issue passes to reporters seeking to join the conquering troops in Richmond. Page wrote:

> The course of the War Department towards newspapers and their correspondents during the whole war had been marked by petty tyranny, by a caprice that would be funny if it had not been so troublesome, and by the most consummate ignorance, short-sightedness, and folly. Perhaps the conglomerate word "pig-headedness" well sums up my indictment. The procurement of passes for correspondents has always developed on the part of some one or another of its officials with whom one came in contact the above-mentioned quality. . . .
>
> Bearing the past in mind, I was not at all surprised, on calling at the Department at noon on Monday, to find that, from Secretary [Stanton] down, no one had authority to grant passes. "The late successes so changed the circumstances that probably a new policy as to passes would be required," and would I "call tomorrow?" I determined I would not call to-morrow, particularly as I thought I could find an old pass, "By authority of General Grant," bearing the endorsement, last May.

Page set off for the front aboard one of "General Ingall's line of steamers." Joining him aboard the steamer were three other veteran correspondents—the *Cincinnati Gazette*'s Whitelaw Reid, the *New York Times*' Lorenzo Crounse, and the *New York World*'s Richard Colburn. It wasn't exactly the old Bohemian Brigade, but it was at least a formidable squad. The steamer stopped at Grant's depot at City Point (where Crounse, for unfathomable reasons, dropped off), and then continued to Varina Landing, fifteen miles from Richmond.

The three Bohemians were preparing to walk all the way to Richmond when the private carriage of General Weitzel, commanding officer of the occupation forces in the capital, drove up. "It had come down from the city with a party of ladies, escorted by Major Graves, of Weitzel's staff," Page wrote. "Luckily the major was an acquaintance of mine, and our greetings were cut short by my initiating negotiations for seats in the wagon on its return passage. . . . We three, with all the flourish of an old-time stage coach, and to the no small envy of a dozen others, rattled off on the corduroy road."

But the driver refused to drive at night, fearing rebel mines still primed in abandoned fortifications "might be exploded and *kill his horses!* The sublime self-abnegation of that driver, and his great love for his horses, begat our respect." They bedded down in General Weitzel's abandoned headquarters, "ten miles on the hither side of Mecca."

No reporter in the war was better at this kind of writing than Page. Here's how he described the evening he and his fellow Bohemians spent in Weitzel's camp (politically incorrect asides and all):

> We at once established ourselves in Weitzel's own tent, and by the potency of greenbacks soon had the entire population of the village working and contriving for our comfort. One proceeded to cook our supper. A second started a cheerful wood-fire. A third foraged for furniture, producing three cushioned and two rocking chairs, a center table, and three sofas—originally the spoils of deserted houses in the neighborhood. Awaiting supper we spied out the vicinity. On our return Sergeant Ebony informed us that he had brought us . . . our toilet water and towels, but "I'se not got no comb, na' no harbrush, na' no toof-brush," and his surprise was open-mouthed when each of us in turn produced from his own diminutive traveling bag these articles. A supper of coffee, bacon, and pones, alias corndodgers, was to us as nectar and ambrosia. My own subsequent cigar (knowing that my companions never smoked, I took care to offer each a prime Havana from my own store) had a perfume sweeter than odors of Oriental gardens, and indeed a reveried satisfaction more blissful than dreams of hasheesh eaters.

After supper, the Bohemians gathered around the camp fire and began reminiscing about the marches and sieges, battles and campaigns, "of adventures ludicrous or dangerous, ending with one accord in expressions of satisfaction that they were all soon to become things of the past—that now, at last, the war was almost over." But the storytelling, of course, was just beginning; it would go on and on, for years, for the rest of their lives.

They set off at five the next morning for Richmond. Page wrote:

A jolly ride, that. The sun rose with a glory that crimsoned the whole East, and the balm of the air, and the green of the fields, and the buddings of the tree—and we Mecca-bound. It was intoxicating. On the left, now near, . . . was the [James] river. And there were our gunboats above Dutch Gap, above Drury's Bluff, ay, within shot of the farthest house in Richmond. All around, everywhere, were the yellow parapets of the concentric lines, so well defended, . . . the great guns still planted upon them, but the host of the enemy gone. . . .

Up Main Street, and up a long hill,—for Richmond, like Rome, sat upon her more than Seven Hills,—and making a wide detour to avoid the burned district, we reached the Spottswood House.

"Onward *into* Richmond," Page wrote, in his first dispatch from the capital, "and the representative of the Tribune is at the Spottswood."

White Reid wrote his first dispatch celebrating the surrender of Richmond on April 4, and he was grumpier than ever. In his first paragraph, he complained about "years of maundering drivel called Strategy," about "campaigns that wasted the armies of the Republic," about "games of 'blindfold' in which we stumbled about to seek for fit leaders."

For all of that, he admitted, "Washington was aflame with its triumphant glow. The War office was surrounded with a great multitude clamoring for more news, cheering, waving hats, singing 'Rally Round the Flag,' embracing each other, and making the most formidable efforts to embrace—Stanton!"

And then this vignette:

"I forgive ye all yer sins, ye old buzzard!" shouted a jubilant soldier at the Secretary; while Stanton shook him by the hand till the radical and conservative had melted into one in the nervous, spasmodic grin; and tears stood in Stanton's eyes as he turned from one to another to acknowledge the rush of blood-hot congratulations that had suddenly transformed him—revival though it was of the age of miracles—into the most popular man in Washington.

Reid noted in his story that he was joined on the trip from Washington to City Point by Crounse, Page, Colburn, and Coffin. "So we were to meet in the rebel capital," he said, "so many of the 'Old Guard' of Army Correspondents, who four years ago had met in the young romance of the war in the fields of the Southwest."

The band aboard the ship played national airs, "the forts along the Potomac thundered out their stormy salutes, Mount Vernon gleamed in a passing glimpse of sunshine from its green eminence, Acquia Creek was deserted, the Potomac flotilla was idle or absent—its occupation gone—and so we steamed into the night and the Chesapeake."

In one of the most dramatic incidents of the war—any war anywhere—Lincoln entered Richmond on Tuesday, April 4. Coffin was there to greet him. His dispatch, written on the fourth, appeared in the *Boston Morning Journal* on the tenth. He wrote:

> President Lincoln is in Richmond. The hated, despised, ridiculed, the brute, the beast, the baboon of the Yankee nation, as the Richmond editors have named him, is here in the house from which Jeff. Davis fled in haste and terror on Sunday last! The thought sets one's brains in a whirl, and yet it is my business to write coolly of the great events now transpiring in the city.

Coffin was once again at the right place at the right time. "I was standing upon the bank of the [James] river, viewing the scene of devastation, when a boat, pulled by a dozen sailors came up. It contained President Lincoln and his son [Tad, celebrating his twelfth birthday], Admiral Porter," and several other officers. Coffin described the scene:

> Somehow the Negroes on the bank of the river ascertained that the tall man wearing a black hat was President Lincoln. As he approached I said to a colored woman,
>
> "There is the man that made you free."

"What, massa?"

"That is President Lincoln."

"Dat President Lincoln?"

"Yes."

She gazed at him a moment, clapped her hands, and jumped straight up and down. "Glory, glory, glory!" till her voice was lost in the cheering.

Coffin ended his story with these words:

No wonder that President Lincoln who has a child's heart, felt his soul stirred; that the tears came almost to his eyes and he heard the thanksgivings to God and Jesus, and the blessings attended for him from thankful hearts. . . . He came not as a conqueror—not with bitterness in his heart, but with kindness. He came as a friend, to alleviate sorrow and suffering—to rebuild what has been destroyed.

Page watched the proceedings with more detachment.

Crowds—thousands—rushed out for a glimpse of his tall figure, as he walked into the city attended by a few friends and an escort of a score or two of soldiers. The enthusiasm was, however, confined to the negroes, the foreigners, and exceptional Virginia-born citizens. But the joy of the negro knew no bounds. It found expression in whoops, in contortions, in tears, and incessantly in prayerful ejaculations of thanks. The President proceeded to General Weitzel's headquarters, the late residence of Jeff. Davis. I do not imagine he went there for the sake of any petty triumph, but simply because it was the headquarters of the general commanding. Many officers and citizens of Richmond came to pay their respects, after which he rode about the city. He slept on board one of the gunboats, and last night returned to City Point.

Page dined that evening at the Spottswood Hotel. "The chivalry," he wrote,

used to rate this house as we do the Fifth Avenue and the Brevoort, though I do not see how, if it were in New York, it could ever have been considered more than a fourth-rate hotel. The dinner was not inviting. Among the guests were Honorable Roscoe Conkling [a powerful New York politician], Assistant Secretary [of War] Charles A. Dana [former managing editor of the *New York Tribune*] and wife, and C. C. Coffin, of the Boston Journal, who, since the war began, has always managed to be at the point of interest, whether it were Vicksburg, Chattanooga, the Wilderness, Savannah, Charleston, Wilmington, or Richmond. Near Mr. Dana sat [Edward] Pollard, late of the [Richmond] Examiner, though I think neither ex-editor was aware of the other's presence.

The *New York World*'s George Alfred Townsend and Jerome B. Stillson took rooms at the Spottswood, too. Before retiring for the night, they walked through the city. "From the pavements where we walk far off into the gradual curtain of the night, stretches a vista of desolation," Townsend wrote. Overwrote, perhaps. "The hundreds of fabrics, the millions of wealth, that crumbled less than a week ago beneath one fiery kiss, here topple and moulder into rest. A white smoke-wreath rising occasionally enwraps a shattered wall as in a shroud. A gleam of flame shoots a grotesque picture of broken arches and ragged chimneys into the brain. . . . We are among the ruins of half a city."

In Richmond, too, was a correspondent of "Colonel" John W. Forney's *Philadelphia Press.* His name was Thomas Morris Chester, and he was the Civil War's only black correspondent for a major metropolitan daily. He was born in Harrisburg, the Pennsylvania capital, in 1834. His mother had been a slave in Virginia; his father, George, owned a downtown restaurant that served as the city's abolitionist headquarters. Young Chester was educated at a private academy near Pittsburgh and, when he was eighteen, emigrated from the United States to take part in the controversial black colonization program in Liberia. He returned, a disappointed young man, the next year, and completed his education at Thetford Academy in Vermont. The *Philadelphia Press*'s managing editor, John Russell Young, hired him as a war correspondent in the spring of 1864.

The *Press* wasn't a very good newspaper, chiefly because its proprietor, Colonel Forney, was a timid fellow who hated spending very much money on covering the news. Forney was secretary of the U.S.

Senate and spent most of his time in Washington, drinking brandy, smoking cigars, and generally enjoying convivial company. Why this man and this newspaper chose to employ a black war correspondent has never been explained.

Chester became a champion of the black soldiers in the Union army, though their role had never been a major concern of his newspaper. Chester's biographer, R. J. M. Blackett, said that he "paid specific attention to the actions of black soldiers in the field." His reports "highlighted and repeated accounts of bravery and dedication to the cause, for Chester was determined to dispel the myth that blacks would not fight."

Chester wrote under the byline of Rollins. His stunning dispatch began this way:

> Hall of Congress, Richmond, April 4, 1865.
>
> Seated in the Speaker's chair, so long dedicated to treason, but in future to be consecrated to loyalty, I haste to give a rapid sketch of the incidents which have occurred since my last dispatch.

Chester chose not to tell what happened to him while he was writing that story seated in the speaker's chair. Coffin and Page told the story for him. Chester, Coffin said, was "tall, stout, and muscular. God had given him a colored skin, but beneath it lay a courageous heart." While he was writing his dispatch in the speaker's chair in what had been the Confederates' unicameral legislative hall, a paroled Confederate officer entered the room. Coffin described the scene:

> "Come out of there, you black cuss!" shouted the officer, shaking his fist.
>
> Mr. Chester raised his eyes, calmly surveyed the intruder, and went on with his writing.
>
> "Get out of here, or I'll knock your brains out!" the officer bellowed; and rushing up the steps to execute his threat, found himself tumbling chairs and benches, knocked down by one well-planted blow between the eyes.
>
> Mr. Chester sat down as if nothing had happened. The Rebel sprang to his feet and called upon Captain Hutchins of General Devens's [Brigadier General Thomas Devin's] staff for a sword.

"I'll cut the fellow's heart out," said he.

"O no, I guess not. I can't let you have my sword for any such purpose. If you want a fight, I will clear a space here, and see that you have fair play, but let me tell you that you will get a tremendous thrashing," said Captain Hutchins.

The officer left the hall in disgust.

Page told pretty much the same story. He said the rebel officer—"scion of a first family"—ordered "Mr. Chester" to "kim out of thar." When the officer laid hold of him to take him out, "Chester planted a black fist and left a black eye and a prostrate Rebel." Page said Captain Hutchins offered to referee a fair fist fight,

> at the same time expressing the opinion that he [the rebel] would "get thrashed worse than Lee did the other day."
>
> The scion bottled his wrath and skulked away; meanwhile Chester was coolly writing.

In his story, Chester gave a vivid description of the Union army entering Richmond.

> The citizens stood gaping in wonder at the splendidly equipped army marching along under the graceful folds of the old flag. Some waved their hats and women their hands in token of gratitude. The pious old negroes, men and women, indulged in such expressions: "You've come at last;" "We've been looking for you these many days;" "Jesus has opened the way;" "God bless you;" "I've not seen that old flag for years;" "It does my eyes good;" "Have you come to stay?" "Thank God," and similar expressions of exultation.

In Chester's accounts—and in his alone—black men and women did not speak in dialect.

The final drama moved from Richmond to the front parlor of Wilmer McLean's two-story brick house in a hamlet called Appomattox Court House. There, on April 9, 1865, Robert E. Lee met Ulysses S. Grant to negotiate the surrender of his army. Cadwallader was there. He seemed to suggest in his memoirs he was inside Mr. McLean's cottage during the talks. In fact, he was outside, with the rest of the press corps.

"General Lee," he wrote,

was much older in appearance, but soldierly in every way. He was over six feet in height, rather heavily built in these later years of his life, and wearing an elegant costly sword by far too valuable for field service. . . . His manners and bearing were perfect, and stamped him a thoroughbred gentleman in the estimation of all who saw him. His position was a difficult and mortifying one to a proud and sensitive man; yet he comforted himself with that happy blending of dignity and courtesy so difficult to describe, but so befitting to the serious business he had in hand.

Grant, Cadwallader explained,

had been separated from his headquarters train about forty-eight hours. He was compelled to meet Gen. Lee in the ordinary fatigue blouse, a hat somewhat the worse for wear, without a sword of any kind (as he seldom wore one on a march) and with no insignia of rank excepting the Lieutenant-General's shoulder straps on the outside of his blouse to designate him to his own troops. His appearance, never imposing, contrasted strongly with that of Gen. Lee. But his quiet, unassuming deportment rarely failed to impress everyone with his force of character, no matter what his surroundings might chance to be.

The reporters waited impatiently outside Mr. McLean's cottage for news of the surrender talks. One of them was the *New York Tribune*'s Henry Wing, campaigning those last few days with Phil Sheridan. Wing, no longer so innocent or naive, had made an arrangement with a member of Grant's staff. "If Lee did surrender, as was expected, this man, as soon as it was certain, should come out from the house where they were quartered, take off his hat and wipe his forehead three times with a handkerchief," Wing's biographer, Ida Tarbell, wrote. "There were other signals for other contingencies."

When the staff officer signaled that Lee really had surrendered, Wing jumped on his horse—Jesse, undoubtedly—and galloped off to the nearest telegraph station to file his last dispatch as a war correspondent.

He was back home in Litchfield, Connecticut, when he heard the terrible news that his friend, Abraham Lincoln, had been shot at Ford's Theater by an assassin on Good Friday, April 14, 1865. The president died the next morning.

Epilogue

THE CIVIL WAR was the central event in the lives of almost all of the members of the Bohemian Brigade. Yet many of them had lots of other interesting things still to do. More or less in the order in which they appear in this book, here's what happened to some of them.

Bull Run Billy Russell continued his interest in the war from his position as the editor of his own publication, the weekly *Army and Navy Gazette*, read almost exclusively by members of the British armed forces but followed closely by editors of mainstream daily journals.

"The world has never seen anything in the war so slow and fatuous as Grant's recent movements, except it be those of Sherman," he wrote in the *Gazette* on August 8, 1864. "The Northerners have, indeed, lost the day solely owing to the want of average ability in their leaders in the field."

Not many days later, Sherman entered Atlanta.

Good reporters don't always make good pundits, and Russell's performance gave weight to that notion. But good reporters know how to retreat, as if they had never advanced at all. Russell made an amazing retreat in the *Gazette* on September 24. "General Sherman," he said, "has fully justified his reputation as an able and daring soldier; and the field operations by which he won Atlanta are not the least remarkable of the series which carried him from Chattanooga . . . into the heart of Georgia."

Russell took the field again to cover the Franco-Prussian War in 1870–1871 and the Zulu War in 1879–1880. But it wasn't the same. He was never comfortable writing pithy dispatches for the telegraph, preferring those long, discursive "letters" that had served him so well in the Crimean War in 1854 and 1855. He was embarrassed in the Franco-Prussian War by the brilliant work of his rival, Archibald Forbes of the *London Daily News*. George Smalley, who covered only one major battle in the Civil War (Antietam), but covered it so well he earned a considerable reputation, was the *New York Tribune*'s man in London during the war between France and Prussia. In alliance with Forbes's *Daily News*, he created an extraordinary news-reporting machine. He organized the coverage of the war so effectively, "using the cable and telegraph freely, that the paper could claim with some justice the best reporting of the event by any newspaper on either side of the Atlantic," according to his biographer, Joseph J. Mathews. That's hardly fair to the *Daily News*, which, after all, employed Forbes, perhaps the finest war correspondent who ever lived.

Russell visited the United States again in 1881, stopped by the White House, and had a nice chat with the president, James A. Garfield. Russell's wife, Mary, had died in 1867; in 1884, he married Antoinette Malvezzi, a thirty-six-year-old Italian countess. He received a knighthood in 1895 and was inducted into the Royal Victorian Order in 1902. His final years were happy and prosperous. Sir William died in 1907.

The best reporter at the first battle at Bull Run was the *New York World*'s Edmund Clarence Stedman. Like Smalley, though, he was a one-battle correspondent. He left the field to work in the attorney general's office in the capital and then moved to New York City to open his own brokerage office. He churned out dozens of volumes of poetry and criticism, most of it, by modern standards, pretty dreadful. In his day, though, he was a major figure in American literature. He died on January 18, 1908.

Horace Greeley turned over editorial control of the *Tribune* to Whitelaw Reid in 1869. Always ambitious for high office, Greeley ran for president against Grant in 1872 as the candidate of the Liberal

Republicans and the Democrats. He barely campaigned after Mary, the wife he had neglected for so many years, died on October 30, in the final days of the campaign. Grant won, with 3,600,000 votes to Greeley's 2,800,000. The defeat was a crushing blow, and Greeley's mind began to fail. He was put into a home for mental patients and died on November 29. General Grant attended his funeral, riding in a carriage just behind those containing members of the Greeley family.

Reid was a much more predictable editor and he ran the *Tribune* in a thoroughly professional way. He hired good people—Mark Twain became a contributor—and he began to turn a profit. Reid was politically ambitious, too. He was Benjamin Harrison's running mate in 1892; the ticket lost to Grover Cleveland and Adlai Stevenson by fewer than 500,000 votes. Reid was serving as the American ambassador in London when he died on December 15, 1912. His body was returned to the United States in a British warship. He was succeeded as editor by his son, Ogden Mills Reid.

The *New York Herald*'s James Gordon Bennett, born in Scotland in 1795, was the oldest of the three great proprietors. His health began to fail in 1871, when he was seventy-six years old. "In slippered feet and dressing gown, he puttered about his garden, chatted to his collection of birds (each of whom bore the name of some politician, preacher or newspaperman), [and] dozed in the warm summer sun," his biographer, Oliver Carlson, wrote. On May 21, 1872, he summoned Archbishop McCloskey to his bedside, made his confession, and took the church's last sacrament. "He had returned to the church of his fathers," Carlson wrote. He died in his sleep June 1.

No member of "the three graces" died more dramatically than the *New York Times*' Henry Raymond. He spent the evening of June 17, 1869, with friends, and then about ten o'clock excused himself to hold a "political consultation." The consultation he had in mind was with his mistress, the actress Rose Eytinge. About midnight, a carriage pulled up outside Raymond's home at 12 West Ninth Street, and two men who were never identified delivered his unconscious form to the front door. Raymond's daughter, Mary, discovered her father's body at the doorstep and called for help. The victim of a stroke, he died early the next morning. He was only forty-nine years old.

The Civil War reporters—the Bohemians—had a more difficult time adjusting to a nation at peace than the wealthy proprietors. Most of them went home when the war was over and became editors and general-assignment reporters. When they found the time, many of them wrote their memoirs. Franc B. Wilkie, the mischievous western correspondent, returned to Chicago and became something of an institution with Wilbur F. Storey's *Chicago Times*. Storey—Sylvanus Cadwallader's first boss—had always been cheap—"so close," Wilkie said, "that, to save a trifling use of Fabers, he provided tong-like arrangements that would clasp the end of a pencil and permit a further use of it after it had become too short to be held in the fingers." As the years went by, he became increasingly eccentric. His third wife introduced the old man to spiritualism, and his constant companion became the spirit of an Indian girl he called "Little Squaw." Wilkie said, "She followed him everywhere, night and day, giving him suggestions as to the origin of his ill-health, how to dispose of his property, who were his friends and who were his enemies."

The two reporters who escaped from a rebel prison, Albert D. Richardson and Junius Henri Browne, worked on newspapers and wrote books. Richardson wrote a biography of General Grant, though Sylvanus Cadwallader said he supplied most of the details. Browne wrote a book about Horace Greeley.

Henry Villard, Mr. Bennett's star reporter during the early years of the war, married Fanny Garrison, the only daughter of the abolitionist William Lloyd Garrison, in 1866. He first became interested in railroads in 1873, when he became one of the owners of the Oregon & California Railroad Company and the Kansas Pacific Railroad Company. He asked his friends and supporters to contribute to a "blind pool" in 1881 without telling them what the money would be used for. He spent their $20 million and everything he had of his own to win control of the Northern Pacific Railroad. He completed the line in 1883 (but was forced to resign in 1884 when the railroad was unable to pay off huge debts; he resumed control four years later). He acquired control of the *New York Evening Post* in 1881 and declared— splendid example for the present owners to emulate—that he wouldn't interfere with his editors in setting the paper's editorial positions. He kept his word, too. He died on November 12, 1900.

Bradley Sillick Osbon, the outstanding specialist in naval affairs, took to the sea a few times after the war was over. He served briefly in the Mexican navy, taking part in operations against forces supporting the French emperor, Maximilian. He founded a successful magazine, *Nautical Gazette,* and sold it for a tidy profit. As late as 1898, during the Spanish-American War, he served aboard a ship that poked around the Caribbean, looking for enemy warships. He found one or two near Curaçao and filed his observations with the secretary of the navy. From his "snug harbor" at the foot of Twenty-fourth Street, in New York City, he wrote a number of books and pamphlets, including a useful "Handbook of the Navy." As the years went by—he lived to a very old age—his stories became better and better.

Grant's favorite reporter, Cadwallader, headed the *Herald*'s Washington bureau after the war. His wife didn't like Washington and remained behind in Milwaukee, Cadwallader sharing a house in the capital with his old friend (and best source), General Rawlins. He must have seen his wife from time to time because the Cadwalladers had a son in 1866, whom they named Rawlins. Cadwallader left the *Herald* in 1868 and moved back to Milwaukee, accepting appointment as the assistant secretary of state in Madison, the state capital. He was named quartermaster general of the State of Wisconsin in 1874, and preferred to be called General Cadwallader thereafter. Toward the end of his life he and his family moved to Fall River Mills, a remote village in Shasta County, in northern California. He wrote his memoirs there when he was seventy years old.

Members of the Jolly Congress went home, some of them during the war, some after it was over, and wrote books, too. Francis Lawley left the *Times* following the war (when the paper was under attack for the way it had supported the Confederacy) and worked briefly for the *Daily Telegraph.* He spent his remaining years scrabbling to make ends meet. He died on September 18, 1901, a forlorn and forgotten figure. Frank Vizetelly sailed from New York to Ireland in August of 1865 to cover the laying of the Atlantic telegraph cable. He covered the rise of the Mahdi's religious movement in the Sudan in 1883 for the *London Graphic.* He was with Colonel William Hicks's rabble of an army when it was annihilated by the Mahdi's troops in November. His body was never found. A plaque was erected in St. Paul's Cathedral in London on June 16, 1888, memorializing Vizetelly and the other six war correspondents who died in campaigns in the Sudan.

FitzGerald Ross, the Austrian hussar, retired from his regiment in 1868 and returned to England. He remained close to his old colleagues, Heros Von Borcke and James Arthur Lyon Fremantle, and played a key role in making sure the giant Prussian wrote his memoirs. Von Borcke fought with distinction in the Austro-Prussian War in 1866, before retiring to his farm. He returned in triumph to the old Confederacy in September of 1884, but he was already in failing health—he never recovered entirely from his Civil War wounds—and he died shortly after he returned home. The Prussian Justus Scheibert fought in the Franco-Prussian War, and was badly wounded *three* times. He lectured and wrote about military affairs until his death in 1904.

That Christian gentleman, Charles Carleton Coffin, understood the newspaperman's adage—if you've got a good story, recycle it, tell it again and again. Coffin wrote about his Civil War experiences in so many books it is hard to keep count of them all. He published the same books three and four times (one of them, *Four Years of Fighting*, was published in 1866, 1881, 1891, and 1896). He simplified some of his books and made them available to young people. He wrote biographies of Garfield and Lincoln; he wrote novels; he delivered more than two thousand lectures. He was elected to the Massachusetts state assembly in 1884 and the state senate in 1890. He played the organ at the Shawmut Congregational Church in Boston. His friends gathered around as he and his wife celebrated their fiftieth wedding anniversary at their home in Brookline in February of 1896. The most energetic, productive, and reliable of all Civil War correspondents, he died two weeks later, of apoplexy, on March 2, 1896. He was seventy-two years old.

Henry Wing returned to Litchfield, Connecticut, and bought a piece of the local newspaper, the *Enquirer*. He gave that up in 1872 and became a Methodist preacher, spending twenty years of his ministry in Iowa before returning to Connecticut. He was eighty-four years old when he told his story to Ida Tarbell, the muckraker who spent a lifetime puncturing the reputations of famous men. She fell for old Henry Wing, just as Abraham Lincoln had succumbed to the innocent charms of the young Henry Wing. He died at his home in

Bethel, Connecticut, in 1926, just before Ms. Tarbell's book was published. She said he was "clear in mind and serene and cheerful in spirit" to the end.

Charles A. Page, the Civil War's best feature writer, was appointed U.S. consul in Zurich, Switzerland, by President Andrew Johnson in 1865. Zurich, he found, was surrounded by rich dairy farms. He organized the Anglo-Swiss Milk Company in 1866 to sell condensed milk in Great Britain and the United States. It was a huge success, but Page didn't live long to enjoy it. He died in London in May of 1873. He was thirty-five years old.

Thomas Morris Chester, the war's only black correspondent, was an extraordinary man. After the war, he traveled to London and took a law degree at the Middle Temple. He toured Europe as a sort of roving ambassador for the Liberian government, dining one evening in Moscow with the czar of all the Russias. He returned to the United States in 1871 and gave a series of lectures in Kentucky and Louisiana. In May of 1873, he was appointed a brigadier general in the Fourth Brigade, First Division, of the Louisiana state militia. In 1883, he became president of the Wilmington, Wrightsville, and Onslow Railroad in North Carolina, owned entirely by blacks. But the company couldn't raise enough money to build the railroad, and it went out of business the next year.

In his final years, a discouraged and frustrated Chester practiced law in New Orleans; his wife taught at an all-black school. He died at his mother's home in Harrisburg on September 30, 1892, and was buried in a segregated graveyard. He was fifty-eight years old.

The *New York World*'s George Alfred Townsend became something of a literary sensation following the war with the publication of his best-known novel, *The Entailed Hat, or Patty Cannon's Times*, the story of an evil woman who kidnapped free Negroes in Delaware and sold them into slavery in Virginia. With the proceeds from his literary output Townsend bought one hundred acres of wooded land in Maryland at Crampton's Gap on South Mountain, scene of the fighting that opened the bloody battle of Antietam. He built an entire cluster of unusual buildings and called the complex Gapland.

But he also built nearby a fifty-foot-high stone monument commemorating most of the men who covered the Civil War for the

George Alfred Townsend's memorial to the Bohemian
Brigade near Antietam Battlefield.

North. "In shape," Lida Mayo, the editor of his memoirs, wrote, "it
is like the gateway to a castle. On a Moorish arch are superimposed
three Roman arches and a turret. Flanking the main arch are marble
tablets containing the names of one hundred and fifty-seven Civil
War correspondents and artists."

Townsend collected $5,000 to build it from dozens of wealthy
Americans, including J. P. Morgan, George Pullman, Joseph Pulitzer,
John Wanamaker, and Thomas A. Edison. It stands there today, lonely
and neglected, reaching out to the occasional tourist who stops by to
look at it in wonder and amazement. It is the only monument ever
built to honor the memory of the Bohemian Brigade.

Bibliography

Standard Works

Battles and Leaders of the Civil War. Edited by Robert Underwood Johnson and Clarence Clough Buel. 4 vols. New York: 1884–1887.

Catton, Bruce. *The Centennial History of the Civil War:*

———. *The Coming Fury.* New York: Doubleday, 1961.

———. *Terrible Swift Sword.* New York: Doubleday, 1963.

———. *Never Call Retreat.* New York: Doubleday, 1965.

Foote, Shelby. *The Civil War: A Narrative:*

———. *Fort Sumter to Perryville.* New York: Vintage Books, 1958.

———. *Fredericksburg to Meridian.* New York: Vintage Books, 1963.

———. *Red River to Appomattox.* New York: Vintage Books, 1974.

McPherson, James. *Battle Cry of Freedom: The Civil War Era.* New York: Oxford, 1988.

War of the Rebellion: A Compilation of the Official Records of the Union and Confederate Armies. 128 vols. Washington, D.C.: 1880–1901.

War of the Rebellion: A Compilation of the Official Records of the Union and Confederate Navies. 30 vols. Washington, D.C.: 1894–1922.

Manuscripts and Papers

James Gordon Bennett Papers, Library of Congress
Sylvanus Cadwallader Papers, Library of Congress
Horace Greeley Papers, Library of Congress
DeBenneville Randolph Keim Papers, Library of Congress
Thomas Knox Court-Martial Papers, File LL554, National Archives
Whitelaw Reid Papers, Library of Congress

Newspapers

Boston Daily Journal

Charleston Daily Courier

Chicago Daily Tribune

Chicago Times

Cincinnati Daily Gazette

Cincinnati Enquirer

New York Daily Tribune

New York Herald

New York Times

New York World

Philadelphia Inquirer

Philadelphia Press

Savannah Republican

Times (London)

Books and Articles Written by Civil War Correspondents and Editors

Brooks, Noah. *Mr. Lincoln's Washington.* Edited by P. J. Staudenraus. New York: Thomas Yoseloff, 1967.

Browne, Junius Henri. *Four Years in Secessia.* Hartford, Conn.: O. D. Case, 1865.

Cadwallader, Sylvanus. *Three Years with Grant.* Edited by Benjamin P. Thomas. New York: Alfred A. Knopf, 1955.

Chester, Thomas M. *Black Civil War Correspondent: His Dispatches from the Virginia Front.* Edited by R. J. M. Blackett. Baton Rouge: Louisiana State University Press, 1989.

Coffin, Charles Carleton. *The Boys of '61, or Four Years of Fighting.* Boston: n.p., 1881.

———. *Four Years of Fighting: Personal Observations with the Army and Navy.* 1866. Reprint, Boston: Estes and Lauriat, 1881.

———. *Marching to Victory.* New York: n.p., 1888.

———. *My Days and Nights on the Battlefield.* Boston: n.p., 1887.

Crounse, Lorenzo Livingston. "The Army Correspondent." *Harper's New Monthly Magazine* (October 1863).

Dana, Charles A. *Recollections of the Civil War.* New York: D. Appleton, 1898.

Dawson, Francis W. *Reminiscences of Confederate Service.* Edited by Ben Wiley. Baton Rouge: Louisiana State University Press, 1993.

De Fontaine, Felix Gregory. "The First Day of Real War." *Southern Bivouac* (July 1886).

———. *Marginalia, or Gleanings from an Army Notebook.* Columbia, S.C.: Steam Power Press, 1864.

———. Scrapbook. University of South Carolina, 1861–1864.

———. *Shoulder to Shoulder: Army Letters of "Personne," 1861–1865.* Charleston, S.C.: The XIX Century, 1896–1897.

Fremantle, James Arthur Lyon. *The Fremantle Diary.* Edited by Walter Lord. Boston: Little Brown, 1954.

Greeley, Horace. *Recollections of a Busy Life.* New York: J. R. Ford, 1868.

Knox, Thomas W. *Camp-Fire and Cotton Field: Southern Adventure in Time of War.* New York: Da Capo Press, 1969.

Osbon, Bradley Sillick. *A Sailor of Fortune: Personal Memoirs of Captain B. S. Osbon.* Edited by Albert Bigelow Paine. New York: McClure, Phillips, 1906.

Page, Charles A. *Letters of a War Correspondent*. Edited by James R. Gilmore. Boston: L. C. Page, 1899.

Reid, Whitelaw. *Ohio in the War: Her Statesmen, Generals, and Soldiers*. 2 vols. Cincinnati: Moore, Wilstach and Baldwin, 1868.

———. *A Radical View: The "Agate" Dispatches of Whitelaw Reid, 1861–1865*. Edited by James G. Smart. 2 vols. Memphis: Memphis State University, 1976.

Richardson, Albert Deane. *The Secret Service, the Field, the Dungeon, and the Escape*. Freeport, N.Y.: Books for Librarians Press, 1971.

Ross, FitzGerald. *Cities and Camps of the Confederate States*. Edited by Richard Barksdale Harwell. Urbana: University of Illinois Press, 1958.

Russell, William H. *My Diary, North and South*. Edited by Fletcher Pratt. New York: Harper & Brothers, 1954.

———. "Recollections of the Civil War in North America." *North American Review* (February–June, 1868).

———. *William Howard Russell's Civil War: Private Diary and Letters, 1861–1862*. Edited by Martin Crawford. Athens: University of Georgia Press, 1992.

Scheibert, Justus. *Seven Months in the Rebel States during the North American War, 1863*. Edited by William Stanley Hoole. Tuscaloosa, Ala.: Confederate Publishing, 1958.

Shanks, William F. G. "How We Get Our News." *Harper's New Monthly Magazine* (March 1867).

———. *Personal Recollections of Distinguished Generals*. New York: Harper & Brothers, 1866.

Smalley, George W. *Anglo-American Memories*. New York: n.p., 1911.

———. "Chapters on Journalism." *Harper's New Monthly Magazine* (August 1894).

———. "Notes on Journalism." *Harper's New Monthly Magazine* (July 1898).

Stedman, Edmund Clarence. *Life and Letters of Edmund Clarence Stedman*. 2 vols. Edited by Laura Stedman and George Gould. New York: Moffat, Yard, 1910.

Swinton, William. *Campaigns of the Army of the Potomac*. New York: n.p., 1866.

Taylor, Benjamin S. *Pictures of Life in Camp and Field*. Chicago: S. C. Griggs, 1875.

Townsend, George Alfred. "Campaigning with General Pope." *Cornhill* (December 1862).

———. *Campaigns of a Non-Combatant and His Romaunt Abroad during the War*. Edited by Lida Mayo. New York: Blelock, 1866.

Villard, Henry. "Army Correspondence." *Nation* (July–August 1865).

———. *Memoirs of Henry Villard, Journalist and Financier, 1835–1900*. 2 vols. Boston: Houghton Mifflin, 1904.

Von Borcke, Heros. *Memoirs of the Confederate War for Independence*. 2 vols. New York: Peter Smith, 1866.

Wilkie, Franc B. *Pen and Powder*. Boston: Ticknor, 1888.

———. *Personal Reminiscences of Thirty-five Years of Journalism*. Chicago: n.p., 1891.

———. *Walks about Chicago, 1871–1881, and Army and Miscellaneous Sketches*. Chicago: n.p., 1882.

Wing, Henry. *When Lincoln Kissed Me: A Story of the Wilderness Campaign*. New York: Eaton and Mains, 1913.

Young, John Russell. *Men and Memories.* New York: F. Tennyson Neely, 1901.
————. "Men Who Reigned: Bennett, Greeley, Raymond, Prentice, Forney." *Lippincott's Monthly* (February 1893).

Books about Correspondents and Editors

Adams, Ephraim Douglas. *Great Britain and the American Civil War.* 2 vols. New York: Russell and Russell, 1924.

Andrews, J. Cutler. *The North Reports the Civil War.* Pittsburgh: University of Pittsburgh Press, 1955.

————. *The South Reports the Civil War.* Pittsburgh: University of Pittsburgh Press, 1970.

Atkins, John Black. *The Life of Sir William Howard Russell.* London: John Murray, 1911.

Blacket, R. J. M. *Thomas Morris Chester, Black Civil War Correspondent.* Baton Rouge: Louisiana State University Press, 1989.

Brogan, Hugh. *The Times Reports the American Civil War.* London: Times Books, 1975.

Brown, Francis. *Raymond of the Times.* New York: W. W. Norton, 1951.

Bullard, Frederic Lauriston. *Famous War Correspondents.* New York: Beekman, 1974.

Carlson, Oliver. *The Man Who Made the News: James Gordon Bennett.* New York: Duell, Sloan and Pearce, 1942.

Cortissoz, Royal. *The Life of Whitelaw Reid.* 2 vols. New York: Charles Scribner's Sons, 1921.

Fahrney, Ralph. *Horace Greeley and the Tribune in the Civil War.* Cedar Rapids, Iowa: Torch Press, 1936.

Fermer, Douglas. *James Gordon Bennett and the New York Herald.* New York: St. Martin's Press, 1986.

Fiske, Stephen Ryder. "Gentlemen of the Press." *Harper's New Monthly Magazine* (February 1863).

Goldsmith, Adolph G. "Reporting the Civil War: Union Army Press Relations." *Journalism Quarterly* 33 (1956).

Griffis, William Elliott. *Charles Carleton Coffin, War Correspondent, Traveler, Author, and Statesman.* Boston: Estes and Lauriat, 1898.

Hale, William Harlan. *Horace Greeley, Voice of the People.* New York: Harper & Brothers, 1950.

Harrison, Constance Cary. *Recollections Gay and Grave.* New York: Charles Scribner's, 1911.

Hindes, Ruthanna. *George Alfred Townsend.* Wilmington, Del.: privately published, 1946.

Hodgson, Pat. *The War Illustrators.* New York: Macmillan, 1977.

Hoole, William Stanley. *Lawley Covers the Confederacy.* Tuscaloosa, Ala.: Confederate Publishing, 1964.

————. *Vizetelly Covers the Confederacy.* Tuscaloosa, Ala.: Confederate Publishing, 1957.

Iseley, Jeter Allen. *Horace Greeley and the Republican Party.* Princeton, N.J.: Princeton University Press, 1947.

Lorr, Ella. *Foreigners in the Confederacy*. Gloucester, Mass.: Peter Smith, 1965.

Malone, Henry T. "Atlanta Journalism during the Confederacy." *Georgia Historical Quarterly* (September 1953).

Mathews, Joseph J. *George W. Smalley: Forty Years a Correspondent*. Chapel Hill: University of North Carolina Press, 1973.

Parton, James. "The *New York Herald.*" *North American Review* (April 1866).

Peckham, Harry Houston. *Gotham Yankee: A Biography of William Cullen Bryant*. New York: Vantage, 1952.

Seitz, Don Carlos. *Horace Greeley, Founder of the New York Tribune*. Indianapolis: Bobbs-Merrill, 1928.

Sisler, George. "The Arrest of a *Memphis Daily Appeal* War Correspondent on Charges of Treason." *Western Tennessee Historical Society Papers*, 11 (1957).

Tarbell, Ida M. *A Reporter for Lincoln: The Story of Henry E. Wing, Soldier and Newspaperman*. New York: Macmillan, 1927.

Vizetelly, Henry. *Glances Back through Seventy Years*. 2 vols. London: Kegan Paul, Trench, Turner, 1893.

Wolseley, Garnet J. *The Story of a Soldier's Life*. London: Archibald Constable, 1903.

Wykoff, George S. "Charles Mackay, England's Forgotten Civil War Correspondent." *South Atlantic Quarterly* (January 1927).

Books and Articles about the War and about the Press

Anderson, Bern. *By Sea and by River: The Naval History of the Civil War*. New York: Alfred A. Knopf, 1962.

Andrews, J. Cutler. "The Pennsylvania Press during the Civil War." *Pennsylvania History* (January 1942).

———. "The Press Reports the Battle of Gettysburg." *Pennsylvania History* (April 1964).

Baker, Thomas H. "Refugee Newspaper: The *Memphis Daily Appeal.*" *Journal of Southern History* (August 29, 1963).

Bates, David Homer. *Lincoln in the Telegraph Office*. New York: Century, 1907.

Bosse, David. *Civil War Newspaper Maps*. Baltimore: Johns Hopkins University Press, 1993.

Crozier, Emmett. *Yankee Reporters*. New York: Oxford University Press, 1956.

Daniel, John M. *The Richmond Examiner during the War*. New York: n.p., 1868.

Dorsett, Lyle W. "The Problem of Ulysses S. Grant's Drinking During the Civil War." *Hayes Historical Journal* (Fall 1983).

Fellman, Michael. *Citizen Sherman: A Life of W. T. Sherman*. New York: Random House, 1995.

Grant, Ulysses S. *Personal Memoirs*. New York: Library of America, 1990.

Howarth, Stephen. *To Shining Sea: A History of the United States Navy, 1775–1991*. New York: Random House, 1991.

Hudson, Frederic. *Journalism in the United States, from 1690 to 1972*. New York: Harper & Row, 1969.

Joseph, Alvin M. *The Civil War in the American West.* New York: Alfred A. Knopf, 1991.

Knightley, Phillip. *The First Casualty: From the Crimea to Vietnam: The War Correspondent as Hero, Propagandist, and Myth Maker.* New York: Harcourt Brace Jovanovich, 1975.

Lewis, Lloyd. *Sherman: Fighting Prophet.* New York: Harcourt, Brace and World, 1960.

Marszalek, John. *Sherman's Other War: The General and the Civil War Press.* Memphis: Memphis State University Press, 1981.

Mathews, Joseph J. *Reporting the Wars.* Minneapolis: University of Minnesota Press, 1957.

McNamara, John. *Extra! U.S. War Correspondents in Action.* Boston: Houghton Mifflin, 1945.

Nevins, Allan. *The Evening Post: A Century of Journalism.* New York: Russell and Russell, 1922.

Randall, J. G. "The Newspaper Problem in Its Bearing Upon Military Secrecy during the Civil War." *American Historical Review* (January 1918).

Sandburg, Carl. *Abraham Lincoln: The War Years.* 4 vols. New York: Harcourt, Brace, 1939.

Sass, Herbert Ravenel. *Outspoken: 150 Years of the News and Courier.* Columbia: University of South Carolina Press, 1953.

Sherman, W. T. *Memoirs.* New York: Library of America, 1990.

Sloan, Edward William, III. *Benjamin Franklin Isherwood, Naval Engineer.* Annapolis, Md.: U.S. Naval Institute Press, 1965.

Starr, Louis M. *Bohemian Brigade: Civil War Newsmen in Action.* New York: Alfred A. Knopf, 1954.

Thompson, Robert Luther. *Wiring a Continent.* New York: Arno Press, 1972.

Thompson, W. Fletcher, Jr. *The Image of War: The Pictorial History of the American Civil War.* New York: Thomas Yoseloff, 1959.

Weisberger, Bernard. *Reporters for the Union.* Boston: Little, Brown, 1953.

West, Richard. "The Navy and the Press during the Civil War." *U.S. Naval Institute Proceedings* (January 1937).

Wilson, Quintus C. "Confederate Press Association: A Pioneer Press Agency." *Journalism Quarterly* (June 1949).

Index

Aberdeen, Lord, 2
Alexander, George W., 164
Alexander, Peter Wellington, 25, 34, 198–200
Alexandria, Va., ix, 232, 236
Anderson, Finley, 249
Anderson, Robert, 92–94, 112
Andrews, J. Cutler, x, 38, 175, 204
Antietam, battle of, 200, 221, 279, 284
Appler, Jesse J., 122
Appomattox Court House, Va. surrender at, 275–76
Archer, James, 210
Argentine revolution, 89–90
Army and Navy Gazette, 278
Atkins, John Black, 8–9
Atlanta, Ga., 160–62, 254

Baltic (Union ship), 93, 94
Baltimore, Md., 9, 19, 32, 186, 187, 206, 213, 256
Banks, Nathaniel P., 136, 140, 227
Bartow, Francis, 24
Battles and Leaders of the Civil War, 122–23
Beaman, George W., 69

Beauregard, Pierre Gustave Toutant, 11
ban on battlefield reporters, 34
and Bull Run, 18, 21, 22–23, 26
and Shiloh, 122, 130, 132
Bee, Barnard, 24–25
Bennett, Henrietta Cream, 53
Bennett, James Gordon, xi, 43, 44, 56, 245, 255
character and career of, 49–55
in Charleston, 49–51
and Gettysburg coverage, 204
and Keim, 177
and Knox court-martial, 153
message to Lincoln, 54–55
news philosophy, 21
Osbon as naval correspondent, 87, 94
postwar activities, 280–81
view of war, 58
and Villard, 37, 53–55, 113, 200
See also New York Herald
Bennett, James Gordon, Jr., 53, 54–55
Benton, Thomas Hart, 61
Blackett, R. J. M., 274
Blackford, William W., 194
Blackwood's (magazine), 186
Blair, Frank Jr., 139, 151

Blair, Montgomery, 151
Bohemian Brigade, 66, 78, 81, 205
  and fall of Richmond, 268–69
  first deployment of, 36
  first formal appearance, 69
  members' imprisonment and escape,
    69, 156–73
  members' postwar activities, 144,
    278, 281, 285
  spirit of, 59–60, 69–73
  See also names of specific members
Bollmeyer, J. F., 125
Boston, Mass., 49, 260, 283
Boston Morning Journal, x, 41, 73, 80
  Bull Run headline, 31–32
  and fall of Richmond, 271, 273
  and Fredricksburg, 200
  and Gettysburg, 204
  and Savannah relief, 260–61
Brady, John, 263
Bragg, Braxton, 120, 160–61, 209, 223,
  237–38
Brandy Station engagement, 208
Breckenridge, John C., 120, 129, 168
Brisbane, Arthur, 46
Brogan, Hugh, 2
Brooklyn (Union ship), 101, 105
Broome, John, 106
Brown, John, 262
Browne, Junius Henri, 69, 71, 77,
  78–79, 84–85
  imprisonment and escape, 156–73,
    249
  postwar activities, 281
  and Vicksburg campaign, 137, 174
Brownell, Francis, ix
Brownson, Edward P. (Ned), 255
Brownson, Orestes A., 255
Brownson, Sarah, 255
Buchanan, James, 78
Buckner, Simon Bolivar, 78, 79
Bucyrus Forum (newspaper), 125
Buell, Don Carlos, 116, 120, 122,
  131–33
Buford, John, 210
Bulkley, Solomon T., 164

Bull, O. A., 161
Bull Run, first battle at, 19–42, 55,
  63–64, 73, 80, 96
  details of, 22–28, 33, 34, 38–40
  New York editors' reaction, 43–44
  Raymond and, 28, 36, 38–39, 56–57
  reporters at, 25, 33–42, 48, 202
  reporting errors, 31–33
  Russell and, 20–23, 25–31, 123, 185
  Sherman at, 24, 39, 112
  sketched by Vizetelly, 187
  Stedman's as best coverage, 279
Bull Run, second battle at, 142
Burnside, Ambrose E., 125, 142, 175,
  187, 243
  and Fredericksburg, 195, 200–202
  and Petersburg, 253
Butler, Benjamin F., 100, 136, 226,
  262–65
Byington, A. Homer, 216–17

Cadwallader, Mary Paul, 257, 282
Cadwallader, Sylvanus, 240, 254–59
  and Crapsey incident, 251–52
  and end of war, 275–76
  and Grant drinking incident,
    178–83
  and last campaign, 262–65
  and Missionary Ridge, 237–40
  postwar activities, 281, 282
  on Swinton, 254–55
  and Vicksburg, 174–78
  and Wilderness, 241–46
Cairo, Ill., 18, 19, 71–73, 85, 133, 140,
  204
Calhoun, John C., 49
Cameron, Simon, 114–15, 117
Carleton, Edmund, 254
Carlson, Oliver, 49, 53, 280
Carondelet (Union ship), 74, 77–78
Carrick's Ford, battle at, 126–27
Cary, Constance, 13, 189–91
Castle Thunder (Richmond prison), 164
Catton, Bruce, 120, 216, 227, 238–39
Cayuga (Union ship), 103, 107
Chamberlain, Joshua, 216

Chambersburg, Pa., 205, 208–9
Champion Hill, battle of, 177
Chancellorsville, battle of, 203, 207, 208, 211–12
Chapman, Frank G., 78, 240, 243
Charleston, S.C., 6, 11–12, 16
  Bennett's time in, 49–51
  fall of, 261–62, 267, 273
Charleston Daily Courier, 11, 25, 34, 49, 199
Charleston Mercury, 34
Chase, Salmon P., 55
Chattanooga, battle of, 223, 237–39, 250, 273, 278
Chattanooga, Tenn., 223, 237, 245
Chesnut, James, 11
Chesnut, Mary, 11
Chester, George, 273
Chester, Thomas Morris (Rollins), 273–75, 284
Chicago Times, 174–75, 177–78, 237, 240, 281
Chicago Tribune, 142–44, 175
Chickamauga, battle of, 161, 223
Chickasaw Bayou, battle of, 139–41, 144
Cincinnati (Union ship), 74
Cincinnati, Ohio, 125, 133, 144, 206
Cincinnati Commercial, 70, 125
  and Sherman "insanity," 110, 113, 117–18
Cincinnati Daily Gazette, x, 40, 69, 70, 172, 268
  Reid as correspondent, 125–27, 252
  reporter's imprisonment, 165
  and Sherman's "insanity," 118–19
Cincinnati Enquirer, 125
Cincinnati Times, 239
Circleville Watchman, 125
City Point, Va., 263, 268, 271, 272
Clay, Henry, 111
Cleveland, Grover, 123, 280
Cobb, Thomas R. R., 196, 199–200
Coe, Juan Halsted, 90
Coffin, Charles Carleton, x, 25, 41, 73, 80–81

and fall of Richmond, 266–67, 271–74
and Fredericksburg, 200–201
and Gettysburg, 204–6, 210, 212–13, 216, 220–21
and Petersburg, 254
postwar activities, 283
and Savannah relief, 260–62
Colburn, Richard T., 69, 153
  capture and imprisonment, 156–63
  and fall of Richmond, 268, 271
  and Vicksburg campaign, 174
Cold Harbor, battle of, 246, 249, 250, 252
Columbus (Ohio) *Crisis*, 125
Colvill, William, 216
Confederate Press Association, 198
Confederate States Penitentiary. *See* Salisbury prison
Conkling, Roscoe, 273
Continental (Union ship), 137, 148, 151
Corinth, Miss., 120–22, 136
Crampton's Gap, Md., 284
Crapsey, Edward, 243, 250–52
Crawford, Martin, 30
Crimean War, 1–2, 17, 111, 205, 279
Crounse, Lorenzo Livingston, 38, 207, 216, 268, 271
Crump's Landing, 127, 128
Curtis, Samuel R., 81–82
Custer, George Armstrong, 266

Dana, Charles A., 43, 48–49, 273
  and Grant drinking incident, 178, 180
  and Wing, 232, 235
Dandridge, Stephen, 192
Danville, Va., 266
Davis, J. C. Bancroft, 9, 10, 11, 18
Davis, Jefferson, 14–15, 34, 126, 163
  and fall of Richmond, 266, 268, 271–72
Davis, Joseph, 210
Davis, Varina Jefferson, 14
Davis, William E., 165–73
Dayton Empire, 125

DeCourcy, John F., 139, 142
de Fontaine, Felix Gregory, 11, 25, 34, 198
Delane, John Thadeus, 2–3, 5, 8, 20, 29, 186
Devin, Thomas, 274
Dickens, Charles, 56, 190
Dickinson, Anna E., 123
Diligence (steamboat), 178–80
Dill, Benjamin F., 160–61
Dorsett, Lyle W., 182–83
Douglas, Stephen A., 60
Drayton, Percival, 96–98
Drayton, Thomas F., 96, 97
Dubuque Herald, 60, 64, 65
Duff, W. L., 241
Duncan, David Grieve, 34
Du Pont, Samuel F., 95–97

Eads, James B., 74
Early, Jubal, 212, 217
Edison, Thomas A., 285
Ellis, Dan, 170–72
Ericsson, John, 87
Essex (Union ship), 74, 75
Evans, Nathan G., 23–24
Ewell, Richard S., 34, 211–12, 215
Ewing, Maria Boyle, 111
Ewing, Philemon, 118
Ewing, Thomas, 111–12
Ewing, Thomas, Jr., 113
Eytinge, Rose, 280

Farragut, David G., 100–103, 105–8, 254
Fayel, William, 82
Fellman, Michael, 117
Field's Ford, Va., 230
Fitzpatrick, J. C., 243
Five Forks, battle of, 265–66
Floyd, John B., 78, 79
Foote, Andrew H., 73, 74, 77, 79
Foote, Shelby, 81, 103, 105, 182
    on Fredericksburg, 194
    on Gettysburg, 219
    on Petersburg, 253

on Shiloh, 120, 130
Forbes, Archibald, 279
Forney, John W., 153, 273–74
Forrest, Nathan Bedford, 78, 79, 136, 136–37
Forsyth, action at, 62–63
Fort Beauregard, 96
Fort Donelson, 73, 74, 119, 143, 213, 240
    action at, 77–81, 85
    Forrest's escape from, 79, 136
Fort Fisher, 263–64
Fort Henry, 73–77, 81, 119
Fort Jackson, 100, 105
Fortress Monroe, 98–99
Fort Saint Philip, 100
Fort Stedman, 265
Fort Sumter, 6, 107, 109
    campaign, 9–10, 12, 15, 92–94, 112
    retaken by Union, 261, 267
Fort Walker, 96–98
Forty-eighth Pennsylvania, 253
Foster, F. C., 143
Fourier, Charles, 46
Fourteenth Ohio, 126–27
Four Years of Fighting (Coffin), 283
Fox, Gustavus, 92–94, 95, 109
Franco-Prussian War, 279, 283
Frank Leslie's Illustrated Newspaper, 69, 70, 85, 144
Franklin, Benjamin, 49
Franklin, William B., 195
Frederick, Md., 206
Fredericksburg, battle of, 142, 143, 194–97, 199–202, 221, 225, 250
Fredericksburg, Va., 186, 195, 243–44
Fremantle, James Arthur Lyon, 184, 189
    and Gettysburg, 208–10, 214–15, 217–18, 221
    postwar activities, 283
Frémont, Jessie Benton, 61
Frémont, John C., 61, 65, 67–70
French, Francis M., 88
Fuqua, J. A., 166

Garfield, James A., 279, 283
Garibaldi, Giuseppe, 187, 193
Garnett, Robert S., 126–27
Garrison, Fanny, 37, 281
Garrison, William Lloyd, 37, 281
Gay, Sydney Howard, 216
Gettysburg, battle of, 185, 204–22, 223, 250–51, 266
Gettysburg Address, 221
Gladstone, William E., 185
Glenn, Joseph, 40, 70
Governor (Union transport), 96
Graham, Sylvester, 45
Graham, "Wash," 180–81
Grant, Frederick, 182
Grant, Julia, 182
Grant, Ulysses S., 20, 73–77, 79
  alcoholism of, 182–83
  and Cadwallader, 178–83, 240, 257, 282
  and Chattanooga, 237–39
  and Cold Harbor, 250
  final campaign, 261–64, 266
  and Fort Henry attack, 74–75
  and Isham arrest, 176
  and Knox court-martial, 151, 154, 155
  and Lee surrender, 275–76
  managerial talent, 195
  and Petersburg, 252–53
  presidential campaign, 278–82
  Richardson relationship, 76–77
  Sherman friendship, 119–20
  and Shiloh, 122–23, 127–28, 130, 132–33
  as supreme commander, 226, 251, 254–55
  and Vicksburg, 135–37, 140, 163, 174, 208, 223
  and Wilderness, 227–29, 232–35, 240–43, 245, 248
  Yazoo drinking incident, 177–83
Greeley, Horace, xi, 123, 178, 200, 202, 226
  and Bull Run, 23, 43–44
  and capture of correspondents, 156, 159, 174
  career and character of, 44–48
  and Gettysburg coverage, 204
  postwar activities, 279–81
  and Raymond, 55, 56
  Russell's impression of, 6
  view of war, 58
  See also New York Tribune
Greeley, Mary Cheney, 47, 280
Greene, George, 216
Grenada Appeal (newspaper), 148
Grey, T. C., 224
Greyhound (Confederate ship), 260
Griffis, William Elliott, 261

Hale, William Harlan, 47
Halleck, Henry, 73, 116–17, 119–20, 126, 136
Halstead, Murat, 110, 113, 117–18, 125, 146
Hammond, J. H., 142, 144, 149
Hampton Roads, Va., 95, 98
Hancock, Winfield Scott, 225, 247, 255
Hardee, William J., 120
Harper, Robert S., 125
Harper's Ferry, Va., 23, 193
Harper's Illustrated Weekly, 44–45, 69, 98, 99
Harriet Lane (Union ship), 92–93, 108
Harrison, Benjamin, 123, 280
Harrison, Burton, 189
Hartford (Union ship), 101, 103, 105–7
Hayes, Joseph, 247
Hayes, Rutherford B., 182
Hayes Historical Journal, 182
Heintzelman, Samuel P., 23
Heisler, George, 105
Hendricks, S. A., 164
Heth, Henry, 210–12, 217
Hickok, Wild Bill, 82
Hicks, William, 187, 282
Hill, A. P., 210–11, 215, 220
Hill, Henry, 39
Holly Springs, Miss., 136, 140, 149
Hood, John Bell, 209, 215, 254
Hooker, Joseph, 195, 203, 207, 209, 237
Hoole, Wm. Stanley, 186

House, Edward Howard, 36–39, 43
Howard, Oliver O., 212–13, 221
Hudson, Frederic, 56, 94, 98, 100, 153, 240, 245
Hunt, Henry, 221
Hunter, David, 23, 39
Hurlbut, Stephen A., 122, 129–30

Illustrated London News, xii, 26, 184, 187, 194
Iroquois (Union ship), 86, 101
Isely, Jeter Allen, 45
Isham, Warren P., 175–76
Isherwood, Benjamin Franklin, 95
Itasca (Union ship), 102

Jackson, James W., ix
Jackson, Miss., 75, 149, 160–61
Jackson, Stonewall, 20, 24–25, 136, 142, 195, 203
Jefferson City, Mo., 69, 70, 71
Jesse (horse), 229–31, 235–36, 276
Jewett, Helen, 52–53
John Adams (Union ship), 86
Johnson, Andrew, 284
Johnston, Albert Sidney, 73, 120, 122, 129–30, 227
Johnston, Bradley T., 192
Johnston, Joseph, 23, 26, 32, 266
Jolly Congress, 184–98
   backgrounds of members, 184–89
   and Fredericksburg, 194–98
   and Gettysburg, 185, 204, 208, 213
   infatuation with "Lost Cause," xii, 184–85
   members' postwar activities, 282–83
   See also names of specific members
Joslyn, Ed, 71

Kees, John W., 125
Keim, DeBenneville Randolph, 144, 177
Kelly's Ford, Va., 230
Kennebec (Union ship), 101
Kershaw, Joseph, 200
Keyes, Erasmus, 24, 39

Knox, Thomas W., 62–64, 66–69
   with Curtis, 81, 82–84
   Sherman's arrest and court-martial of, 62, 110, 145–55, 161
   and Vicksburg campaign, 137, 139, 144

Lawley, Francis Charles, 184–90, 192–94, 208
   background and early career of, 185–86
   and Fredericksburg, 196–97, 202
   and Gettysburg, 204–11, 213–19, 221
   and "Lost Cause", xii
   postwar activities, 282
Lawley-Thompson, Paul Bielby, 185
Lee, Fitzhugh, 190–91, 244
Lee, Robert E., 20, 142, 183, 184, 191, 198, 224
   and Cold Harbor, 250
   and fall of Richmond, 266
   final campaign, 265, 267, 275
   and Fredericksburg, 194–96
   and Gettysburg, 185, 204–5, 208–10, 215–17, 219, 221, 223
   and Petersburg, 252–53
   surrender by, 275–76
   and Wilderness, 227–28, 230, 233, 235, 242
Lewis, Lloyd, 117, 118, 119, 120
Libby Prison (Richmond), 162–64, 244
Life and Adventures of Martin Chuzzlewit, The (Dickens), 56
Lincoln, Abraham, 92, 160, 260, 283
   assassination of, 109, 277
   call for volunteers, 54
   defense of Grant, 133
   and Frémont, 68–69
   and generals, 195, 207, 223, 264
   and Greeley letter, 43–44
   and Knox court-martial, 153–55
   Missouri policy, 61, 82
   and Osbon's innocence, 109
   press opposition, 125, 254
   press support, 58, 175
   Richmond visit, 271–72

Russell's reportage of, 6, 7–8
and Sherman "insanity," 119
and Villard, 55, 201–2
and Wing, 224–25, 233–36
Lincoln, Tad, 271
Linebaugh, John H., 160–61
Litchfield *Enquirer*, 283
London Daily News, 279
London *Daily Telegraph*, 282
London Graphic, 282
London *Times*. See *Times* of London
Long, A. L., 215
Longstreet, James, 189, 195, 209–10,
    215–18, 220
Lord, Walter, 189
"Lost Cause," xii, 184–85
Louisiana (Confederate ship), 100–101
Louisville (Union ship), 77, 78, 240
Louisville, Ky., 116, 117–18, 206
Lovie, Henri, 69, 85, 144
Lyon, Nathaniel, 61, 63, 68
Lyons, Lord, 15

Mackay, Charles, 185
Mahoney, Dennis, 60
Mallory, Stephen Russell, 87
Manassas (Confederate ship), 100,
    106–7
Manassas Junction, Va., 21, 232. *See
    also* Bull Run, first battle at
Manning, John Laurence, 11
*Marginalia, or Gleanings from an Army
    Notebook* (de Fontaine), 198
Marszalek, John F., 112
Matanzas (Union ship), 95–96
Mathews, Joseph J., 279
Mayo, Lida, 285
McClanahan, John R., 160
McClellan, George Brinton, 126–27,
    150, 195, 254, 265
McClernand, John A., 79, 122, 130,
    135–36, 140
McCormick, Richard Cunningham, 38
McCullagh, Joseph B., 69
McCulloch, Ben, 63, 81, 82
McDougall, Harry, 178, 180

McDowell, Irvin, 21, 23, 35, 36, 38–40,
    57
McFeely, William S., 182
McLaws, Lafayette, 208, 215
McLean, Wilmer, 275–76
McPherson, James B., 177, 195
Meade, George Gordon, x, 226–27,
    229, 257
    and Crapsey, 250–52
    and Gettysburg, 207, 209–10, 217, 223
Meagher, Thomas, 39
Medill, Joseph, 175
Memphis, Tenn., 135–36, 153
Memphis Daily Appeal, 34, 160–61, 198
Meredith, Solomon, 212
Merrimac. See *Virginia*
Milliken's Bend, La., 137–38, 174
Milwaukee, Wis., 37, 257, 282
Milwaukee Daily News, 176
Mississippi (Confederate ship), 101
Mississippi (Union ship), 101, 103, 107
Missouri Valley Register, 62
Mobile, Ala., 16, 17
Mobile Bay, battle of, 103, 254
Monitor (Union ship), 87, 100
Montgomery, Ala., 7, 13–15, 16, 160,
    161
Montgomery Daily Advertiser and Register,
    34, 198
Morgan, George W., 137, 139–40, 142
Morgan, J. P., 285
Morris, Mowbray, 5
Morse, Samuel F. B., 32
Mosby, John, 230
Mount Vernon News, 246
Mulligan, James A., 65, 66
Murphy, R. C., 136

Nashville, Tenn., 79, 239, 245
Nautical Gazette (magazine), 282
naval warfare, 86–98
Nelson, William, 131–32
New Orleans, 9, 17, 18, 71, 136, 264,
    284
    Union campaign against, 99–108
New York Associated Press, 113, 199

New York City
  competition among three major
    newspaper editors, 21, 43–58
  Russell in, 5–6, 9, 18
  Villard postwar mansion, 37
New York *Courier and Enquirer*, 48, 51,
  56
New York *Enquirer*, 51
New-Yorker (publication), 56
New York Evening Post, 38, 281
New York Herald, xi, 11, 44, 70, 144
  Bull Run coverage, 31, 33, 36, 41–42,
    43
  Cadwallader as correspondent, 175,
    237, 240, 243–46, 255–59, 282
  Chapman as correspondent, 78
  Gettysburg coverage, 204, 216–17
  history of, 51–54, 56
  imprisoned correspondents, 164
  Knox as correspondent, 62, 81, 82–84
  and Knox court-martial, 110, 145–46,
    149, 151, 153–54, 155
  and last campaign, 262–63
  merger with *Tribune*, 123
  Osbon as naval correspondent, 87,
    91–104
  position on war, 58
  postwar Washington bureau, 282
  Russell's disparagement of, 21
  sensationalist stories, 52–54
  Shanks as correspondent, 114, 239,
    245
  Southern newspaper exchange,
    262–63
  taunting of Raymond, 57
  and Vicksburg, 137
  Villard as correspondent, 36, 37, 54,
    131, 202
  and Wilderness, 248–49
  See also Bennett, James Gordon
New York *Herald-Tribune*, 123
New York Times, 44, 55
  Bull Run coverage, 28, 29, 36, 57
  and fall of Richmond, 268
  Gettysburg coverage, 204, 206, 207,
    216, 222

  and Knox court-martial, 153
  New Orleans campaign coverage, 107
  and Port Royal expedition, 95
  and Raymond's death, 280
  Raymond's founding of, 48, 56
  Saint Louis representative, 62
  support for Lincoln, 58
  Swinton as correspondent, 177, 200,
    254–55
  Vicksburg coverage, 137, 138, 140,
    142
  Wilderness coverage, 248–49
  Wilkie as correspondent, 62–68, 74,
    80
  See also Raymond, Henry Jarvis
New York Tribune, 6, 35, 70
  Browne as correspondent, 69, 84–85
  and Bull Run, 23, 36, 43–44
  correspondents' imprisonment and
    escape, 156–73, 174
  Dana and, 43, 178, 232, 273
  and fall of Richmond, 270
  and Fredericksburg, 200–202
  Gettysburg coverage, 204, 216
  history of, 45, 47–48
  and Knox court-martial, 153
  merger with *Herald*, 123
  Page as correspondent, 246
  Pea Ridge coverage, 84–85
  position on war, 58
  postwar activities, 279–80
  Raymond as early editor, 48, 56
  Reid and, 123
  Richardson as correspondent, 66, 84
  Vicksburg coverage, 137
  Wilderness coverage, 248–49
  Wilkeson as correspondent, 114–15,
    224, 253–54
  Wing as correspondent, 224, 226,
    228–29, 235, 244, 276
  See also Greeley, Horace
New York World, 40, 69, 70
  Bull Run account, 33–34, 35–36
  Colburn as correspondent, 153
  Colburn's capture and release,
    156–59, 163

and fall of Richmond, 268, 273
Fort Donelson correspondent, 77
Osbon as naval correspondent, 87,
    91, 94, 107
Pea Ridge coverage, 84
Stedman as correspondent, 279
Townsend as correspondent, 265,
    284
Norfolk, Va., 9, 10, 11
Northern Pacific Railroad, 281
North Reports the Civil War, The (An-
    drews), x
Nott, Eliphalet, 60

Old Capitol Prison (Washington, D.C.),
    224
Oneida (Union ship), 101
Ord, Edward O. C., 264
Osband, E. D., 177–78, 180
Osbon, Bradley Sillick
    arrest and trial, 109, 146
    background and early career, 87–91
    Bennett's hiring of, 94
    and Fort Sumter, 92–94, 107
    as journalist, 87, 91–92
    and *Merrimac*, 98–99
    and New Orleans campaign, 99–108
    and Port Royal expedition, 95–98
    postwar activities, 282
Osterhaus, Peter, 82
Our Whole Union (publication), 62

Page, Charles A., 246–50, 267–72,
    274–75, 284
Painter, Uriah H., 25, 39, 40, 206, 236
Parton, James, 47–48, 51, 52
Patrick, Marsena, 241, 251
Patterson, Robert, 23
Paul, George, 257, 259
Pea Ridge, battle of, 82–84, 136
Peerless (Union ship), 96
Pemberton, John C., 136–37, 161, 177,
    223
Pender, William Dorsey, 217
Pensacola (Union ship), 101
Pensacola, Fla., 17, 175

Perry, Matthew Calbraith, 107
Perryville, battle of, 161, 223
Perryville, Ky., 223
Petersburg, battle of, 253, 255
Pettigrew, James, 217
Philadelphia, Pa., 100, 250
Philadelphia Inquirer, 39, 40, 206, 243,
    250
Philadelphia Press, 55, 153, 273
Pickett, George E., 216–17, 219–20,
    266
Pike, Albert, 81
Pillow, Gideon, 78, 79
Pinola (Union ship), 102
Pittsburgh (Union ship), 78
Pittsburg Landing, 121, 123, 127–28,
    132
Plympton, Florus B., 113
Pocahontas (Union ship), 96–98
Polk, Leonidas, 120
Pollard, Edward, 273
Pope, John, 116–17, 142
Porter, David Dixon, 100–101, 109,
    137, 145, 264, 271
Port Royal, S.C., 261
Potter, Robert, 262
Powhatan (Union ship), 16
Prentiss, Benjamin M., 122, 129–30
Price, Sterling, 61, 63, 65–66, 69, 81,
    116–17
prisoners of war, reporters as, 69,
    156–73, 174, 249
Pryor, J. P., 34
Pulitzer, Joseph, 285
Pullman, George, 285
Punch (magazine), 15
Pyle, Ernie, 246

Radziwill, Prince von, 188
Rappahannock Station, Va., 231
Rawlins, John A., 152, 179, 182, 245,
    264, 282
Raymond, Henry Jarvis, 44–45
    and Bull Run, 28, 36, 38–39, 56–57
    career and personality of, 48, 55–58
    death of, 280

Raymond, Henry Jarvis *(continued)*
  founding of *Times* by, 48, 56
  and Wilkie, 62, 63, 64, 65, 67
  See also New York Times
Raymond, Mary, 280
Rebecca Barton (Union ship), 244
Reid, Marion Ronalds, 123
Reid, Ogden Mills, 123
Reid, Robert Charlton, 123
Reid, Whitelaw, x, 198, 203, 236
  background and career, 123–27
  and Crapsey incident, 251–52
  and fall of Richmond, 268, 270–71
  and Gettysburg, 205–8, 212, 216,
    219–21
  postwar activities, 279–80
  and Sherman's "insanity," 118–19
  Shiloh coverage, 127–34
Reynolds, John F., 207, 210
Richardson, Albert D., 66–70, 84
  at Fort Henry action, 75
  and Grant relationship, 76–77
  imprisonment and escape, 66,
    156–73, 249
  and Knox court-martial, 153–54
  postwar activities, 281
  and Vicksburg campaign, 174
Richmond (Union ship), 101, 105
Richmond, Va., 16, 38, 162, 164, 165,
    198, 263
  fall of, 266–75
  as reporters' destination, 187, 188,
    189, 202
  social scene, 189–91
  as Union objective, 195, 251
Richmond Daily Dispatch, 34, 198
Richmond Daily Enquirer, 25, 198
Richmond Examiner, 273
Richmond Whig, 198, 266
Roanoke Island, expedition to, 187
Rodgers, John, 98
Rolla, Mo., 64, 82, 84
Roman, Alfred, 18
Rosecrans, William, 223
Ross, FitzGerald, 184, 189, 191
  and Gettysburg, 208–9, 214, 217

postwar activities, 283
Russell, Antoinette Malvezzi, 279
Russell, Mary, 279
Russell, William Howard, 19, 111, 198,
    205
  background and personality, 1–4
  Bull Run dispatch, 20–31, 123, 185
  criticism of New York press, 20–21
  postwar activities, 278–79
  tours of North and South, 4–20
  Union indignation at Bull Run ac-
    counts by, 22, 29–30, 31

Saint Louis (Union ship), 74, 77
Saint Louis, Mo., 62, 64, 65, 66, 70–71,
    74, 81–82
Saint Louis Missouri Democrat, 69, 82
Saint Louis Republican, 66, 78
Salisbury Prison (N.C.), 69, 164–67,
    173
San Francisco *Sunday Times*, 112
San Jacinto (Union ship), 86
Saunders, John, 190
Savannah, fall of, 260, 273
Savannah Republican, 25, 34, 198
Scheibert, Justus, 184, 188
  and Gettysburg, 208, 214, 217
  postwar activities, 283
Schenectady *Evening Star*, 60
Scott, Winfield, 21, 22–23
Sedalia, Mo., 116–17, 118
Seventy-ninth New York, 39
Seward, William H., 6–7, 9, 10, 45
Shakespeare, William, 144, 158
Shanks, William F. G., 114, 239–40,
    245
Shepardson, William G., 34
Sheridan, Philip, 20, 223, 265–66,
    276
Sheridan, T. W., 90–91
Sherman, Charles, 111
Sherman, Ellen Ewing, 111–12,
    116–17, 119
Sherman, John, 116, 119
Sherman, Mary, 111
Sherman, Thomas W., 95, 119

Sherman, William Tecumseh, 20, 73, 206, 237, 251
  arrest of Isham by, 176
  Atlanta's fall to, 254
  background and early life, 111–12
  at Bull Run, 24, 39, 112
  and Cameron, 114–15
  campaign in South, 260–61, 278
  on capture of correspondents, 159
  Grant friendship, 119–20
  hatred of reporters, x, 59, 62, 66, 110, 112–13, 134, 176
  "insanity" of, 110, 115–19
  and Knox court-martial, 62, 110, 145–55, 161
  and Shiloh, 120–23, 129–30
  and Vicksburg campaign, 135–45, 177
  and Villard, 113–15
  western command, 223–24, 226
Shiloh, battle of, 116, 120–23, 127–34
Sigel, Franz, 82, 226
Simplot, Alexander, 69
Sisler, George, 160–61
Smalley, George W., 200, 279
Smart, James G., 126
Smith, A. J., 137, 139, 148
Smith, Adam, 16
Smith, C. F., 79, 80
Smith, M. L., 137
Smith, Richard, 125
Sons of America, 165
Sons of Temperance, 182
Southern Confederacy, 161–62
Southern Illustrated News, 13
Spotsylvania, battle of, 246
Spratt, Leonidas, 34
Springfield, Mo., 63, 64, 70
Stager, Anson, 32
Stanton, Edwin McMasters, 49, 114, 178, 240, 256
  and end of war, 268, 270–71
  and Vicksburg campaign, 135
  and Wing, 224, 232–33, 235
Stark County Democrat, 125

Stedman, Edmund Clarence, 33–41, 39–40, 43, 279
Stedman, Laura, 35
Steele, Frederick, 137, 139, 151
Stephenson, Luther S., 212
Stevens, Melvina, 172–73
Stevens Bomb-proof Floating Battery, 91–92, 94
Stevenson, Adlai, 280
Stillson, Jerome B., 273
Stones River, battle of, 223
Storey, Wilbur F., 175, 281
Stuart, J. E. B., 20, 190–91, 206, 209
  Jolly Congress and, 185, 192
Sturges (Union boat), 157
Sturgis, Sam, 65
Sumner, Charles, 30
Sumner, Edwin V., 195–96
Susquehanna (Union ship), 96
Sweeney, Bob, 192
Swinton, William, 177, 200, 254–55

Tarbell, Ida Minerva, 224–26, 228, 233, 235–36, 276, 283–84
Tattnall, Josiah, 97, 100
Taylor, Zachary, 111
Tecumseh, 111
telegraph, 32–33, 34, 232, 233
Terry, Alfred, 264
Thackeray, William Makepeace, 1
Thayer, John M., 140, 147
Thomas, Benjamin P., 178
Thomas, George H., 223, 237–38
Thurston, Charles, 167
Tilghman, Lloyd, 74
Times of London, xii, 282
  correspondents, 184, 185, 186
  Gettysburg coverage, 204, 208
  praise for Browne story, 84
  Russell as correspondent, 1–5, 7–8, 13–18, 22
Times Reports the American Civil War, The, 2
Townsend, George Alfred, 265–66, 273, 284–85
Trimble, Isaac, 217

Turner, Thomas P., 163
Twain, Mark, 280
Tyler, Daniel, 23, 38, 39

Union College, 60

Vallandigham, Clement L., 125, 206
Van Dorn, Earl, 81–82, 136
Van Rensselaer, C., 147
Varina Landing, Va., 268
Varuna (Union ship), 101
Vicksburg, Miss.
    campaign for, 135–45, 148–49, 153,
        174, 273
    capture of, 163, 222–23
    Confederate capture of correspon-
        dents, 156, 160, 163
    siege of, 177, 178, 180
Vicksburg Whig, 149
Villard, Henry
    background, 37
    and Bennett, 37, 53–55, 113
    and Bull Run, 25, 36–38, 40–42, 43
    and Fredericksburg, 200–202
    on journalistic standards, 205
    postwar activities, 37, 281
    and Sherman "insanity" story,
        113–15, 117–18
    and Shiloh, 131–33
Virginia (Confederate ship), 74, 87, 98
Vizetelly, Frank, 26, 192–97, 208
    background and career, 187–88
    description of, 190
    and "Lost Cause," xii, 184
    postwar activities, 282–83
Vizetelly, Henry, 187–88
von Borcke, Heros, 184–85, 188–96,
    208, 283

Wabash (Union ship), 95–97
Wallace, Lew, 130, 131
Wallace, W. H. L., 122, 130, 132
Wall Street Journal, ix, 52
Wanamaker, John, 285
Warre, Frederick Richard, 22, 25
Washburne, Elihu, 254

Washington, D.C., 40, 41, 51, 206, 226,
    274
    response to fall of Richmond, 270–71
    Russell in, 6–9
Washington, Martha Dandridge Custis,
    192
Watts, N. G., 160, 163
Webster, Daniel, 111
Weed, Thurlow, 45
Weitzel, Godfrey, 262–63, 268–69, 272
Welborn, John R., 165, 167
Welborn, Mrs. (Welborn's mother),
    167–68
Welles, Gideon, 86, 92, 95, 234
W.H.B. (Union boat), 74
Wigfall, Louis T., 15
Wilcox, Cadmus, 221
Wilderness campaign, 41, 228, 249,
    252, 255
    coverage of, 233, 245, 246, 273
Wilkeson, Samuel, 114–15, 117
    Gettysburg coverage, 206, 222
    and Petersburg, 253–54
    and *Tribune*, 224, 235
Wilkie, Franc Bangs, 59–81, 84–85
    background and early life, 60–61
    early war experiences, 61–73
    as epitomizing Bohemian Brigade, 59
    and Fort Donelson action, 77–81,
        213
    and Fort Henry action, 73–76
    and Knox court-martial, 147, 152,
        153
    postwar activities, 281
    and Reid after Shiloh, 133–34
    and Vicksburg campaign, 137,
        138–42, 144–45
    and Vicksburg siege, 177
Wilkie, Nellie Morse, 60
Willard's Hotel (Washington, D.C.), 8,
    201, 256
Williams, T. Harry, 223
Willington, Aaron Smith, 49
Wilmington, N.C., 11, 264, 273
Wilson, Charles, 246
Wilson, Henry, 201

Wilson, James H., 238
Wilson, Quintus C., 198
Wilson's Creek, battle of, 63–66, 68, 120
Wing, Ebenezer, 224
Wing, Henry E., 224–26, 244, 253
   and end of war, 276–77
   postwar activities, 283–84
   and trek to Washington, 228–36
Winser, Henry Jacob, 107, 249
Wissahickon (Union ship), 101

Wolfe, Thomas E., 166
Wolseley, Garnet Joseph, 186–88
Woods, W. B., 147–49
Wool, John E., 99

Xenia News, 124

Yellow Tavern, battle of, 191
Young, John Russell, 55, 273
Young's Point, La., 147, 153